Presented to:

From   Date

John R. Rice
Bible Stories

John R. Rice
Bible Stories

SWORD OF THE LORD PUBLISHERS
Murfreesboro, Tennessee 37130

ISBN 0-87398-712-8

Printed and bound in the United States of America.

Introduction

The Bible has only a few sermons; it is made up principally of stories. Jesus could make plain His love for sinners by illustrating a lost sheep which the shepherd sought and carried home on his shoulders; the lost coin for which a troubled woman lighted a candle and swept the house diligently until she found it; the prodigal son who ran away from home and came to want and ruin but, coming to himself, returned to a loving father who watched for him and forgave him.

Here we have stories of Adam and Eve, Cain and Abel, Noah and the Flood, Abraham, Isaac and Jacob, Joshua and David. We have the episodes from the life of the Prophet Samuel and other prophets; tales of God's deliverance of His people. We tell the story of Jonah, the birth of Christ, the beginning of Jesus' ministry, all the apostles, wonderful happenings in Jesus' life. Then there is Gethsemane, Jesus' trial, crucifixion and resurrection. And we learn from the book of Acts about Pentecost and Spirit-filled preachers going everywhere preaching. We recall the ministry of Paul the apostle, his imprisonment and at last his death. Then we take you to the book of Revelation and deal with the last judgment and God's last sweet invitation.

We pray these chapters will make the Bible more precious to you and that you will read it daily, love it and live by it.

God bless every person who looks upon these pages, and every heart that is opened to these wonderful truths from the Bible.

John R. Rice

November, 1979

TABLE OF CONTENTS

Old Testament

1. Beginning of Creation 17
   Genesis 1

2. Man Falls Into Sin 20
   Genesis 2,3

3. Two Boys Are Born.................................... 25
   Genesis 4

4. A World Full of People—Good and Bad............................ 29
   Genesis 4-6

5. The Flood—One Year and Ten Days
   of a World in Convulsion 33
   Genesis 6-8

6. After the Flood God Gives
   His Covenant of the Rainbow 37
   Genesis 9

7. Starting a New World................................. 40
   Genesis 8,9

8. Abraham Says Goodbye to Ur 44
   Genesis 13

9. Sarah the Princess, Wife of Abraham.............................. 48
   Genesis 12-22

10. Lot, the Compromising Christian 52
    Genesis 13-19

11. Isaac, the Son God Promised 57
    Genesis 21-24

12. Jacob, the Precocious Twin 62
    Genesis 25-28

13. Working Seven Years for a Bride,
    Then Being Deceived 66
        Genesis 28-33

14. Joseph, Ambitious, Inspired and Hated 69
        Genesis 37-40

15. Joseph, From Slave, Prisoner, to
    Prime Minister of Egypt 72
        Genesis 41-50

16. Moses Was Pulled Out of the River
    to Save a Nation 78
        Exodus 2-14

17. Daily Care for Millions for Forty Years 84
        Exodus 16

18. The Thirsty Nation Israel Gets Water
    From the Rock at Meribah 90
        Exodus 17

19. Laws for God's Nation Israel 93
        Exodus 20

20. Disaster—the Broken Law 98
        Exodus 32

21. How the Tabernacle in the Wilderness and
    Its Furniture Pictured Jesus 102
        Exodus 35-40

22. Twelve Spies See the Land and Report 107
        Numbers 13.14

23. A Cure for Snakebite 111
        Numbers 21

24. The Talking Donkey 116
        Numbers 22-25

25. Goodbye Wilderness: Israel Enters Canaan 119
        Joshua 1-7

26. When the Sun Stood Still for Joshua 123
        Joshua 10

27. Samson, the Mighty Judge of Israel 126
        Judges 13-16

28. Gideon and His Wonderful 300 133
        Judges 7

29. Ruth, the Beautiful Young Widow,
    Finds a Godly Husband..138
        Ruth

30. Samuel, Given in Answer to Prayer;
    the Last Judge of Israel..142
        I Samuel 1-16

31. David, the Shepherd Boy 148
        I Samuel 17

32. David, the Giant Killer 150
        I Samuel 17

33. David Hides From King Saul 153
        I Samuel 21—II Samuel 5

34. David's Great Sin..156
        II Samuel 11,12

35. Absalom's Rebellion 161
        II Samuel 15-19

36. God Reveals to David the Site
    for Solomon's Temple 164
        II Samuel 24

37. Solomon Becomes King 168
        I Kings 1

38. Solomon and the Queen of Sheba 170
        I Kings 10

39. Elijah and Fire From Heaven 173
        I Kings 18

40. Wicked King Ahab and Naboth's Vineyard......................179
        I Kings 21

41. The Prophet Elisha Called and Anointed 183
        II Kings 2

42. Naaman the Syrian Healed of Leprosy 189
        II Kings 5

43. God Delivers Jerusalem From
    King Sennacherib..193
        II Kings 18,19

44. A Beautiful Jewish Girl Queen in the
    Media-Persian Empire Who Was Used to
    Save Her People 198
        Esther

45. Daniel, Jewish Slave in Babylon 203
       Daniel

46. Three Hebrew Young Men in the
       Fiery Furnace 208
       Daniel 3

47. Belshazzar's Feast 212
       Daniel 5

48. Daniel in the Lions' Den 216
       Daniel 6

49. Jonah and the Whale 219
       Jonah

New Testament

1. The Birth of John the Baptist 227
       Luke 1

2. The Virgin Mother Mary 231
       Luke 1,2

3. The Angel's Christmas Message 236
       Luke 2

4. The Baby Jesus Is Dedicated 239
       Luke 2

5. Wise Men From the East Come to
       Worship Jesus 244
       Matthew 2

6. Jesus at Twelve Years of Age 248
       Luke 2

7. The Baptism of Jesus 251
       Matthew 3, Mark 1, Luke 3, John 1

8. Jesus Tempted at the Beginning of His Ministry 254
       Matthew 4, Mark 1, Luke 4

9. How Jesus, Our Pattern, Was Filled
   With the Holy Spirit 258
      Matthew 3, Mark 1, Luke 3, John 1

10. Andrew Wins His Fisherman Brother
    to Christ 262
       John 1

11. Jesus' First Miracle.. 264
       John 2

12. Jesus Calls Four Fishermen to Be
    His Apostles 267
       Matthew 4, Mark 1, Luke 5, John 1

13. Jesus Heals Peter's Mother-in-Law............................... 271
       Luke 4

14. Jesus Tells a Member of the Sanhedrin,
    "Ye Must Be Born Again" 273
       John 3

15. Jesus and the Samaritan Woman at Sychar 277
       John 4

16. A Roman Tax Collector Is Called to Be
    Christ's Apostle 281
       Mark 2, Luke 5

17. The Blesseds: Jesus Tells Eight
    Ways to Be Happy and Fortunate 284
       Matthew 5

18. The Palsied Man Had Four Friends Who
    Brought Him to Jesus... 290
       Matthew 9, Mark 2, Luke 5

19. At the House of a Pharisee, Jesus Meets
    and Saves a Sinful Woman 294
       Luke 7

20. Jesus Raises the Daughter of Jairus
    From the Dead and Heals a Persistent
    Woman Who Intervenes... 297
       Matthew 9, Mark 5, Luke 8

21. The Feeding of Five Thousand With
    One Boy's Lunch 301
       Matthew 14, Mark 6, Luke 9, John 6

22. Jesus Walks on the Water: Tells Peter
to Come to Him 306
    Matthew 14:27; Mark 6:50; John 6:20

23. The Home of Mary and Martha at Bethany......................308
    Luke 10:38-42

24. Jesus Tells the Story of the Prodigal Son 311
    Luke 15

25. Jesus Heals the Maniac of Gadara 315
    Mark 5

26. Wicked King Herod Has John the Baptist
Beheaded...318
    Matthew 14, Mark 6

27. Jesus Heals the Devil-Possessed Daughter
of a Woman of Canaan 321
    Matthew 15

28. Peter's Great Confession at Caesarea Philippi....................324
    Matthew 16, Mark 8, Luke 9

29. Jesus Transfigured to Appear as He Will at
His Second Coming..327
    Matthew 17, Mark 9, Luke 9

30. The Rich Young Ruler Who Wanted to Be
Saved by Good Works...331
    Mark 10

31. Zacchaeus Who Climbed a Tree to See Jesus 333
    Luke 19

32. Lazarus Raised From the Dead 335
    John 11

33. Jesus Makes Triumphant Entry Into Jerusalem..................339
    Matthew 21, John 12

34. The Ten Virgins: Bridesmaids for the Marriage..................343
    Matthew 25

35. The King's Wonderful Marriage Feast
for His Son 345
    Luke 14

36. Mary of Bethany Anoints the Saviour 349
    John 12

37. Jesus Eats the Last Supper With Disciples 351
    Matthew 6, Mark 14, Luke 22

38. Judas, the Disciple Who Was a Traitor 354
    Matthew 26-28, Mark 14, Luke 22, John 18

39. Jesus Sweats Bloody Sweat in Gethsemane......................359
    Matthew 26, Mark 14, Luke 22

40. How Shocking That Simon Peter Should Deny
    Jesus and Curse and Quit the Ministry! 363
    John 19,21

41. Jesus Condemned to Die...367
    Matthew 27, Mark 14,15; Luke 23, John 18,19

42. The Crucifixion of the Lord Jesus 371
    John 19, Luke 23

43. The Burial of the Lord Jesus 376
    Matthew 27, Mark 15, Luke 23, John 19

44. The Resurrection of Jesus Christ 380
    Matthew 28, Mark 16, Luke 24, John 20

45. The Saviour Goes to Heaven, Promising
    to Return..384
    Acts 1

46. The Wonderful Enduement of Power
    at Pentecost 390
    Acts 2

47. Paul and Barnabas Called to Be Missionaries....................395
    Acts 13

48. Missionary Joys and Troubles 400
    Acts 14

49. Must One Keep the Mosaic Law to Be Saved? 404
    Acts 15

50. Paul and Silas: Another Missionary Journey 408
    Acts 15,16

51. The Gospel in Great Cities of Greece 413
    Acts 17

52. Paul and the Idol Makers at Ephesus 417
    Acts 18,19,20

53. Paul Must Go to Rome 422
    Acts 21-26

54. Paul Faces Shipwreck and Savages at Rome 427
    Acts 27,28

55. The Apostle Paul at Rome 433

56. Exiled on Patmos, the Apostle John Writes the
    Last Book in the Bible...435
        Revelation

57. Sinners Face Jesus at the Last Judgment of
    the Unsaved Dead 439
        Revelation 20

58. The Last Invitation in
    the Bible 444
        Revelation 21

Beginning of Creation

God looked down upon His handiwork, the things He had created, and said, "It is good! It is good!"

God had made a world. He had collected the waters into seas and saw that the dry land appeared. We suppose He had collected the water that is above the earth into a vapor or canopy that would let the sun through for all the wonderful things God does for birds, animals and mankind. We suppose that canopy filtered out any rays of sun that would make man grow old.

Oh, God had things planned out just right. He covered about three-fourths of the earth's surface with water so there would always be enough moisture in the air for plants to grow and so the surface of most of the earth would not be left desert.

"Let's make this earth a great ball nearly eight thousand miles thick lest man be too heavy from being held down by the gravity of a mighty sphere," God said, "because there must be enough gravity to hold the atmosphere which man must breathe to about fourteen pounds' weight per square inch at sea level." "Oh, this is just right," God said. And God set the sun to be a light by day with the earth going around the sun at just the right distance so it would not be too hot nor too cold.

But man will need a night, too, so God put the moon to circle the earth every twenty-eight days. God has it all planned out right for days, months and years, for times and seasons.

And now the plants! Did God enjoy making the

microscopic beauty in the tiny flower, with petals, pistils and stamen, in planning that each plant should bloom and go to seed so the earth could be continually filled with beauty? Then, besides, there were the giant trees and ten thousands of plants whose leaves rustle softly in the wind, with green chlorophyll which God put into leaves to feed the growth and development of every plant.

Then there was food of every kind, not only the grass for wild beasts and cattle, but fruit trees of every kind. Tropical plants here? Oh, yes, God made them all. And in the Garden where they grew, there would never be a frost to kill the peach bloom. Seeds of every kind, food and forage for every kind of animal, every bird and beast. Oh, God thought of everything!

And the animals—He made them all, from the scurrying ground squirrel and the lizard on the rock, to the rabbit in the field and the squirrel in the tree, to the fox in his den. And the cattle peacefully feeding on luxuriant grass. Oh, God thought of everything! And not an animal in there hated or feared man. Lions! Oh, they were as gentle as pussycats! The cumbersome hippo, "river horse," would clamber out of the river's mud to be near man and gaze upon him with docile eyes. A squirrel would chatter to call man's attention to the nut he had found. And the long-necked, ungainly-looking giraffe would reach his head down for man to scratch about the stubby horns. I don't wonder that God said it was good.

And a man was there. The red or yellow or green or blue of the macaws and parrots, the white of the egret and the heron—all these showed their colors through forest glades to be near man.

But, alas, there was no mate for man. What is it, Adam? Among all the animals there was none to laugh as Adam laughed; none to dream as Adam dreamed, none with high hopes and visions. These human traits could not enter the consciousness of these animals. Adam needed a mate. And there was not found on the earth any person, animal or thing that would be the comfort Adam needed, his joys to share.

There was no one to help propagate the race.

But remember that God had made Adam out of the dust of the earth. Can you imagine: He formed the strong handsome face, the delicate fingers, the well-proportioned body and even the tiny details of hair and color! And then God breathed into the body made from dirt, and it became a living soul. God had made a man, made him in the image of God.

And now Adam must have a mate. Did God make the woman out of dirt as He did Adam? Oh, no. There must not be two kinds of creation. The man and woman must be of one body, one flesh, one bone; so God performed the first surgical operation in the world. Adam was put into a deep sleep and God opened his body and took out a rib and from that rib He made a woman to be a mate, a helper, a companion. Now when Adam woke from his sleep he beheld this woman. Oh, she was the prettiest thing he ever saw! They talked and laughed and looked each other over. Why? They were meant for each other! They saw they must have each other forever. So God had the first wedding ceremony there in the Garden of Eden.

How wonderful was life in that Garden of Eden! There is nothing to grieve God, nothing to hurt man. The roses, I think, had no thorns. And it may be Adam and Eve slept on a bed of rose petals. If there were mosquitos, they probably just joined in the symphony orchestra and didn't go about puncturing people with their tiny hypodermic needles.

And best of all, God Himself came every day and walked in the Garden and talked with Adam. There was no sin, no evil talk, no hate, no envy, no irreverence to displease a holy and loving God!

Man Falls Into Sin

GENESIS 2 and 3

One day in Heaven there was a startling thing. An archangel rebelled against God. All the amazing wisdom and power God had given to him did not keep him from unholy envy and ambition. "I want to make myself above God, above the stars of God," said Lucifer.

But yonder in this beautiful planet earth where God had formed a Garden and let man and woman keep it and enjoy it, Satan saw an opportunity to break the heart of God. He would deceive, he would defile, he would seduce these perfect creatures; he would poison a race of men.

Among all the animals, the most subtile and intelligent, before God put a curse on snakes, was the serpent. So Satan entered into this serpent and talked to Eve. He may have said, "Good morning, Lady, it is a wonderful garden and park you have here. I suppose you have all you need, all you can eat."

"Oh, yes," Eve replied. "And we can eat of the fruit of every tree except the tree of the knowledge of good and evil in the center of the Garden. That, God says, we must not eat of, or we will die."

I can imagine that serpent chuckled a little and said, "Why, Lady, you won't die if you eat of that tree. God just knows that you will be wise like Himself. You need not heed His warning."

Oh, that is an old, old trick of the Devil. Now he tells foolish men that God's Word is not really true. He tells men that God did not really create this whole universe from

nothing as He said He did; that He did not make man by the direct act of God. No, Satan wants people to believe that all things, including man, simply developed, evolved and grew by natural and amazing ways from little one-celled animals to man, the crown of creation. So Satan said, "You shall not surely die. God wants to keep you from becoming really wise."

Eve, sadly we say it, was deceived. That serpent was so bright-colored, and spoke so charmingly, and the fruit did look as if it would make people wise. So she took and ate of that forbidden fruit. Then she gave it to Adam who had not been deceived and persuaded him to eat of it. Oh, calamity! Oh, greatest tragedy that ever happened to mankind! Adam and Eve have sinned! Instead of the pure innocent beings who could talk with God and who had never grieved Him— now they are sinful and the taint has entered into their souls. Now every child who will be brought into the world will have this fallen, guilty nature. How sad!

Now Adam and Eve were conscious that they were sinners. They looked upon themselves with shame. "Why, we are naked!" Of course the truth is, every poor, sinful being in the

world is someway conscious of his sin and knows that he needs a covering. Adam hid from God when God came visiting in the Garden. When He called, "Adam, where art thou?" Adam would not come. Before he had met God so gladly and they had talked so freely; now he is a stranger, a guilty sinner. He would not feel he could serve a holy God.

But God called him and now he admitted the sin. He someway knows that spiritual death has come upon him and upon Eve and that physical death will inevitably follow. Adam explained, "The woman whom Thou gavest to be with me, she gave me of the tree, and I did eat." So God announced what had befallen mankind.

Now, instead of gathering the fruit and foodstuffs so easily, with never a weed nor a thorn nor an insect pest nor a storm of hail nor a parching drought to hinder, God has cursed the ground. It brings forth thorns and thistles. There are insect bugs that will eat the fruit. Plant diseases will hinder. Man can now live only by the sweat of his brow. Now there is enmity between man and all kinds of beasts. To Eve God said, "I will greatly multiply thy sorrow and thy conception; in sorrow thou shalt bring forth children; and thy desire shall be to thy husband, and he shall have the rule over thee." Before sin came in man needed no ruler but God. But now parents must supervise children. Wives are to be subject to husbands. Cities and countries must have rulers. Laborers must have bosses. Man is a sinful being.

Now that is a sad picture. God sets an angel with a flaming sword to drive out Adam and Eve from the Garden of Eden. They must not be allowed to eat of the tree of life and live forever as sinful beings. We suppose that marvelous Garden where the ground was cursed, as it had been outside, soon became a wilderness of tangled vines, noxious weeds, grasshoppers and beetles, insect pests and varmints. There can be no paradise for sinful man till God makes a way to cover his sin and restore man to fellowship with God.

Ah, but God will do that. So for the shame-faced naked man and woman, God made garments of skin. They had tried to cover their nakedness before each other and God

God sets an angel with a flaming sword to drive out Adam and Eve from the Garden of Eden.

with fig leaves. But these aprons would soon dry up and fall apart. God killed innocent animals to make robes to cover the skin of these naked sinners.

So God provides us the dear Lord Jesus, God's dear Son who took part with Him in the creation, to be born into this world and die to pay for men's sins. Those innocent animals were pictures of the coming Saviour. Those garments of skin were pictures of His righteousness which shall be applied to our (the sinner's) account when we put our trust in Him for forgiveness and salvation.

Then God gave the great promise. To the serpent He said, "I will put enmity between thee and the woman, and between thy seed and her Seed; it shall bruise thy head, and thou shalt bruise His heel." So there is yet to come, Eve, a Saviour. He will be born of a woman without a human father. He shall crush the serpent's head. At long last the Saviour is to bring man eternal victory over Satan.

Have you who read this, put your trust in the Saviour whose blood cleanses from all sin? Do you have on the robe, spiritually, of Christ's righteousness which He imputes to all who trust Him for salvation?

Two Boys Are Born

Outside the Garden of Eden where Adam must toil to provide for and to protect his own, of course there would be many evidences of the calamity of sin which is on all mankind. Now Adam finds himself tired after the day's toil. We think he said to Eve, "I was never tired, no matter how long the day, when we lived in the beautiful Garden." And Eve's face sometimes had tired lines and I am sure she found she was sometimes fretful.

But they had a promise from God about the Seed of the woman. Adam had seen other animals bring forth their young. Now he and Eve were conscious of her first pregnancy. A little nausea in the morning, a slow enlargement of her belly—I can imagine it was a fascinating thing for these two to see the process of how a child was to come into this world. Of course there was some pain, some distress, for God had said, "I will greatly multiply thy sorrow and thy conception; in sorrow thou shalt bring forth children. . ." (Gen. 3:16).

The baby was born. And what a wonder, the first little baby this world had ever seen! How delicate his little fingers; and Eve nursed him at her breast and rocked him and said, "I have gotten a man from the Lord" (Gen. 4:1). Is this the one, I wonder, who will bruise the serpent's head? No, Eve, for this is a child of a human father, not only the Seed of the woman.

In due season another son was born—Abel. And he loved the flocks and herds and looked after the lambs and kids and led them to better pastures. But Cain liked the plowing and sowing and reaping. My, what luscious tomatoes and melons and cabbages! What peaches, oranges and apples!

We may be sure that Adam and Eve had told the babies very early of the Garden of Eden and of their own shameful fall. They knew they must worship God. So each on certain days brought sacrifices to present before God.

Cain, let us suppose, arrayed the most beautiful of his vegetables and fruits, with ears of fresh corn from the field, to offer before God. Cain knew that one needs to serve and honor God. So he did. Alas, he missed the point. There must be some bloody sacrifice to pay for sin before anybody can be acceptable to God.

So by faith Abel offered a more excellent sacrifice. And by faith means, I am sure, that he knew of the coming Messiah that God had promised, the Seed of the woman that should bruise the serpent's head. And by faith in that Saviour, Abel, a believing, trusting, forgiven sinner, offered solemnly a lamb for a sacrifice. He knew this pictured the Lamb of God that would take away the sin of the world.

But Cain was angry. God seemed not pleased with all his labor, with all this beautiful fruit of the ground that he had brought to God. And God told Cain, 'If your sacrifice is not well pleasing, it is because sin lieth at the door' (Gen. 4:7).

None of us poor mortals can be welcomed gladly into the presence of God except as we face the fact that we are sinners, and trust in the dear Saviour God has provided to pay for sins.

Did Cain take well the rebuke of God? No. He was angry. How many men today boast of their good deeds. They want a religion without a bloody sacrifice. They want men to be good and often claim that men are naturally good. But, alas, human experience and the Bible prove that "all have sinned, and come short of the glory of God" (Rom. 3:23).

Here is a remarkable thing about that younger brother, Abel. He was not only a Christian in the sense that he had personally trusted the Saviour who must come, but he was a prophet of God, as Jesus said in Luke 11:50. He felt he must

Cain seized a club, smote and killed his brother Abel.

earnestly urge Cain to trust in the Saviour. But as he pressed the matter, Cain grew more angry. And because he was wicked, he hated his brother Abel who had trusted in the goodness of the Saviour and had been made righteous in his heart.

One day as they talked, the rebellion in the heart of Cain, rebellion against God, against the Gospel, against his righteous brother, burned hot in Cain's heart. He seized a club and smote his brother and killed him.

Let us imagine that it is eventime. Eve calls her grown sons: "Cain, Abel, supper is ready." Only Cain comes. He has downcast eyes. He has hate and guilt in his heart. "Where is your brother Abel?" Adam asked. God had asked the same question and Cain answers it with anger, "Am I my brother's keeper?" O Cain, that is a murderer's question!

Let us imagine that Eve, now distressed and fearful, runs down the path toward the sheepfold to find Abel. She found him—head crushed, eyes vacant and staring. Sobbing, she takes that still form in her arms and weeps. Oh, what sin brings to troubled mankind!

A World Full of People— Good and Bad

My, how the human race multiplied! God had commanded Adam and Eve, ". . .multiply and replenish the earth." So after Abel was dead, God gave another son, Seth.

Eve said, "Oh, he will take the place of my Abel!" Then Adam lived nine hundred and thirty years and begat sons and daughters. We are told that "Eve was the mother of all living." So when Cain would marry and go away into the land of Nod, he took as wife one of his sisters or perhaps a daughter of some brother, and they built a city.

Seth is counted among the godly people who served the true God.

How long people lived in those days! Adam lived nine hundred and thirty years, Methuselah, nine hundred and sixty-nine. A fine civilization appears even before the Flood. Men built cities, so you may be sure that all the arts of the mason, the carpenter, the finisher, were used. Some men developed flocks and herds; others were skilled in agriculture and horticulture. One family developed men who were skilled in metal working in iron and brass and silver and gold. Another family developed musicians. They made beautiful musical instruments, stringed instruments like the harp, guitar, violin, and wooden instruments like the flute, and even the amazing skill to develop organs and wind instruments. So we know that they had already found the chords of music which God has put into nature.

But sadly I must tell you the race became more and more wicked. As far as we know, no human government had been established to punish crime. Wickedness and unbelief spread everywhere through the ungodly seed of Cain.

And now there came a great tragedy. In the nature of the case, godly fathers and mothers tended to rear godly children and to keep company with godly people. But now one of the men of Seth's line saw a beautiful girl among the descendants of Cain. So he courted her and took her to be his wife. Other young men did the same.

And there rose among the line of Cain many vigorous young men who saw the daughters of the godly line of Seth, and they courted them, loved them, and took them as wives. Now we find the bad and good are intermixed. From these mixed marriages came out a race of people without the old faith and convictions. Now the godly line of Seth has mixed in with the ungodly heathen world, and the whole world becomes corrupt.

I am sure this broke the heart of God. God had looked on mankind He had made in the world, and said, "It is very good"; but now that has changed. God saw that the wickedness of man was great on the earth and that "every imagination of the thoughts of his heart was only evil continually." It grieved God's heart, of course.

What would God do? God said, "I will start over. Here is one man, Noah, and his family, who serve me with a whole heart. There was godly Enoch who walked with Me and I took Him to Heaven. So he cannot help down here. So I will bring a Flood to cover the whole earth. I will blot out every man, woman, child, every animal that has breath, except Noah's family, and I will destroy mankind whom I have made. Then I will start over with Noah and his family."

Oh, Noah had found grace in the eyes of the Lord. So God had Noah to build a great ark, or ship, or barge, and Noah was warned that he had only a hundred and twenty years to build this great ark while he preached the Gospel to men about him.

At long last the big boat is finished. It is about 450 feet

long, 75 feet wide, 45 feet deep. It will hold as much or more than 500 railroad boxcars. They have stored up foods of every kind for man and animal. Now God has animals selected— two of every kind—who present themselves and walk into the ark. Of some kinds Noah takes seven so there will be animals for sacrifices.

God said to Noah, "Come thou and all thy house into the ark," and God shut the door. Then there came a Flood to destroy the whole earth.

What about those millions of people who perished in the Flood? But remember God said, "My spirit shall not always strive with man, for that he also is flesh. . . ." Remember that Noah had preached to these people for 120 years, and Noah was called the preacher of righteousness. We are glad to read also that Christ came and preached to these people through the Holy Spirit as Noah preached to them. So un- saved men were warned time after time, but they did not turn. They were enlightened, they were convicted, but with rebellious hearts they continued in sin, rejecting salvation.

The sad truth is that in this poor race of sinners all must die, for "it is appointed unto men once to die, but after this the judgment" (Heb. 9:27). It is not of special moment that millions of people perished, let us suppose, in the first day or two of the Flood. Ah, if they did not die then, they would die later. If they died unforgiven, they would be lost forever. It is not by the wickedness of God that lost people die. Those who will not repent must perish. I think the marvel is that God waited 120 years before He sent the Flood.

Can you imagine a godly preacher preaching day after day to all the crowds he could gather for 120 years, warning them of judgment to come, and yet they would not hear? The marvel is that God's mercy called so long to men who did not turn, did not repent, did not seek God. Even today men hear the Gospel, and they think, I have plenty of time. They think, Well, many others do not take that to heart, so why should I? So men ignore God's mercy and eventually must meet God's judgment on unrepentant sinners.

The Flood—One Year and Ten Days of a World in Convulsion

GENESIS 6-8

"How do you feel, Noah, shut up here in this mighty vessel with only yourself, your wife, the three sons and their wives, with a host of animals?" Noah is still tormented, we think, by the faint cries of those who hammer on the closed doors outside, and say, "I believe you now, Noah! A terrible rain is coming! I wish I had listened to you!"

Ah, Noah hears the pounding of the rain on the ark, the great vessel shivers under the mighty winds that began to blow, and then the water rising in the valley begins to lift one end of the ark. Now it is afloat. O Noah, where will this ark go? How can you escape when the whole race outside is perishing? But it was "by faith" that Noah built the ark. That is, he believed God. He trusted in the coming Saviour. He had followed God's instructions. So I am sure he was saved. And the Scripture says, "And God remembered Noah." And all through these terrible days ahead he may know that the angels of God watch over him and his wife, his three sons and the daughters-in-law who may have been frightened.

The mighty rain continued "forty days and forty nights." Also "were all the fountains of the great deep broken up." We suppose that the canopy of water vapor that surrounded and covered the earth was added to the flood waters. This physical earth was convulsed. Waters rose to cover the highest mountains, over twenty feet. As waters came forth from ocean beds, tidal waves, hundreds, perhaps thousands,

of feet deep, rushed around the world. Every human habitation, every mark of mankind's presence, was washed away so that the Scripture says, "Whereby the world that then was, being overflowed with water, perished" (II Pet. 3:6).

Seashells from ocean beds were scattered in layers over the highest mountains. Giant forests were uprooted, then covered with great layers of mud and gravel to make the coal beds. Multiplied millions of animals, dead in the Flood, were covered by the great flow of mud and water, often buried far deep, to make the oil deposits and the fossils, now so abundant.

But now there is water that covers the face of the whole earth. So God must lower the ocean bottoms to make room. The pressure makes volcanoes that spew out their molten lava, mountain ranges rise, but God sets the boundaries for the waters and sees that they shall not return to overflow the earth.

Now we find the earth covered with layers of mud, gravel, sand, seashells and fossils, and coal beds. A giant volcano belches forth from the hot inside of the earth and the layers of soft ground may be pressed into waves or hills, and that mud will become stone. Inland seas break through the mud boundaries, and the Colorado River, for example, cuts through layers of the mud and gravel which would soon become stone, and so cuts out the Grand Canyon. This turbulence in earth goes on for one year and ten days, from the 17th day of the first month of Noah's 601st year, to the 27th day of the first month of the second year (Gen. 8:13,14).

How hungry Noah must have been to set foot on solid earth again! But by faith he waits on God. How Noah's sons and their wives must have longed to see the sunshine, birds, flowers, and trees again!

The waters have receded, going back to the boundaries God has set. So Noah opens the window of the ark and sends forth a dove. She returns. He sends forth a raven, and that bird of prey never returns. No doubt it has found enough decaying carcasses to feed on. Again Noah sends forth a dove and it returns with an olive leaf in her bill. Oh, vegetation is

They go in—two of a kind.

Noah sends forth a dove. She returns with an olive leaf.

beginning to sprout. So again we will have olive orchards, vines, fruit trees, and fields of corn and wheat, and forests of oak and pine! Now God is ready, and Noah and his family come forth to start again in a brand new world with every man, every city, every river, every road removed from the earth.

Noah starts to live in the new earth. He offers a sacrifice and God calls his attention to a glorious promise. "See that rainbow in the sky? Before the Flood you did not have rain nor a rainbow. That rainbow is a bow of promise. I have promised there will never again come a flood that will destroy the whole earth."

After the Flood God Gives His Covenant of the Rainbow

When Noah, his wife, his three sons (Shem, Ham and Japheth) and their wives came out of the ark, they came to an entirely different world. After being shut up in the ark over a year while the whole earth was covered and washed with tidal waves, while mountains were moved and earthquakes and volcanoes had part in the convulsions that shook the whole earth, I can imagine that these come out of the ark very deeply stirred and much concerned. Every city in the world had been washed away, every house had been destroyed, and every human being but these eight in the ark had been killed. That was true also with the animals that were over the face of the earth. Now they are washed away and will become fossils buried in the mud and debris after the Flood.

God gave some rules to Noah and his sons: They were to multiply and replenish the earth. They were to set up governments so that "whoso sheddeth man's blood, by man shall his blood be shed" (Gen. 9:6). Noah set up an altar and worshiped God.

No doubt those eight people talked a great deal about what had happened. Remember, there had never been rain before the Flood, but a mist went up from the ground and watered the plants.

Let us suppose that one day when the rain began again, they trembled. Perhaps Mrs. Noah said, "O Noah! Will the earth be covered with water again? What will we do?"

But God promised them that no more would He cover the earth with water and destroy all mankind.

"And God spake unto Noah, and to his sons with him, saying, And I, behold, I establish My covenant with you, and with your seed after you; And with every living creature that is with you, of the fowl, of the cattle, and of every beast of the earth with you; from all that go out of the ark, to every beast of the earth. And I will establish My covenant with you; neither shall all flesh be cut off any more by the waters of a flood; neither shall there any more be a flood to destroy the earth. And God said, This is the token of the covenant which I make between Me and you and every living creature that is with you, for perpetual generations: I do set My bow in the cloud, and it shall be for a token of a covenant between Me and the earth. And it shall come to pass, when I bring a cloud over the earth, that the bow shall be seen in the cloud: And I will remember My covenant, which is between Me and you and every living creature of all flesh; and the waters shall no more become a flood to destroy all flesh. And the bow shall be in the cloud; and I will look upon it, that I may remember the everlasting covenant between God and every living creature of all flesh that is upon the earth. And God said unto Noah, This is the token of the covenant, which I have established between Me and all flesh that is upon the earth."—Gen. 9:8-17.

They looked, and, behold, they saw a strange and beautiful thing they had never seen before! As the sun shined down through the falling rain, there was a beautiful arch in the heavens, a bow made of seven colors. The light shining through the drops of water was divided into the seven colors and so made a lovely rainbow. Sometimes the rainbow is double. Now a rainbow would always be a sign that God had promised the world was never to be destroyed again by water.

So when you see the rainbow in the sky, you must remember the mercy of God. He loves us. He protects us. And His loving mercy is so great that He will not destroy us with a flood as He destroyed the people in Noah's time. The rainbow is God's signature in the sky. It is formed as sunlight shines through raindrops. But since there was never any rain before the Flood, there was never a rainbow until after the Flood. What a beautiful sign of God's constant care!

Starting a New World

Noah and his sons set out to repopulate the earth and to subdue it. We know that Noah was a good man, but he found many changes in this new world. For one thing, the climate varies. Before the Flood there were all kinds of tropical plants and animals even in the Arctic Circle. And elephants or mammoths have been found frozen in the far reaches of Siberia and Alaska. Before the Flood, no doubt, the whole world was under a semitropical climate, protected by that canopy of "waters above the earth," as we suppose. Now it will be colder toward the poles and warmer at the equator.

So Noah planted a vineyard and made grape juice. I do not know if he had ever tasted wine before the Flood. But now he drank this wine after it fermented and he became drunken. And I give him the benefit of the doubt, but at any rate he lay drunken in his tent. His son Ham saw him naked in his tent. It was a shocking thing, of course, for children to see their own father or mother naked. And the other two sons took a covering and backed into the tent so they could not see the father's nakedness and covered Noah. But a curse came on the son, Ham, because he had looked upon his naked father.

Now God has given all the animals for food for man. In ceremonies the Jews were allowed to eat only certain animals as clean beasts. But that restriction is removed in the New Testament, and now we are told "every creature of God is good, and nothing to be refused, if it be received with thanksgiving: For it is sanctified by the word of God and prayer" (I Tim. 4:4,5). Before the Flood, we suppose, men had only a vegetable diet.

There were three sons of Noah, and from their families came all the peoples of the earth. I wonder, were Cain and Abel colored alike? Was one of them blond, perhaps, and one of them brunette? We do not know. But we know that in Adam and Eve all the genes were carried that will produce all the races of the earth.

It is a fact we must not forget that the whole world went into terrible sin before the Flood, so now God must set some laws and put some authority in government to somewhat restrain and guide and protect men from criminal tendencies. So God told Noah, "Whoso sheddeth man's blood, by man shall his blood be shed" (Gen. 9:6). From this time on that will involve governments throughout the world and God holds these governments responsible to maintain law and

"We will build a tower and make it strong and high so we will be safe from any flood in the future." So these rebellious people built the Tower of Babel.

order and to punish the wicked and protect the innocent.

And now what a scattering of people! God has a whole earth to cover. Noah lived 350 years after the Flood; a total of 950 years. And his sons were prolific and eventually there was a great mass of people, not all of them devout, not all of them believing or God-fearing. So as the sons scattered, some of the sons of Ham went to the continent of Africa. And there is a tradition that Mizraim, the second son of Ham, became the first Pharaoh of Egypt.

One descendant of Shem was Eber and he had two sons. One was Peleg; "for in his days was the earth divided" (Gen. 10:25). The earth was divided? Perhaps that means that up to this day all the continents were connected. That string of the Aleutian Islands was then, no doubt, an open pathway between Asia and North America. No doubt down from Indonesia and the Philippines to Australia there were land connections. And God so arranged it so the animals from the Flood multiplied and scattered over the whole earth and men likewise scattered to inhabit all the earth. We know that in the early days men made voyages from Sweden and Iceland to America. There is good evidence that from the West Coast of South America people sailed frail boats all the way down to the Polynesian Islands. But one day the earth was divided and the passageway was cut off from Australia to other continents. So some kinds of animals are in Australia that died out in other parts of the world.

But many people still remembered the Flood. They remembered it with fear and perhaps with anger. No doubt, some were rebellious against God and they said, "We are not going to risk God about this flood business. We will build a tower and make it strong and high so we will be safe from any flood in the future." So they built what was called the Tower of Babel. Their intentions were not good. But God intended that this beautiful earth He had made should be inhabited and used and blessed by the people of mankind everywhere. So God came among the people there and changed their languages. Strangely now one man could not understand others, but only a few of his own household or tribe! So people then went out to separate according to tribes and dialects around the world.

Thus far God has been dealing with the race as a whole, but now, after Genesis 11, we will be reading more and more about one particular section of mankind and that will include Abraham and his descendants.

Abraham Says Goodbye to Ur

GENESIS 12

The first 11 chapters of our Bible are concerned with all the races of the world, those destroyed in the Flood, and those who followed, some going into heathen idolatry or barbarianism and others into idolatry of every kind. But now the interest in the Bible will be on Abraham and his children, God's promise to Israel, and when it talks about Jews in captivity in Babylon, Abraham's children are still the center. And so with the restoration and all the other events until Jesus comes.

Let's imagine one bright morning Abraham (his name was Abram then, but God changed it to Abraham and so we will call him by that name) came out of his great home (for he was rich) in Ur of the Chaldees and looked over his land, his flocks and herds. Ur was a prominent city then, even having a library. But Abraham felt some need to get alone; God was calling. So God told him, "Abraham, are you ready to leave all this? I want you to leave your kindred, your land, and come to a far country that I will show you. There you will live in tents, but eventually you will have a son, and I will give you a great land and a multitude of seed."

This is written in the Holy Land. Outside my window now is a Bedouin tent—just as the Arabs and all the Nomads of this country have used for centuries. The tent is large, made out of goat's hair and stretched across ropes and poles. I am sure they cook on little camp fires. They sleep on padded pallets of goat's skin and fur. A camel grazes outside. Abraham and Sarah had to give up comforts and luxuries to go into a

far unknown country to live in tents as God had said.

By faith, Abraham consented to leave all the settled comforts of Ur. But should he leave his old father Terah? Perhaps he should, because God told him to leave his kinfolks. But old Terah went with him, and Lot, his nephew. Lot was a young man and his father was dead. So kindhearted Abraham took Lot and his family, too.

They came to Haran where old Terah refused to go further. So there they stayed until Terah died.

Then Abraham, now seventy-five years old, took his caravan, along with servants, oxen, donkeys, camels, sheep and goats, down into the land of Canaan. God said to Abraham, "All the land which thou seest, to thee will I give it, and to thy seed for ever." And he had Abraham walk through the land—north, south, east and west. The Canaanites and the Perizzites and other heathen people were in the land, but Abraham and Isaac and his descendents were to live in tents as sojourners, temporary dwellers, until God should set the time to drive them out. God had Abraham view the starry heavens at night and said, "So shall thy seed be." He had Abraham consider the sand of the seashore and said that would represent his seed, too. We suppose the sand pictured literal, physical descendants. We suppose the stars pictured spiritual descendants, those who would have Abraham's faith. But once, when God made His promise to Abraham He said, "For all the land which thou seest, to thee will I give it, and to thy seed for ever"—not seeds, many, but one Seed. Oh, that would be Christ!

Abraham now remembered all these sacrifices he had been taught to make, sacrifices that godly men had made from Abel down through Enoch and Noah to Abraham, the tenth generation after the Flood. Now he saw that the lamb on the altar pictured a coming Sacrifice, a Lamb of God. That would be the "seed of the woman" promised Eve. That would mean that, like innocent beasts were slain so coats could be made to cover Adam and Eve, Someone would die who would provide robes of righteousness for those who trust in Him.

So, with the Spirit helping, and believing the promise, the Scripture says, "Abraham believed God, and it was imputed unto him for righteousness" (Jas. 2:23). Now we can understand how the Bible says that "By faith Abraham. . . ." Ah, Abraham trusted in the coming Saviour, as we trust in the One who has already come.

But Abraham had a sorrow. God had promised him a son. Now he is seventy-five years old. The years go by and Sarah is never pregnant. Sarah thought that since she was barren, God might allow another wife to bear Abraham the promised seed, and through him eventually would come the Saviour. So she urged Abraham to take Hagar, her Egyptian maid, as a wife.

A son, Ishmael, was born through this union. But, no, they find Ishmael is not the promised one.

At long last, when Abraham was one hundred years old, and when Sarah was ninety, God visited Abraham. Abraham's tent was pitched close to the oak of Mamre. And as he sat in the shade, here came three men—no, not men— too grand for that. Two were angels and one was God in human form. God told Abraham now at long last his prayer was heard; Sarah would bear him a son within a year. Now the old man, made young and strong, was to become a father at last!

Abraham was a godly man. He believed God and it was counted to him for righteousness. Oh, may we, too, trust in the same Saviour. And Abraham was willing to make a great sacrifice to go into an unknown country, to live in tents instead of palaces, and to wait and pray until God gave the son Isaac whom He had promised.

Sarah the Princess,
Wife of Abraham

GENESIS 12-22

Yes, her name was first Sarai. But when God promised that through Sarah and Abraham should come the Messiah, God changed her name to Sarah, meaning princess. Abraham would be the father of many nations and Sarah a mother of multitudes.

Terah, Abraham's father, had more than one wife. When Abraham was ten years old there was born into the family from another wife a beautiful baby girl. Ah, she learned to follow Abraham everywhere. And when they were older, Abraham married Sarah his half-sister.

She must have been a beautiful woman. Abraham later told her she was so fair to look upon that he dared not announce that she was his wife lest one kill him to get her. When they went down into Egypt, the nobles marveled at the beauty of Sarah. They reported it to Pharaoh. Pharaoh sought her to be his wife but God delivered her. And later, when she was ninety years old and pregnant at last, her youthful beauty was so restored that Abimelech was captivated by her beauty and wanted her for his wife.

I suppose she had many lovely things at Ur of the Chaldees, for Abraham was rich. I can imagine the laces and silks, the jewels, the beautiful hanging curtains, the lovely furniture of a large home. But God has told Abraham to go to a far country, an unknown country. And there they were to live in tents. I can imagine that Sarah trembled a bit at the idea. What about my beautiful pots and pans? What about my silverware and my nice china? How will I keep my fine dresses and how will I look living in a tent and sleeping on pallets of goat's skin? But Sarah met that problem like many another Christian woman meets it when she plans to go to the foreign mission field. Oh, how she loved Abraham! She "obeyed, calling him lord." What Abraham wanted was law for Sarah. What Abraham believed Sarah believed, too. What Abraham was willing to give up, she was willing to give up also. So we never find a question that Sarah would raise against the will of God.

Oh, but if only she could have a son! Her godly, strong, wise husband—his heart was set on children. And God had promised children to Abraham. Yet the years went by and Sarah was still barren.

We must not criticise her if she began to wonder. Maybe God wanted to give Abraham a son by another wife. Oh, Abraham never looked toward another woman. No, he loved Sarah with all his heart. He never wanted anyone else.

One day we suppose Sarah said to Abraham, "What do you think about this lovely Egyptian girl Hagar you bought for me down in Egypt for a handmaid? Isn't she beautiful?"

"Oh, I suppose so. Yes, she looks good enough, I think, but I never thought about her looks much," answered Abraham.

"But, Abraham, since God has shut up my womb and will not let me bear the son you want, maybe God wants you to take Hagar as a wife. And I will give her to you for that if you wish. Remember, my lord, our father had more than one wife."

So, at the pleading of Sarah, Abraham took Hagar as his wife and Ishmael was born. Ishmael was to become the father of the Arab races.

"No, no," God said. No, the child of promise is to come from Sarah.

And one glad day when God and two angels came to visit with Abraham under the oak of Mamre, God promised that in the time of life, within a year, Sarah would bear him the promised son. Sarah, inside the large goatskin tent, heard it and laughed. Was it a giggle? To think of the preposterous thing that she, an old woman of ninety, long since past the child-bearing age, with flabby breasts and wrinkled face— would she laugh at that ridiculous idea? Maybe it was a laugh of faith.

And God said to Abraham, "Why did Sarah laugh?"

"Oh, I didn't laugh," Sarah denied. But she did. Probably she didn't know whether to laugh or cry. Could she believe

Sarai, so fair to look upon, that Abraham dare not announce that she was his wife, lest one kill him to get her.

it? Oh, she must believe it, for the Scripture says it was "through faith also Sara herself received strength to conceive."

Now a strange thing happened. Abraham, now one hundred years old, is suddenly vigorous and active like a strong man again. And after some scores of years, when Sarah has died, he will marry and have more children. And Sarah! The lines are gone out of her face. Her hair has the lustrous beauty it had before the gray crept in. Her body was made young again with functions of a young woman.

Now she conceived. Now she is beautiful like a young woman. Now kings will desire her.

In the fullness of time a child is born. What laughter, what happiness for them when they held their tiny newborn son in their arms! How beautiful he was! What shall we name him? Oh, name him Isaac, which means laughter. Now Sarah says that every woman who hears this will laugh with her at God's blessing (Gen. 21:6).

Lot, the Compromising Christian

GENESIS 13-19

We remember that when God told Abraham to "leave thy father's house and thy kindred," good old Abraham did not leave Lot behind. Lot was his nephew. Lot's father was dead, and Abraham felt he must look after the young fellow.

We know that Lot was a "righteous man" and we take it that he knew about Abraham's God and put his trust in the Saviour, so often pictured in Abraham's sacrifices, and so clearly promised to be Abraham's Seed.

But like many Christians today, Lot was not a strong Christian.

By Abraham's sponsorship and protection, Lot soon accumulated great flocks and herds and now there began to be a jealousy between the herdsmen of Abraham's cattle and of Lot's cattle. With so many, they would have to drive out a good ways from camp to find grass enough, and each herdsman would like to get the use of every little verdant valley. So they quarrelled. Abraham said, "I see our possessions are too many for us to dwell together. We are kinfolk. There must be no quarrelling." So Abraham said, "Lot, you choose the land you like. If you go to the right hand, I will go to the left. If you go to the left, I will go to the right." Good, generous Abraham; but Lot was money-minded. He saw the rich Jordan valley around the lower end of the Dead Sea. "My, the grass would be belly-deep to a steer! Why, I could sell beef and wool to those cities, Sodom, Gomorrah, Admah, Zeboiim and Zoar!" mused Lot.

So Lot chose the valley of Jordan and drew near those

cities. Ah, but those are wicked, wicked, idolatrous people. Yet for convenience and profit, Lot pitched his tent toward Sodom and then moved into Sodom.

Trouble came. Four strong kings, Amraphel, Arioch, Chedorlaomer and Tidal, came in a terrifying raid on Sodom. These cities had been tributaries, paying taxes to the great kings of the east, and probably they neglected to pay their taxes and insisted on their independence. So when the city of Sodom was sacked and its fine goods stolen away, these kings took Lot, rich Lot, and his family and servants and goods.

But Abraham heard of it and gathered his servants, 318, he had trained with bow and spear. With him all other Bedouins joined. Now on swift camels they followed the trail of the invaders. On north they went, nearly 200 miles, and there near Damascus these great kings and their victorious armies camped secure, they thought. But with avenging fury, Abraham and his servants and neighbors set upon the kings and killed them, seized the goods they had carried away, seized the kidnapped wives and children. And here was Lot and his family intact. So Abraham returned them to their city.

Abraham gave tithes to Melchizedek, refused to take any part of the spoil, and went back to his wilderness tents in peace.

But the wickedness, the idolatry, the lewdness of Sodom and the neighboring cities, Admah, Zeboiim, Zoar and Gomorrah, continued. When God, with two angels, came to visit with Abraham at Mamre, and they had eaten dinner of the calf that Abraham prepared, God had the two angels go before and he talked seriously with Abraham. This is when he had promised the son, Isaac, would be born next year.

But God told Abraham the angels kept reporting great wickedness in Sodom. He must destroy the city.

Abraham pleaded, "But Lot lives there. He is a righteous man. Would You destroy the righteous with the wicked?" And then with holy argument Abraham pleaded his case for his beloved but worldly nephew, Lot. "If there be only fifty righteous there, would You spare the city for fifty?" God said yes, He would.

Abraham did not have much faith that Lot would have won fifty people. If all his family, his children, his in-laws, his herdsmen and hired help were saved, that might have been fifty. But Lot wasn't much of a testimony. Lot wasn't much of a soul winner. And would God spare the city for only forty-five? Yes, He would.

So Abraham was bolder. "God, would You spare it for forty?" Yes, He would. "Would You spare it for thirty?" God agreed. Now Abraham, more boldly, insisted, "But, Lord, maybe there is only twenty—would You spare it for only twenty lives?" Yes. Oh, God was as anxious to spare it as Abraham was.

But now Abraham makes his last request. "Lord, if there is only ten [I suppose he meant Lot and his wife, his two single daughters and perhaps three married daughters and their husbands—that would be ten], would You spare it for ten lives?"

But, alas, the angels found not ten righteous, but only one. Lot had not won his wife, nor his single daughters, nor his married daughters and sons-in-law. So the angels came to Sodom and prepared to destroy it.

Lot met them. His hospitality insisted on their coming to his house. It may be that is why the Scripture says, "Be not forgetful to entertain strangers: for thereby some have entertained angels unawares" (Heb. 13:2), and these angels looked like men.

But, oh, the wickedness of Sodom! The men of the city lusted after these angels. Pounding on the door, they insisted that these angels be brought out for their sexual abuse.

Lot pleaded with them. Shamefully he tried to appease these wicked men and called them "brethren." He even offered to surrender to them his own virgin daughters! Now Lot's wicked neighbors pressed sore upon him and would seize upon him to abuse him. But the angels caught him, pulled him inside and closed the door, and struck with blindness these vicious sinners outside.

Now they must leave the city. Tomorrow morning the fire of God will fall to destroy it. Lot rushed to the homes of his sons-in-law, but to them he was only as one that mocked. Shameful that sinners ever feel that way about a Christian loved one!

The little procession started to leave the doomed city with the angels leading Lot, his wife and two daughters. "Hurry! We cannot do anything at all until we get you out of danger," said the angels. But Lot's wife had her heart set in Sodom. There were her married daughters. There were the ladies of her culture club, those with whom she chatted daily. Despite the clear warning of the angel of God, she lingered and looked back and became a pillar of salt!

Now Lot and his two daughters were hurried out and made their home in a Judaean cave. I am sad to tell you that these two daughters got their father drunk and had two sons who headed separately the tribes of Moab and Ammon by their incest with their father.

Poor Lot! What a warning against compromise and bad company! How sad to put money or property or jobs before a

godly environment. And we have the warning of God in the Scripture, "Remember Lot's wife." All who linger with love for the world and its ways and its people, as far as personal fellowship goes, is in great danger.

Isaac, the Son God Promised

The little boy Isaac started to grow up now, in a family that had grown richer and richer. Abraham owned many servants, men and women; he owned great flocks of cattle, sheep, goats, camels, donkeys. I suppose the tents of his group would make a small village. My, how Abraham and Sarah adored this lad for whom they had prayed thirty or forty years!

But there was one shadow on this happy scene. Hagar's son Ishmael was fourteen years older and he mocked and teased young Isaac. This was a grief of heart to Sarah. But God soon took Hagar and her son away.

Isaac was accustomed to the regular offerings his father made. He knew that God came and talked to his father Abraham, and God repeated the promise that one day the seed of Abraham would possess all this land of Canaan. We can imagine that being the favored son, loved and served and praised by all the leaders in the camp who were glad to honor him, Isaac might have become proud and snobbish.

But one day God said to Abraham, "Abraham, take now thy son, thine only son Isaac, whom thou lovest, and take a three days' journey down from Hebron up to Mount Moriah, and there on a place I will show you, you offer Isaac for a sacrifice." Consternation! What strange quirk in the plan of God is this? Abraham knew God had promised that through this son Isaac should come great nations. Is God forgetting His plan? No, if Isaac dies, God must raise him from the dead to keep His promise.

I do not think Abraham told Sarah about the plan. First, they must cut wood and load it on the donkey, for there must be a fire, and wood is a picture of the works of mankind, as we see in I Corinthians 3:12-15.

They take their journey toward that ridge Moriah which runs through the Old Jerusalem. At one end is the place where Solomon would later build his Temple. At the other is a great cut in the ridge leaving a mound shaped like a skull where the Lord Jesus would later be crucified.

I can imagine that as they went along, Isaac, the young teenager, may have picked wild flowers or thrown rocks at the rabbits. Did Isaac know that God had commanded Abraham to kill his own son? I doubt it. And I can imagine the first night when they camped Abraham raised his hand outside the goatskin pallet and let the sand trickle between his fingers. Oh, God had said, "My seed through Isaac should be as the sand of the sea." What will you do if Isaac dies? And perhaps the next night he looks at the starry skies and remembers again the promise. Then God must raise Isaac from the dead!

So they came to the hill Moriah. The servant and donkey are left down below. Abraham takes his son, the wood, a big package. Abraham takes some of the wood and ties it on the back of Isaac. He has, perhaps, a copper pot with coals kept burning. And they come at last to the hilltop. Abraham builds an altar of stone. There he explains to the boy, "Son, God told me to offer you as a sacrifice. You must give yourself to God for this day." I believe that startled yet believing young Isaac, who had great faith in Abraham and in Abraham's God, willingly allowed himself to be tied and placed on the altar, on the wood spread out. Then Abraham raises his knife. His hand trembles. The tears run down his face. With a groan of sorrow he prepares to plunge the knife into the breast of his son.

"Wait!" God said, "I know now that you love Me and that you will do what I say. Unbind the boy. Here is a sacrifice to take his place." And they found a ram caught by his horns in the brush and the ram was put on the altar instead of Isaac.

Oh, Isaac will never forget this! There must come One some-day who will take the sins of the world on His back and carry it up to Mount Calvary, just like Isaac carried the wood to this mount. Some innocent Sacrifice must substitute for all his poor sins. The Bible does not tell us that Isaac now believed in Christ and the coming Messiah and was saved. But I think surely he was saved.

Oh, the trip back home I am sure was much more speedy. What a great tale they had to tell Mamma!

How Isaac loved his mother. But when he was about thirty-six years old, Sarah died. Now his lonely heart began to think more and more that he ought to have a wife to love him, he ought to have a family of his own. But all about him were heathen women. And when he talked with his father,

Abraham builds an altar of stone. . .places Isaac on the altar. Abraham raises the knife. But God intervenes. A ram was put on the altar in the place of Isaac.

his father agreed they must make some plans for a godly wife for Isaac.

The years went on. Isaac became forty years old. Ah, he was not to marry one of these heathen girls in the land; he must marry a girl with a godly heritage. So Abraham sent Eliezer, an old trusted servant in charge of all his property, with ten camels, back the long trail to Padan-aram. There Abraham's people still lived. Abraham had been insistent, "You must not take my son Isaac back to that country. You must find the woman God has for him and bring her to be his bride."

And so old Eliezer departed. He took along fine jewels and garments; but how is he to find the right woman? As they drew near the city the camels were thirsty for water after the long desert trek. His own lips were parched with thirst. And so he prayed. Surely God can show him the right one or he must go back with the task unfinished. So he made a little plan in his prayer to God. He will say to some likely young woman, "Will you give me a drink?" And if she is the right one, then she must say, "Yes, and I will take a water pitcher down the steps, dip it in the water and bring it back to the trough again and again until all the camels are full." And Eliezer said, "Lord, if she be the right one, let it be so."

Well, here came tripping down to the well a beautiful young woman. And when Eliezer asked for a drink, she responded. She held her pitcher for him to drink and said, "I will draw water for all your camels also." Oh, that was the one!

Who is this beautiful girl? Her name is Rebekah. Her father is Abraham's nephew Bethuel. How gladly they received Eliezer into the home place. The camels are fed. The feast is prepared. "But first, I must tell you my errand," said Eliezer. And he told how God had blessed Abraham, how Isaac was the heir to his riches; what a handsome, sensible and godly man he was. Now, would Rebekah go back with him to marry Isaac? Eliezer had put jewels upon her hands, earrings upon her ears. There is much evidence that Isaac was well-to-do, that he was God's man. Would

Rebekah go? Yes, she agreed to go. And she took her hand-maid. They mounted the camels with Eliezer and the other servants and away they went to meet the bridegroom whom she loved but whom she had never seen.

God provides Rebekah for Isaac.

So Isaac had a bride. And he took her to his mother's tent, loved her, and she became his wife.

We know that in the matter of Abraham's offering Isaac as a sacrifice, Isaac was a type of the Lord Jesus Christ. And it is proper that God intended us to think of Isaac as a type of Christ and He is the Bridegroom and we poor sinners who learn to love and trust Him are His bride, for the Scripture says, "Husbands, love your wives, even as Christ also loved the church, and gave himself for it" (Eph. 5:25).

So, moved in heart toward this strange man she had never seen, she loved him and there sprang up in her heart a deep desire to know him, to be his wife, to join him forever.

So Eliezer here comes like a preacher or like the Holy Spirit, to plead with the sinner, and as Rebekah said, "Yes, I will go," so every reader ought to be glad to say, "Yes, Lord Jesus, I will take You as my Bridegroom, my Saviour, and live for You forever."

Jacob, the Precocious Twin

GENESIS 25-28

How happy Isaac was with his beautiful bride Rebekah! God had worked it out and they were meant for each other. But, alas, twenty years went by and they had no children. Rebekah grew sad and sometimes, when alone, she wept. Isaac took that very much to heart and he earnestly prayed that God would open Rebekah's womb and give a child.

Not one child, but twins were given to Rebekah. As the little ones moved and seemed to struggle in her womb, she wondered about it. There was a struggle between the two children, Jacob and Esau. God had chosen Jacob to head the family and through him to fulfill the promise to Abraham that the Saviour should come through this line and that Palestine was to be given to Abraham and his seed.

Esau was born first. I guess he was a little red-headed baby. His twin, Jacob, later someway knew that God was putting him to be the head of the race, to found the nation Israel.

When the babies were grown up, Esau was the favorite of his father. He was a hunter, an outdoorsman. He would kill a deer, perhaps, and bring in the meat and see that his old father had a good meal. But Jacob was the favorite of his mother. Someway she seemed to have been more spiritually-minded than old Isaac who was growing blind. And Jacob longed to have the birthright, that is, he longed to head the tribe and rear up a nation for God.

Of course the babies had heard their father Isaac and their

grandfather Abraham talk about those wonderful promises of God. But Jacob took them more seriously.

One day he had cooked a fine meal of "red pottage." Do you suppose it was like chili or meat stew with tomatoes that made it red?

After a happy day of hunting, walking for hours, Esau came in. Boy! was he hungry! So he asked if he could have some of that wonderful-smelling stuff that Jacob had prepared. Jacob bargained with him. "I will trade you some of this good-smelling stuff if you will give me the birthright." Esau, rather worldly-minded, we suppose, was more interested in food than the birthright; so he traded. Afterward he saw the great mistake he had made.

Now Isaac was old and the time of death drew near. So he said to Esau, "Go find some venison and cook it and make a delicious meal for me and I will give you the birthright blessing." In those days often the father in the home acted as the priest of God and was given prophetic powers.

Jacob, disguised as Esau, receives his father's blessing.

But Rebekah knew that God had chosen Jacob to be head of the nation Israel and yet fearing that God would fail to bring it about unless she helped Him, she suggested a scheme. She heard Isaac's instructions to Esau. And when Esau took bow and arrow and started out to hunt venison, Rebekah had Jacob kill a kid and she made a lovely meal for old Isaac. And so she instructed Jacob to pretend he was Esau. He went in before his old blind father. The father ate the lovely meal and then put his hands on Jacob and pronounced the blessing. Rebekah had put goat's skin over Jacob's arms so he felt like hairy Esau. And pretending to be Esau, he got the great blessing which God gave Isaac.

Of course Rebekah did wrong to deceive. She meant well, but no one ever has to do wrong to bring things out right. God would have done it well without her meddling.

When Esau came in with his venison and found his father already complacently satisfied and that Jacob had gotten the blessing intended for him, he was angry, very angry. He declared, "When my father dies, I will kill Jacob." Rebekah took to heart these threats.

She said to her old husband, "It would break my heart if Jacob should marry one of these heathen women. Let's send him back to my brother Laban in Padan-aram and let him find there a wife of our own people." So Jacob, fearing his brother and shamed because of his subterfuge, started out alone with a sack and a little food on the long way back to Padan-aram.

One night as he stopped to sleep on the ground, he had a wonderful dream. He saw a ladder reach from earth to Heaven and angels of God ascending and descending. Ah, the only ladder between earth and Heaven is the dear Lord Jesus Christ! Remember He said, "I am the way, the truth, and the life" (John 14:6). And here Jacob saw what all of us should learn with great delight, that the angels of God surround us and protect us. "The angel of the Lord encampeth round about them that fear Him, and delivereth them" (Ps. 34:7). Angels love us and look after us and go to Heaven to report and come back. And God made Himself known to

In a dream, Jacob sees a ladder reaching from earth to Heaven and angels ascending and descending.

Jacob there. He said, "I am the Lord God of Abraham thy father, and the God of Isaac"; and there God repeated the blessed promise that through Jacob would be fulfilled the promise of great nations and the Messiah and ownership eventually of the land of Canaan.

Jacob awoke and how glad he was, a poor, lonely young man running for his life, yet to know God was with him and had great plans for him. So Jacob set up a stone for an altar and said, "This shall be to me the house of God." And he promised that if God would bring him back to his father's house in peace and care for his needs, "Then shall the Lord be my God. . .and I will surely give the tenth unto Thee."

Jacob called the name of that place Beth-el, the house of God, and so it is called unto this day.

Working Seven Years for a Bride and Then Being Deceived

GENESIS 28-33

When Jacob, fearful of Esau, came back to Rebekah's country, he saw flocks of sheep in the fields and inquired of a man, Did the man know Laban the brother of Rebekah? Yes, he did. His sheep were in a flock yonder and were being tended by a beautiful girl, Rachel, younger daughter of Laban.

These other lazy shepherds felt they must wait until all the sheep were gathered and then together they could remove the stone cover from the well and could water the sheep. But vigorous young Jacob removed the cover and called for Rachel to bring her flock, and he watered them. Oh, how beautiful Rachel appeared to this hungry-hearted, lonely young man! He took Rachel in his arms and kissed her. It was love at first sight.

So Jacob came to live with Laban and kept Laban's flocks. He asked for the hand of Rachel. And Laban proposed that he should work seven years for Rachel. Oh, how he loved her! And the years went by, with labor and hope and dreams. And after seven years Jacob now had a right to claim his beautiful bride.

But what a surprise! After proper festivities, Jacob was led into the dark tent and behold, when morning came he found he had wedded Leah, the older sister with weak eyes. He complained at Laban's deception but it was arranged that after fulfilling her week he could marry Rachel and work seven years more. Jacob bargained for one wife and he got two. But eventually these jealous sisters, each anxious to produce more children than the other, gave their handmaids to Jacob as wives also. And from this family God gave twelve sons and a daughter.

The years went by. Scheming Laban changed Jacob's wages ten times, but always God was with Jacob, and after some years he had great flocks and herds of his own. Encouraged by his wives, he felt he must now go back to the land of his father Isaac.

They departed. When Laban pursued them, God warned him to do them no harm. So Laban made a covenant.

Jacob had his trouble. A daughter, Dinah, was seduced and led into sin by a young prince by the name of Shechem. The wild sons of Jacob, with burning hatred, schemed and murdered a whole town full of people. Jacob, with a sad heart, finds God calling him back to Beth-el. And there he went to worship God anew. But he feels he must go back to meet Esau in the country God had promised He would later

Jacob meets Rachel keeping her father's sheep.

give for a permanent possession. He hears shocking news. Esau is coming to meet him with four hundred armed men. Oh, that surely does not mean peace. He knows trouble is ahead. So Jacob selected great flocks of five hundred head of cattle, donkeys, sheep, goats and camels and sends them with his servants to meet Esau and offer this love gift, this gift of peace.

How the heart of Jacob was stirred, partly over the shame of his mistreatment of Esau, partly over the fear of Esau's vengeance. Yet he must have known that now he is God's anointed man and he must account to God. They had come to the brook Jabbok.

Jacob took all his household, the flocks and herds, across the little river and then went back to pray alone all the night. There came an angel of God. He wrestled with the angel and prayed, "Oh, for the blessing of God!" And the angel said, "Let me go, for the day breaketh." And Jacob answered back, "I will not let thee go, except thou bless me." And the angel touched the hollow of Jacob's thigh. For years he will limp on that leg. It is a sign of something wonderful. The angel said, "Thy name shall be called no more Jacob, but Israel [prince]: for as a prince hast thou power with God and with men."

Now gladly, happily, unafraid, Jacob went to meet Esau. They embraced with tears and the old-time boyhood love is restored. Jacob has become Israel, a prince of God.

Joseph, Ambitious, Inspired
and Hated

GENESIS 37-40

Of all the sons of Jacob it is easy to understand that the two he loved best are Joseph and Benjamin, both born of the beloved Rachel. When Rachel went down into the valley of the shadow she had hard labor in bringing forth Benjamin and died on the approach to Bethlehem and was buried there.

But those two sons, Joseph and Benjamin, were special. They seemed to have had more character and to have had more faith than the other sons. Old Jacob had a coat of many colors made for Joseph.

Joseph knew about those wonderful, wonderful promises. His father Jacob had earnestly sought and received the birthright to head the nation. Surely God would use him, too, with a ministry to lead His people.

Joseph dreamed that with his brothers they shocked wheat in the field and the shocks of all the other brothers bowed down to his. God was telling him some of His plans.

Again he dreamed and perhaps he ought not to have told his dream. He dreamed that the sun, moon and the eleven stars all bowed down to his star. Jacob was startled and a little vexed! He said, "Do you think your mother and I and your brothers will all bow down to you?"

And the other brothers, not so spiritual, not so anxious to please their father as was Joseph, hated him. Once the father said to Joseph, "Go see how the flocks and herds are doing

**Pharaoh's butler and baker tell
Joseph of their dreams.**

and bring me a report of how they prosper under the direction of your brothers." Away up at Dothan the older brothers
saw him coming and they said, "Let us kill this dreamer."
But Reuben intervened. After discussion, they decided to sell
him as a slave to an Ismeelite caravan going down to Egypt.
And so they did. But how will they explain to the father
Joseph's disappearance? They took that coat of many colors
and dipped it in the blood of a kid and took it to the father
who thought some wild beast had devoured his son.

But God was with Joseph. In Egypt he was sold to
Potiphar, captain of Pharaoh's guard. But how wise, how
obedient, how industrious, how thoughtful was Joseph. Why,
Potiphar soon found that he could run the whole affair,
direct the servants and handle the property, that God
blessed everything Joseph did.

Potiphar's wife fell in love with this handsome Hebrew
slave and tried to seduce him. Joseph was shocked. He could
not so dishonor his own principles and her husband Potiphar
who trusted him. But the evil woman seized his garment,
tore it from him and held it to show her husband and others.

She accused Joseph that he had attempted to force her. Angry Potiphar believed his wicked wife and so Joseph was put in prison. Poor Joseph—he is first a slave; he is hated by his brothers; he is out of touch with his father and his younger brother Benjamin; and despite his righteousness and vigor, now he is slandered and imprisoned. Ah, but God was with Joseph and made whatever he did to prosper. Strangely enough the warden of the prison was shocked to find that everything Joseph put his hand to, prospered. Soon he ran the whole prison. ". . .and whatsoever they did there, he was the doer of it."

One day two of Pharaoh's honored servants were put in prison. Pharaoh was angry with his butler and his baker.

Joseph came upon them one day and saw how glum and sad they were. Why? They explained that they had each had a dream. And Joseph, who even in prison had stayed so near the Lord, told them God would give them the meaning of the dream.

The butler had dreamed that he would bring three bunches of grapes for wine, press it out and present it to the king as before. And Joseph told them that in three days he would be restored to his position.

The baker had dreamed that there were three baskets of bakemeats on his head and the birds had devoured them out of the baskets. What did it mean? The three baskets were three days. In three days he would be hanged and the birds of the air would eat his flesh, Joseph told him. And so it came to pass. Ah, Joseph, who made sure God was with him in prison, God has greater things for you ahead. To the butler returning to his job, Joseph pleaded, "Remember me to Pharaoh. I have done no wrong. I am in prison under false charges." But the butler forgot all about Joseph. Two years went by before the mighty hand of God appeared again.

Joseph, From Slave, Prisoner, to Prime Minister of Egypt

GENESIS 41-50

Pharaoh was in a dither. What strange dreams these were that troubled him. His wise men could not explain them. In times past, often when there was no Bible, God sometimes revealed Himself in dreams. But troubled Pharaoh could not imagine what the dreams meant.

There was a great hubbub throughout the castle. It reached the ears of the butler. "Ah, I remember my fault now. I promised to remember Joseph and report his case and I did not." So he sent word to Pharaoh that "there is a man in prison in whom is the Spirit of God and he can explain your dreams even as he explained mine. I was returned to my position in three days as he said I would. And the baker was hanged in three days as his dream had indicated. It happened just as Joseph explained the dreams."

How eagerly Pharaoh sent for Joseph! He was allowed to bathe and shave before coming before Pharaoh. He explained, "It is not in me: God shall give Pharaoh an answer of peace."

Here were the dreams. First, there were seven fine full ears of corn (corn to them did not mean our American Indian corn, but wheat, rye or barley). These full ears of corn then were followed by seven scrawny, useless ears and they swallowed up the good ears of corn. What could it mean? What was God trying to tell Pharaoh, the one responsible for the welfare of millions of people? The other dream was this: Seven fine fat cattle came up out of the River Nile to feed in

Joseph presents his brothers
to Pharaoh.

a meadow. They were followed by seven weak, skinny cattle who swallowed up the fat cattle, and they were gone. What could it mean?

Joseph said, "God is revealing to you that there will be seven years of great plenty in Egypt. The land will bring forth by handsful. Then these seven years shall be followed by seven years of famine."

Joseph urged upon Pharaoh to appoint some man to gather up of the abundance in the first seven years of great plenty and store it that the people would not starve in the years of famine.

Pharaoh said, "But where shall I find such a man as this Joseph in whom is the Spirit of God, to put over this matter?"

So Joseph was made prime minister of Egypt. He had one of the king's chariots. He had total control of the economy.

Ah, Joseph's character, his custom of always being cheerful, of always being agreeable, of always trusting God, always trying to do right, has led him to be the most important minister in the greatest nation on the earth. The seven years of plenty go by. Great treasure cities are built to store the surplus. Now Joseph is in charge to see that the food supply is ·wisely used. All over Egypt the people must come to Joseph for their supplies.

But over in Palestine there is a famine, too. One day Jacob said to his older sons, "I hear there is food in Egypt. Take some money and some balm and nuts and honey as a gift to the prime minister and buy us grain that we may live and not die, and our families." Benjamin, the younger son, stayed at home. He was too precious for Jacob to allow too far away.

Now Joseph's brethren down in Egypt came before the august prime minister to buy food. We suppose some seventeen years have gone by. They would not expect their brother, a slave, to now be prime minister. They did not know Joseph, though he recognized them. Joseph spoke to them sternly: "Oh, yes, you are spies come to spy out the land because of the famine!" No, they protested vigorously, they were ten sons of one father. Another son was at home and another son "is not." They insisted they were true, good men. They had brought money to pay for the grain.

Joseph looked upon them with a stern face. He would keep Simeon in prison until they returned and if indeed they were true men, he said, they would bring their younger brother with them. They could buy no more grain in the famine unless they brought with them Benjamin!

The grain sacks of the nine men were filled and, depressed, they were on their way. When they camped at night they found strangely the money had all been returned in their sacks with the grain.

They returned to Palestine and their father. The old man was indignant at the idea that Benjamin must go with them on the next trip. At last the supplies ran low: they must have more grain. The older sons pleaded. Then Judah said, "The

Joseph's brothers bowing before him.

man did solemnly protest unto us, saying, Ye shall not see my face, except your brother be with you. If thou wilt send our brother with us, we will go down and buy thee food" (Gen. 43:3,4).

Again Jacob protested but Judah said, "I will be surety for him; of my hand shalt thou require him: if I bring him not unto thee, and set him before thee, then let me bear the blame for ever" (Gen. 43:9).

The only alternative is to starve or Benjamin must go with them to buy more food. So Jacob consented. How eager Joseph down in Egypt was to see his younger brother Benjamin. So feigning himself as an Egyptian who could not understand the Hebrew language, he spoke to his brothers by an interpreter. But he had all the eleven brothers at his house for dinner. Extra food, extra care was provided for Benjamin.

Again Joseph works his little plot, to bring his brothers to repentance. When the men go on their journey he has arranged his silver cup to be hidden in Benjamin's sack. And before they are far out of the city a man on a fast camel catches them. They are accused of stealing the silver cup. Every sack is opened and at last in Benjamin's sack is that fateful cup. Joseph's messenger pretends that it is the cup by which Joseph divines or sees the future. Sadly, the bedraggled, confounded group go back to face Joseph again. First, he tells them they should all be slaves. But then, apparently relenting, he said, "No," that he would keep only the younger scamp who had stolen the cup; the rest could go home.

Meantime these brethren had been remembering how they had sold Joseph into captivity years before. They have no idea this is Joseph, but they are remembering that sin. But Judah is more agitated. He pleads for a moment alone with this august prime minister. He explains that Jacob will die if he loses this last child of beloved Rachel, and Judah has promised to bear the blame forever or return the child. So he pleads, "Let me, I pray you, remain as a bondservant. I will give up my family and everything else if you will let Benjamin go and let me stay in his place. I cannot face my father without Benjamin."

Joseph is overcome with emotion and goes to a secret place to weep. Then he sends every Egyptian out of the room. He announces himself to his brothers, speaking for the first time in Hebrew. "I am your brother Joseph," he said. He then inquired after his father and the family. They must all go back and take with them wagons of provisions to bring the whole family down to Egypt to live!

So they depart. How glad Jacob was to see Benjamin back home! And when he saw the wagons, as last he believed what the older brothers told him: Joseph was alive. He would see beloved Joseph again. "And Joseph shall put his hand upon thine eyes" (Gen. 46:4).

Now they prepare for the migration to Egypt—seventy souls altogether. In Egypt they were introduced to Pharaoh.

Joseph was allowed to set apart land for them in Goshen where they might keep their herds. And there in Egypt Israel grew to be a great nation. In the fourth generation God will lead them out to Palestine and they are to carry Joseph's bones with them to bury in the Promised Land.

Joseph finds his path to the Egyptian court through the pit into which his brothers threw him.—Talmage.

Moses Was Pulled Out of the River to Save a Nation

EXODUS 2-14

"My! isn't he a beautiful, beautiful boy!" Jochebed said. She was a good woman, a daughter of Levi, and her husband was Amram of the tribe of Levi. Oh, they had been able to save the baby alive. A wicked Pharaoh, alarmed at the ever-growing number of the Jews, had made them slaves. He instructed the midwives that every Hebrew boy born must be put to death. But they pretended that the Hebrew women were so lively that they delivered their babies before the midwife could arrive.

But this baby was a goodly child. Fearfully Jochebed kept him hidden so Pharaoh's officers would not find him and kill him. She felt assured that God had great work for him to do. He must live!

Alas, she decided to commit the child to the Lord, to set him adrift in a little waterproof basket at the edge of the Nile and see what God would do.

Pharaoh's daughter came one day with her maids to bathe in the river. She heard the cry of a child. Her feminine heart was touched. "Oh," she said, "he is one of the Hebrew babies." And she had him drawn out of the river and she decided, "I will keep him for my very own baby." And she called him Moses, because he was drawn out of the river.

Moses' older sister, Miriam, had stood by anxiously to watch what would become of her baby brother. Oh, the princess will keep the baby! Now is her chance. So she came forth and said, "Shall I bring a Hebrew woman to nurse the baby for you?" So Moses' own mother was brought to nurse him, though he grew up in the palace as the son of Pharaoh's daughter.

Ah, Moses was trained in all the arts and learning of the Egyptians. But meantime, that godly mother had stored in his heart words about the true God and how He had promised to deliver Israel, and through Israel would come the Messiah, the promised "Seed of the woman."

Now Moses came to be forty years of age. He saw his own blood kin, the Hebrews, abused by the taskmasters who drove them with whips and had them build the treasure cities, and perhaps some pyramids, for Pharaoh. Once he saw an Egyptian mistreating a Hebrew and he killed the Egyptian and hid him in the sand. He had made his decision. "Choosing rather to suffer affliction with the people of God, than to enjoy the pleasures of sin for a season" (Heb. 11:25). By faith Moses planned his life. He gave up luxury, perhaps a chance at the throne, in order to serve his people and honor God. And the Scripture tells us it was by faith, for he knew God had great plans for Israel and would keep His promises.

Soon it was known that Moses had killed an Egyptian. Pharaoh wanted him hunted down and killed. Moses fled to

Pharaoh's daughter discovers Baby Moses.

the backside of the desert. There he came to live and work with a priest of Midian. He married the priest's daughter; and forty long years he waited.

Oh, that God would open a way for him to deliver His people, Israel!

One day in the desert he saw a strange sight. It was a burning bush. There was no prairie fire. And as the bush burned and burned, he saw it was not consumed. He drew near and, lo, the voice of God spoke. "Draw not nigh hither: put off thy shoes from off thy feet, for the place whereon thou standest is holy ground." There God called Moses to go and deliver His people.

But now Moses was eighty years old. He claimed to be slow of speech. How could he deliver Israel? And how could he contend with all the armies and wealth of the Pharaohs? "What is that in thine hand?" God asked. And Moses replied that it was a staff. God had him throw it down and it became a serpent, and when he took it in his hand again by the tail, it was a staff!

He had Moses put his hand within his bosom and it came out leprous, as white as snow. When it was returned again to his bosom, the skin was as clear as a baby's. "Show that to My people," God said. God warned Moses that it would not be easy, that Pharaoh would harden his heart. It would take great plagues and wonders, but God would be with him. And Aaron, his brother, was now coming to meet him.

What a bold thing it was (and foolish it seemed) to come to demand of Pharaoh: "God said, Let My people go." When Moses showed the sign of his rod miraculously becoming a snake, so Pharaoh's false prophets did also. Pharaoh commanded heavy burdens be put upon the Hebrews. They must make bricks without straw. And God heard the groanings of the people. They were discouraged. But God brought plague after plague on the Egyptians. First, the water of the Nile was turned to blood; people must dig wells to find drinking water. Then a great plague of frogs filled the land—frogs in the bedroom, frogs underfoot, frogs in the bread trays. Pharaoh pleaded and Moses called on the Lord to remove the

Moses sees a fiery bush,
which does not burn away.

frogs and He did. But still Pharaoh would not let the people go.

Then there was the plague of flies. Then a plague of lice on man and beast. Then a plague of great hail that stripped man of his crops and tore loose the branches from the trees. A murrain came among the cattle and many died. But Pharaoh hardened his heart.

Pharaoh said, "They might worship God in the land." "No," Moses insisted; "we must go a three days' journey." After other plagues, then Pharaoh said, "All right, all right. The land is being destroyed. You can go, but leave the women and children." But they would not do it. And Pharaoh compromised and said, "You can go, but leave your cattle here." Ah, but Moses said, "Not a hoof shall be left behind." Ah, God's people ought to make sure that Satan does not get one of ours.

Then there came the plague of midnight darkness. Finally Pharaoh indignantly said to Moses, "You shall see my face no more." Then God pronounced the great passover. Those who believed Moses were to kill a male lamb of the first year and roast it with fire. They were to put the blood on the doorpost and on the lintel above the door. And the death angel that night would pass over Egypt and in every home with no blood on the door, the firstborn son would die.

What catastrophe! What a mourning! From the lowest peasant hut to Pharaoh's palace the firstborn sons died. God had told the Israelites to ask help of sympathetic Egyptians. And they were given gold and gems and clothes and food.

Now they gathered to go to Canaan, the land of promise. We can imagine it was not a well-organized procession as they went toward the east. They came soon to the Red Sea. Perplexed, they waited. Which way could they go? Meantime Pharaoh's nobles said, "Why do you let all these workers, these slaves, go?" And Pharaoh's army, with chariots and horsemen, pursued after the Israelites. But God told Moses to stretch out his rod over the Red Sea and suddenly the water stood up in a wall on each side, opening a way right through the sea. God had a pillar of cloud over them with light in the night, and it came behind them to separate them and protect them from Pharaoh's army. Then they marched on dry ground through the Red Sea.

God afflicted Pharaoh's pursuing army. Wheels came off the chariots. They were hindered by that formidable cloud of darkness before them. And God had Moses to lift up his rod and the sea came tumultuously together again. And Pharaoh's army was destroyed.

We think the last meal in Egypt was the passover lamb. The lamb must be a male lamb of the first year, in prime condition, with no blemish, for it represented the coming Saviour, the Lamb of God who would take away the sin of the world. It must be roasted with fire and no water because there is no alleviation to the suffering of the damned, which suffering Jesus bore for all who trust in Him. The lamb was to be eaten with bitter herbs, picturing the sorrow and pain of Jesus. And that was to be one meal only. Any remains must be burned, for salvation is a one-time event. When Christ died on the cross, He said, "It is finished." One who puts his trust in Christ, then and there, is saved forever.

Oh, there are continuing duties and joy and particularly continual renewing and feeding on Christ.

And so that night of the passover the Jews began a week's feast of unleavened bread, picturing Christ, the Bread of Life, the sustenance and the very life of a Christian day by day.

Now we find Israel across the Red Sea headed for Abraham's land of promise.

Moses was noted for his humility. Right there he fell. He got angry instead of being humble, and fell through lack of humility.
D. L. Moody

Daily Care for Millions
for Forty Years

Can you imagine that great host coming out of Egypt, crossing the Red Sea and now starting out through desert and semi-desert country? There were some 600,000 men of warrior age and we suppose the women and children added would make some 3½ million people.

Mainly they walked, no doubt, and they took their flocks and herds along with them. We suppose some household goods and treasures were hauled in wagons and carts, for later nobles will provide twenty-four wagons to carry the portable Tabernacle and furniture.

They had been wonderfully delivered at the Red Sea which was miraculously opened for them. The Egyptian armies are drowned behind them, but what will this whole nation do for food and water and clothing, traveling through this desert land for months and years?

But God, who commanded them to come, and has brought them safely thus far, will provide for them. First of all, without wheat fields or granaries or grocery stores, God will provide bread from Heaven.

I can imagine what concern, what sense of responsibility, every father would have for his family. But, lo, they woke one morning to find spread everywhere manna from Heaven. It was in small particles like hoar frost. It tasted like wafers made with honey. It was called "angels' food." And the marvel is that God had it all measured out in Heaven before it fell. And when every man gathered what he could and measured it out, there was one omar per day for every man, woman and child.

They were not to save it up for it would spoil and stink. God intended them to trust Him for the next day's food. So we are taught by our Father to pray, "Our Father. . .Give us this day our daily bread," and be free to come tomorrow to pray the same prayer. But since Jews were given a Sabbath to observe on Saturday, God used it mainly to emphasize that, so on Friday two days' food was gathered in the morning and they would eat on the Sabbath day without gathering and the food was perfectly preserved the second day.

What marvel was God's care, that He should feed this multitude every day! God never forgot. His supply never ran low. We are reminded how Paul wrote the brethren in Philippi, "But my God shall supply all your need according to His riches in glory by Christ Jesus."

I do not wonder that God told them to carry a special vessel of this holy food and to put it up in the Ark of the Covenant they would later build, and save it as a miraculous testimony for the future.

It is true that we thus ought to be reminded how wonderfully consistent and faithful God is in caring for His own. So David could say, "I have not seen the righteous forsaken, nor his seed begging bread."

But a greater message is here. That manna pictured Christ, the Bread from Heaven. That is what Jesus told the people, "I am that bread. . . ." For seven days, beginning with the passover supper, the Hebrews should eat bread unleavened. And so we are daily sustained by the sinless Christ. Christ pictures both the passover lamb purchasing salvation (cf. I Cor. 5:6-8) and the unleavened bread picturing Christ our daily Bread and Sustenance.

I wonder how many of that great multitude saw what God was picturing to them every day. The Lord Jesus Christ can be yours simply for the taking and once you have Him as Saviour in your heart, you may happily, safely, feed on His provision and supply every day.

But this nation who were only slaves a few days ago, must

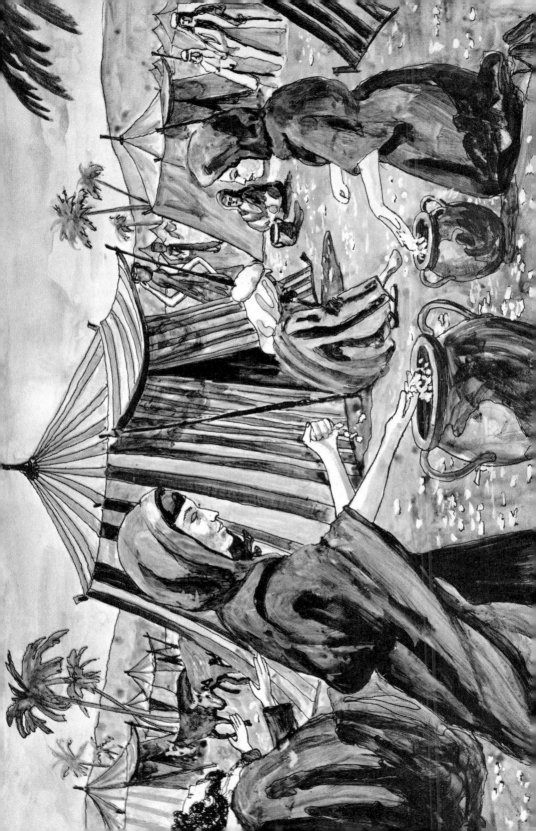

have guidance. There are among them no men who know all this country, none wise enough to select the route and show them where they may safely go and how to go. Oh, but God who led them out of Egypt, will now lead them all these years until they safely enter Canaan. So above the camp in the daytime there is a cloud, and in that cloud the Shekinah Glory, the very Presence of God. And when night comes on, that cloud becomes a pillar of fire—God overseeing His people. And they were instructed that when the cloud moved out they were to quickly assemble their ranks and follow. They need not fret about which way to go and where to camp. When the cloud stopped, they stopped under that cloud and made their camp. And in the night the Presence of God safely guarded them in the pillar of fire.

Once we find that sin and rebellion so grieved God that He had Moses move the tent of meeting outside the camp. And after they had built a golden calf and danced drunkenly around it in idolatry, God had told Moses, "You lead the people to Canaan. They are yours. I will send an angel along but I will not go further." Oh, how the people mourned! And at the pleading of Moses, God restored the leadership of the cloud and fire, and He Himself went with them in it.

So we may sometimes grieve God and may lose the intimate leadership and fellowship of the Holy Spirit. But with confession and earnest seeking, we may have God's leading and conscious fellowship again.

But it was largely desert country through which they traveled. We know that the Sinai Peninsula, the Gaza Strip, the Beer-Sheba country—all that has little water. And when the people came to Meribah, they complained and quarreled and protested: Had Moses brought them out of Egypt to starve them and let their wives and children die without water? Moses appealed to the Lord and he was instructed, "Take the rod of God in thine hand and stand before that great rocky cliff and smite it." Moses did so and out gushed a mighty river of water—enough for 3½ million Hebrews and their flocks and herds.

There are so many pictures of Christ throughout the Old

God fed a multitude every day.
His supply never ran low.

Testament and New. Here He is pictured in two ways. First, He is the Rock, our Safety, our Protection, our Fortress. And we are told, ". . .they drank of that spiritual Rock that followed them: and that Rock was Christ." But, second, Christ is the Water of Life. Water may picture Jesus or picture the Holy Spirit for all three Persons of the Godhead work together saving a soul. So to the woman of Samaria in John 4, Jesus promised that if she only knew who He was, she would ask Him and He would give her an artesian well of everlasting water so that spiritually she need never thirst. So that water pictured salvation through Christ. And it pictures the indwelling and work of the Holy Spirit.

But if that water flowing out from the rock smitten by the rod of Moses, pictures salvation, then it pictures that our salvation can only come when Christ is smitten for us, when Christ suffers for the ungodly, when Christ takes our stripes and our sickness and our sin. The smiting of the rock pictures the crucifixion of the Saviour.

Moses surely knew that, but he must have been so vexed that he forgot it. For again this great host, wandering in the wilderness until they could be fit to go into the land of promise, came to this desert place and again, in the burning heat and dust, they thirsted. Again they complained to Moses, and Moses angrily said to them, "You rebels! Shall I bring you water out of this rock?" and he turned and beat upon the great rock, and again the water came forth. But Moses had dishonored God and had missed the point because Christ is crucified only once and by one sacrifice He had purchased eternal redemption for all who trust in Him. Oh, Jesus need never be crucified again. ". . .there remaineth no more sacrifice for sins" (Heb. 10:26). God gave the water in sympathy for the thirsty people, but Moses had grieved God and lost his ticket to the Holy Land.

One other ever-recurring miracle followed these people through forty years. There were no dry-goods stores in the wilderness. I suppose there was little chance to weave their wool and linen and perhaps their own garments. So God miraculously preserved their garments and "their clothes waxed not old" (Neh. 9:21) through the years. We remember the Lord Jesus Christ told us, "Consider the lilies of the field, how they grow; they toil not, neither do they spin: And yet I say unto you, That even Solomon in all his glory was not arrayed like one of these. Wherefore, if God so clothe the grass of the field, which to day is, and to morrow is cast into the oven, shall He not much more clothe you, O ye of little faith?" (Matt. 6:28-30). Amazing forty years of miracles! daily miracles! As definite creative miracles as when God created the heavens and the earth! Oh, what a teaching for Christians. We, too, can have daily guidance, daily food and drink, daily provision of clothes and houses. We can have whatever we need as we rest in the Lord and serve Him.

The Thirsty Nation Israel Gets
Water From the Rock at Meribah

EXODUS 17

After the children of Israel had come out of Egypt, after they had received the tables of the Law at Mount Sinai, and after they had begun to be fed daily on manna from Heaven, they began to be greatly troubled for lack of water in the wilderness at Meribah.

"And the people thirsted there for water; and the people murmured against Moses, and said, Wherefore is this that thou hast brought us up out of Egypt, to kill us and our children and our cattle with thirst? And Moses cried unto the Lord, saying, What shall I do unto this people? they be almost ready to stone me."—Exod. 17:3,4.

Then the Lord told Moses he should go out before the assembled people, taking with him elders of Israel and that same rod he had had in the wilderness, the same rod that became a serpent when he had thrown it down before Pharaoh, that same rod that opened the Red Sea to let them through when he had held it over it, then how with God's power on that rod, he held it out and the sea closed to destroy Pharaoh's army. God told him to take that rod and smite that wall of stone or rock at Horeb. When Moses did, miracle of miracles happened. The rock opened and a river of water gushed forth, enough to water all the nation Israel (3½ million people) and their cattle!

We know the manna from Heaven pictured Christ, the Bread from Heaven. And that rock pictured Christ, too. The passover lamb pictured Christ, for we are told, "For even Christ our passover is sacrificed for us" (I Cor. 5:7).

Now, when Moses smote that rock, it pictured Christ smitten for our sins, the One who bore our sins, for the Scripture says:

"Surely He hath borne our griefs, and carried our sorrows: yet we did esteem Him stricken, smitten of God, and afflicted. But He was wounded for our transgressions, He was bruised for our iniquities: the chastisement of our peace was upon Him; and with His stripes we are healed. All we like sheep have gone astray; we have turned every one to his own way; and the Lord hath laid on Him the iniquity of us all."—Isa. 53:4-6.

And we read in I Corinthians 10:4, "That spiritual Rock that followed them. . .was Christ."

Out of that great rock there poured out a flood of water. That water pictures the Holy Spirit of God who convicts and regenerates every sinner and makes him a child of God. And then the same Spirit lives within the newborn Christian. When Jesus died and when the soldier thrust his spear into His side, there came out blood and water. The blood was atonement for man's sins; the water was a symbol of the blessed Holy Spirit who comes to every person who puts his trust in Jesus.

What a wonderful lesson to believing Jews when Moses smote the rock and the waters gushed forth.

But a long period, perhaps ten years, go by. The spies have gone into Israel and made their report. But the people have rejected that report and turned back. Now God has promised them they will wander in the wilderness forty years. Again, they come to this Meribah. Again they are thirsty. And again God tells Moses that he is to speak to the rock.

When Jesus died once on the cross, that paid the whole debt of sin. Jesus need not die again. He need not any more pay for the price of sin's redemption. Now anybody who wants salvation has only to look to Jesus, call upon Him for mercy. Romans 10:13 says, "For whosoever shall call upon the name of the Lord shall be saved." So Moses was only to speak to the rock this time and again the water would gush forth to quench the thirst of the multitudes.

But I think Moses was vexed with the people, so vexed and concerned that they had not learned the lesson before. So Moses now, instead of speaking to the rock, smote it again with his rod. Again God let water rush out, but He said to Moses, "You have dishonored Me. You have not kept the picture clear. Christ does not need to be smitten again." So because Moses had thus failed to honor God and had spoiled the type God wanted to show the people about salvation, He told Moses that he could not go into the land of Canaan but would die outside.

Later we find that the children of Israel come to the mountains of Moab, over across the Jordan. They are getting ready to go into the land of Canaan, but God told Moses he must go into the mountain and die there. God gave Moses the privilege of looking from Mount Nebo over across the Jordan Valley to see, in some wonderful way, the whole land of Canaan, but he could not enter it. Then the angels of God buried Moses and no man has ever known where his grave is.

Later, at the transfiguration of Jesus, Moses and Elijah will meet Jesus on the Mount of Transfiguration, but now Moses will not tread in that holy land because he has failed to honor God in smiting the rock the second time instead of speaking to it.

Let us not miss the wonderful message that Jesus Christ has been smitten for us and that now He says, "If any man thirst, let him come unto Me, and drink" (John 7:37). The Holy Spirit, representing Christ, now is to change the heart of every poor sinner who trusts in Him for salvation and then to live in his body and be the Comforter, the Guide, the Representative of the Lord Jesus.

Thank God, Christ was smitten for us, and now everyone may have the Water of Life freely.

Laws for God's Nation Israel

Moral standards of righteousness are in some subtle way planted in the hearts of people everywhere. But people need definite codes of law, fairly interpreted and enforced by human authorities. Since God has set Israel apart to be a nation of His own, now He must give them His laws. Word was sent throughout the great camp that the people were to wash their clothes, they should lay aside all uncleanliness. "Come not at your wives," God said, "and take great care not to go upon the slopes of Mount Sinai." For God today will speak to His people and give them a summary of His laws. How startled, how awed, yes, and how troubled were the people when God Himself spoke aloud to them from Heaven.

"And God spake all these words, saying, I am the Lord thy God, which have brought thee out of the land of Egypt, out of the house of bondage. Thou shalt have no other gods before Me. Thou shalt not make unto thee any graven image, or any likeness of any thing that is in heaven above, or that is in the earth beneath, or that is in the water under the earth. Thou shalt not bow down thyself to them, nor serve them: for I the Lord thy God am a jealous God, visiting the iniquity of the fathers upon the children unto the third and fourth generation of them that hate Me; And shewing mercy unto thousands of them that love Me, and keep My commandments. Thou shalt not take the name of the Lord thy God in vain; for the Lord will not hold him guiltless that taketh His name in vain. Remember the sabbath day, to keep it holy. Six days shalt thou labour, and do

Every nation must have laws. Moses was in a cloud 40 days and nights, and during that wonderful time God gave him the laws by which the children of Israel were to order their lives—the Ten Commandments.

all thy work: But the seventh day is the sabbath of the Lord thy God: in it thou shalt not do any work, thou, nor thy son, nor thy daughter, thy manservant, nor thy maidservant, nor thy cattle, nor thy stranger that is within thy gates: For in six days the Lord made heaven and earth, the sea, and all that in them is, and rested the seventh day: wherefore the Lord blessed the sabbath day, and hallowed it. Honour thy father and thy mother: that thy days may be long upon the land which the Lord thy God giveth thee. Thou shalt not kill. Thou shalt not commit adultery. Thou shalt not steal. Thou shalt not bear false witness against thy neighbour. Thou shalt not covet thy neighbour's house, nor his manservant, nor his maidservant, nor his ox, nor his ass, nor any thing that is thy neighbour's."—Exod. 20:1-17.

These words were addressed particularly to Israel. They are inspired. They are the Word of God, but in this case, particularly, it applies to Israel. Here are summed up not only moral laws, but in some sense ceremonial laws also. When the Bible speaks of the law of Moses, it may refer to the first five books in the Bible. But God sums up a particular outline of laws to be easily memorized and to be earnestly followed.

We look through these commandments and we find the first four commandments express man's duty to God. No other gods, no idols, no taking God's name in vain, and the Sabbath day. The last six commandments guide our relationship to other people: obedience to parents, no murder, no adultery, no stealing, no false witness, no covetousness.

We go through these carefully and we find that nine of these Ten Commandments are carefully repeated in the New Testament. So even now in New Testament times idol gods and idol worship and profane language are sin. Now obedience to parents is still the great commandment with promise, and it is still a sin to murder, to commit adultery, to steal, to bear false witness, to covet. And we are greatly impressed and proud when we see that these Ten Commandments form the basis of all laws in civilized countries.

Why the Sabbath command here, which is not repeated in the New Testament? We are told that the Sabbath was first made known here near Mount Sinai (Neh. 9:13, 14). We are told that the Sabbath was a special command and covenant with Israel, not for others (Neh. 9:14; Exod. 31:13). And Colossians 2:17 reminds us that by the Sabbath command we are not to be judged because it is a shadow or spiritual type referring to Christ. Then why should God put the Sabbath in this list when He especially addresses Israel?

Note again that command. "Six days shalt thou labour, and do all thy work: But the seventh day is the sabbath of the Lord thy God: in it thou shalt not do any work. . . ."

Seven in the Bible pictures God's perfection, so we have seven days in a week. And in nature God uses multiples of sevens in certain life processes. Some bird eggs hatch in two weeks, chicken eggs hatch in three weeks, turkeys, I think, and some other large fowl, have their eggs hatched in four weeks. A woman's menstrual cycle is ordinarily twenty-eight days, four times seven. What does God mean by this seven days here? Six days evidently picture man's life and all his works and good deeds, keeping God's commands. And one who thus does all the work of God perfectly earns Heaven. Here is a plan of salvation by keeping the law, by doing God's commands.

Oh, sadly, we must admit there is nothing wrong with the law, only man has already sinned, has already failed. We are reminded in Romans 10:5, "For Moses describeth the righteousness which is of the law, That the man which doeth those things shall live by them." That is, one should have everlasting life if he perfectly kept the law of God. Alas, no one ever kept these commandments. But here in the midst of the Ten Commandments God puts down the perfect standard. Man who never sins would never need forgiveness. One who was born right and perfect the first time would not need to be born again. One who is not a sinner would not need a Saviour.

So this offer of a heavenly rest to follow a life of perfect service cannot give salvation to anybody. It only shows us as sinful failures. And so "the law was our schoolmaster to bring us unto Christ."

This implied promise of a heavenly Sabbath can only bring me to a sense of my utter need of a Saviour for sinful men who have not kept God's law.

God has a picture of that heavenly Sabbath or rest, too, in the passover supper and the feast of unleavened bread. There the first day of the feast, a high day, the day of solemn assembly, no work was done (Exod. 12). So one who spiritually takes of the passover, Christ our Passover, has claims to Heaven in his heart; has his sins forgiven. And as the six days of man's life proceed, feasting on Christ the Unleavened Bread, again there is the heavenly Sabbath waiting.

Must Christians keep these laws of God? Well, we are still human. When one by the new birth receives a new nature, he finds that he still has the old nature. Still the "flesh lusteth against the Spirit, and the Spirit against the flesh" (Gal. 5:17). Still, like Paul, he will find that "with the mind I myself serve the law of God; but with the flesh the law of sin" (Rom. 7:25).

But a wonderful truth is here for us. God put this in our hearts to love His righteousness and that righteousness is not only imputed to us but imparted in us. So we have the Holy Spirit within to guide and help us "that the righteousness of the law might be fulfilled in us, who walk not after the flesh, but after the Spirit" (Rom. 8:4).

The Jewish people in Paul's day "had a zeal of God, but not according to knowledge. For they being ignorant of God's righteousness, and going about to establish their own righteousness, have not submitted themselves unto the righteousness of God" (Rom. 10:2,3). Paul said, "For Christ is the end of the law for righteousness to every one that believeth" (vs. 4).

Disaster—the Broken Law

After God had spoken from Mount Sinai in awesome tones giving the Ten Commandments, He told Moses to go up into the mountain. Moses must get detailed instructions about the law, the Tabernacle, the offerings. Moses took Joshua, his assistant, with him, and they climbed up that mountain where no one else was allowed to go. Moses received two stone tablets on which God had written the Commandments with His own finger. Oh, those holy days when God talked to Moses face to face!

Down in the camp below the people of Israel waited. What had become of Moses? Remember, they had been a race of slaves. Remember, too, they were used to the idolatry, the Baal worship in Egypt. How often people have an outward form of religion without knowing God personally and without serving Him from a true, loving heart!

The days went by. The people were restive. Some came to Aaron, Moses' brother, high priest in the camp, and said, "Moses is gone. We need some gods to lead us." I suppose they thought God could not help them without Moses and they did not know what had become of Moses.

So Aaron said, "Bring me your earrings, your extra gold." And out of that Aaron made a molten calf or bull and they said, "These be thy gods, O Israel, which brought thee out of the land of Egypt." What blasphemy! Strange that even Aaron was that weak. Here the carnal-minded people have an outward form of religion so they can have ceremonies without heart-moving. So the people drank and then they

Angered at the sight of the Golden Calf, Moses throws down the stone tablets.

danced around the golden calf. Some of them were naked. Oh, what has happened to Israel, the people to whom God has promised the coming Messiah!

Upon Mount Sinai Moses and Joshua started to return to the camp below. Forty days had gone by. Moses carried the two tables of stone on which the commandments were written with the finger of God.

But hark! There is a hubbub, a murmur, a roar. Is it laughter and roistering, or is it war? Joshua said, "There is a sound of war in the camp." "No," Moses said, "it is a sound of shouting and laughter and drunken excess." They drew near and saw the disgraceful scene—drunkenness, idolatry— all of God's laws are broken. Suddenly Moses, in holy indignation, cast the tables of stone down and they are broken.

God said, "Moses, leave this people alone that I may kill them in a moment." But Moses pleaded with God. God said, "But I would make of you and your family the nation I have promised. But let Me blot out this people from all My plans for Israel."

Moses was broken up. He said, "If You blot out this people, blot me out, too." Moses cried, "Lord, if Thou wilt forgive their sin—. . . ." And there is a dash in the Bible (while Moses sobbed, I think). So God agreed to spare the nation. But the open sinners would be brought to judgment.

Moses stood alone and cried out, "Who is on the Lord's side? Let him come unto me." The sons of Levi gathered around him and Moses sent them out with swords to slay the most wicked sinners. Many fell by the wrath of God that day. Moses rebuked Aaron and had that golden calf ground to powder. He strewed that powder on the drinking water and made the Israelites drink it. Then Moses pleaded with God to lead the people still.

First He said, "I will send an angel before thee." But Moses said, "I don't know the name of the angel. If Thy presence go not with me, carry us not up hence." Oh, that is what God wanted anyway; and God agreed. "My presence shall go with thee."

Now Moses will need to go back up on Mount Sinai for

another forty days of fasting, neither eating nor drinking, as at the first. And God will write again the Ten Commandments on the stones. Oh, God's commandments are not done away with because somebody broke them. A forgiving God gives people again and again the chance to start over and do right.

How the Tabernacle in the Wilderness and Its Furniture Pictured Jesus

EXODUS 35-40

When Peter preached to Cornelius in Acts 10 about Jesus, he said, "To him give all the prophets witness, that through his name whosoever believeth in him shall receive remission of sins" (Acts 10:43). Ah, that is one double theme throughout all the Bible. It is Jesus and salvation by faith. So we must not read carelessly in the Old Testament. Christ is there on nearly every page, if we look for Him. And in I Corinthians 10:11 we read, "Now all these things happened unto them for ensamples: and they are written for our admonition, upon whom the ends of the world are come." So a great deal of attention is given in the Pentateuch to the Tabernacle which God had the Hebrews set up for their worship and sacrifices. And all these pictured Jesus.

Now remember that a curtain or fence is set about the Tabernacle and an opening was only at one end. There is only one place to enter and one series of lessons that come in order.

First, there is the great burnt altar where animals are sacrificed. Their blood was poured out. Their flesh was burned. That altar was made of wood overlaid with brass so the altar would not burn up. On it every day was the continual burnt offering, and the fire was never to go out. On that altar they sacrificed the bodies of oxen, sheep, goats, turtledoves and pigeons. All the animals that were used for sacrifices were called clean animals, and we suppose each one had some meaning of its own. But every one pictured Christ. The oxen or bullock pictured Christ the burden-bearing Saviour. The sheep might picture the meek and innocent suffering for the guilty. The mourning turtledoves might picture the sorrow and broken heart of Christ for sinners. But remember, every sacrifice pictured Jesus. The passover lamb once a year for every family was sacrificed to picture Jesus. "Christ our passover is sacrificed for us" (I Cor. 5:7).

Now let us see this. No one has a right to the rest of the places and services in this little compound except he go first by the brass altar of sacrifice. You remember Jesus had said, "I am the way, the truth, and the life: no man cometh unto the Father, but by Me" (John 14:6). The Gospel starts with the crucifixion of Jesus for sinners.

Next, we come to a great basin called a sea which is literally a big tank of water, that those who come to the Tabernacle may wash their feet and hands. We remember the night before Jesus died He girded Himself with a towel and washed the disciples' feet. Peter protested, "Thou shalt never wash my feet." He felt unworthy to have his dirty feet washed by the sinless Saviour, the Creator, God in human form. But Jesus reminded him that all the disciples were clean except Judas, as far as salvation was concerned, but that we walk in a dirty world, so we need daily cleansing. We need to remember that simple part of the Lord's Prayer, "And forgive us our sins; for we also forgive every one that is indebted to us" (Luke 11:4).

Christian, have you been to the great brass altar? Has the sacrifice of Jesus on the cross settled your sin debt forever? Then praise the Lord! But you still need to come to the laver for daily cleansing.

We go now into the Tabernacle. There are two rooms—the Holy Place and the Most Holy Place. We find the Tabernacle covering strangely in three layers. First, above is the pure white linen picturing the unsullied righteousness of Jesus. Then above that is a layer of rams' skin died red. Oh, the Saviour has been crucified. We must never forget the blood.

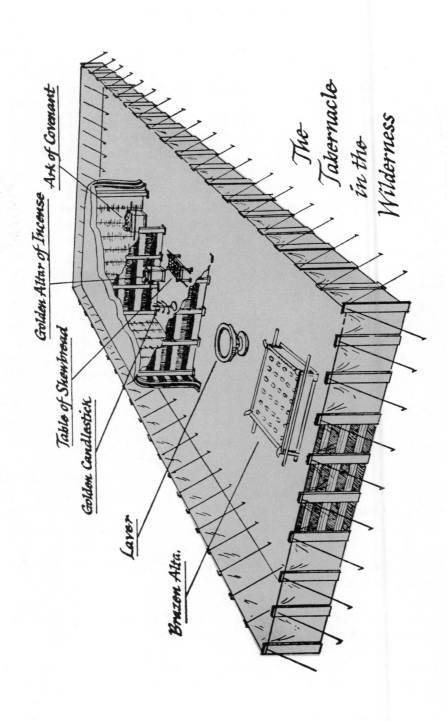

Ark of Covenant

Golden Altar of Incense

Table of Shewbread

Golden Candlestick

Laver

Brazen Alta.

The
Tabernacle
in the
Wilderness

So when we drink of the cup, we do it in remembrance of His death.

And above that is another layer of badger skins, dull, neutral in color. That is the part the outside world can see of the Tabernacle. We recall that it was said of Jesus, "He hath no form nor comeliness; and when we shall see him, there is no beauty that we should desire him" (Isa. 53:2). This world does not love our Lord Jesus. He is called a bastard, son of a Jewish fallen woman. He is called the Galilean Peasant. But one day every knee shall bow to Him and every tongue shall confess that He is Lord.

As we step into the Holy Place I see on the right a table. Here are arranged twelve loaves of bread. They are renewed fresh every Sabbath day. And these loaves picture Christ the Bread of Life. They are called "the shewbread." We have had redemption through the blood at the brass altar. We come daily for cleansing at the laver. And here we find the Bread to sustain us, Christ the Bread of Life. No wonder the people cried out to Jesus, "Evermore give us this bread."

I turn to the left. Ah, what a beautiful piece of furniture! We call it a candlestick, but it is more than that. It is made of solid gold. It is a lampstand with seven lamps. And they burn with pure oil. The seven means deity, perfection. This pictures Jesus the Light of the World. What does the oil mean? That means that Jesus did all His ministry as a Spirit-filled Man, a pattern for us in the power of the Holy Spirit. When Jesus was baptized in the Jordan River, the Holy Spirit came upon Him and He began His marvelous ministry. And as Peter expressed it to Cornelius:

"That word, I say, ye know, which was published throughout all Judaea, and began from Galilee, after the baptism which John preached; How God anointed Jesus of Nazareth with the Holy Ghost and with power: who went about doing good, and healing all that were oppressed of the devil; for God was with Him. And we are witnesses of all things which He did both in the land of the Jews, and in Jerusalem; whom they slew and hanged on a tree."—Acts. 10:37-39.

Oh, we who have Jesus need not walk in darkness. We can have the Light of Life on every footstep.

Now we face a great veil between the Holy Place and the Most Holy Place. We are not allowed to go within the Most Holy Place. Only the high priest once a year, at the day of atonement, can go there.

Men differ about this little golden altar of incense. We think it was before this second veil, before the Most Holy Place. But we have a right to this altar, too, and the sweet incense burned there pictures the praises and prayers we offer to the Lord Jesus. It could picture no one else.

Inside that Most Holy Place would be the Ark of the Covenant. A golden plate covers it, and that is the mercy seat. Every year the high priest will come and sprinkle blood on that mercy seat, on the day of atonement. But he knows, sadly, that he only pictures the atonement. Historically it is not yet completed.

Two carved cherubim are over that mercy seat. Within that box called the Ark of the Covenant covered with gold are the two tables of stone picturing the righteousness of God. There is a bowl of manna picturing God's providential care. And there is a branch of an almond tree that budded in token to God's authority given His prophets.

But, high priest, if you did not know, let me tell you. One day in Jerusalem on a hill shaped like a skull they will hang the long-promised Messiah. And the sun beating down pitifully will suddenly at noon cover her face and leave the world in darkness. And God will reach down with His all-powerful finger to tear apart the veil before the Most Holy Place in the Tabernacle. For now, at long last, when Jesus cries out, "It is finished," and the blood has poured out from His wounded side, the atonement will be finished and no other high priest need ever go through the ceremony of bringing blood to the mercy seat.

The Tabernacle and its furniture all pictured the Lord Jesus Christ.

Amen! Amen! Amen!

Twelve Spies See the Land and Report

NUMBERS 13,14

Much has happened to Israel since they came out of Egypt. They have had the Ten Commandments on Mount Sinai. They have been given the feasts of Jehovah, the passover, the feast of tabernacles, and certain holy days. They have been given clear instructions, and with enormous labor and expense they have been taught to build a rich Tabernacle for the service of God, with its altar, and laver, and table of shewbread, and lampstand, and altar of incense. They have been given the colorful Tabernacle with the rich fabrics, with supports of silver and gold.

Now it is time for God to lead them into the land of Canaan. Are they ready for it? Remember, the Israelites have been slaves in Egypt for many years. They have not grown to be aggressive, bold warriors. How gently God has dealt with them despite their weakness, their murmurings, their lack of faith! But to encourage and prepare them for the wonderland God is giving them, when they had stopped at Kadesh-Barnea, south of the Holy Land proper, God had Moses select twelve spies—one prominent, trusted head man from each tribe.

Moses' assistant, Joshua, of the tribe of Ephraim, and Caleb of the tribe of Judah, are among the twelve. They were instructed to go through and spy out the land of Canaan. They were to view the people. Were they strong and great? or weak? Did they live in tents? in unprotected groups? or did they have walled cities? They were to see if there was plenty of wood in the land. Was the land fertile? And these twelve were to bring fruits of the land.

They returned from searching of the land after forty days. Oh, yes, it was a land flowing with milk and honey. Here was a giant bunch of grapes of Eschol borne on a staff between two men. They brought of the pomegranates and of the figs and reported, "Nevertheless, the people be strong that dwell in the land. And the cities are walled and very great. Moreover, the men—there were giants in the land, sons of Anak. We were in our own sight as grasshoppers, and so we were in their sight." So the committee had reported their findings!

Ten of the spies were frightened and discouraged. They said, "How could we take those walled cities held by giants? How could we defend against armies with chariots?"

But two noble men, Joshua and Caleb, spake out boldly: "The Lord has been with us; He will still be with us. The God who plagued and defeated Pharaoh can defeat these Hittites, Amorites, Jebusites and the Canaanites. Why, those frightened people will be bread for us. God will help us. We can do it. Fear them not."

But the people listened to the discouraging report of the ten rather than to Joshua and Caleb. They said, "Now, aren't we in trouble! We cannot defeat those giants. We cannot take those walled cities. We should never have left Egypt." And the people said, "Let us elect a leader who will take us back to Egypt."

What will God do with His rebellious people? God said, "Moses, let Me destroy this whole nation and take you and your family and start over."

But Moses argued with God: "Lord, if You do that, all these people will say You just don't have strength enough to bring them into the land that You promised to them and so You killed them all." Moses argued on: "Lord God, You have forgiven them again and again; forgive them just one more time. Remember, Lord, Thy mercies are great."

So the Lord agreed not to destroy the nation, but He said, "Every one of these men of fighting age that were numbered

Twelve spies report at
Kadesh-Barnea

from twenty years old and upward when they came out of Egypt, shall die in this wilderness." And the Lord spoke unto Moses and Aaron saying, "Say unto them, Your little ones that you thought would be prey, they shall come and take this land." The people had tried God ten times with their rebellion, their murmuring, their unbelief. Now they will go through forty years of wandering until the last of these rebellious men, save only Caleb and Joshua, are dead. Then their children shall be taken into the land of promise.

Oh, how displeased God was! He sent a plague among the people. And the ten spies who brought evil report died in the plague.

Now some of these hotheads decided they would line up without instructions and start a war to take the land. They were warned not to go, and the Amalekites and the Canaanites smote them and drove them back. Israel must be reconciled to forty years of wandering.

A Cure for Snakebite

What a mass of onery, cantankerous human beings were those Israelites in the wilderness! They complained at the manna even, the angels' food sent them every day from Heaven. They didn't pay for it. We think it was perfectly balanced food, with all the necessary proteins and vitamins and enzymes. They had a normal portion for every day. Nobody went hungry, no one was ill or undernourished. It must have been good for it tasted like wafers made with honey. But these cantankerous Israelites complained at God and Moses and said, "Wherefore have ye brought us up out of Egypt to die in the wilderness? for there is no bread, neither is there any water; and our soul loatheth this light bread." They thought about that fish they had eaten from the River Nile. They had gotten hungry for the leeks, onions and garlic of Egypt.

People are prone to think that what others have must be better than what they have. Every cow wants the grass on the other side of the fence. These complaining hearts were wicked hearts. There are several sins that show their ugly heads in complaining and murmuring. First, how ungrateful they were for all the mercies of God, loving care and food every day. Second, they were rebellious against the will of God and the provisions of God. Children think they know better than their parents and Christians think they know better than God what would be good for them, what would make them happy. Third, there was rebellion against God's man. They "spake against God, and against Moses." That servant of God will be despised when God's way is despised.

What a sin it is to murmur and complain! Johnny at the table may say, "Ah, I don't like green beans," and Susie may say, "Do I have to eat this old oatmeal? You serve it every day." But Christians are commanded, "Whatsoever is set before you, eat, asking no question" (I Cor. 10:27), "For every creature of God is good, and nothing to be refused, if it be received with thanksgiving: For it is sanctified by the word of God and prayer" (I Tim. 4:4,5).

But the Bible commands us, "Do all things without murmurings and disputings" (Phil. 2:14). The Scripture insists that in everything we give thanks. And Paul the apostle, in jail and in poverty, could say, "I have learned, in whatsoever state I am, therewith to be content" (Phil. 4:11).

Well, these complainers, these troublemakers, these critics of God's goodness—they must be taught a lesson, but it is a loving lesson. It points to the way of forgiveness and peace for those who hear.

So God sent fiery serpents among the people "and much people of Israel died." We do not know whether it was some kind of a desert viper, a rattlesnake or a moccasin. Perhaps they were a plague prepared for that very day.

What mourning in the camp! So in many tents there was a cry of loved ones poisoned and dying in pain. What would they do? They came to Moses. I suppose they were penitent now, and they pleaded, "Moses, pray for us," and so good old Moses did so. And God told Moses to make a snake of brass and hang it high on a pole in the midst of the camp. I can imagine there was a little crosspiece on the pole and this brass serpent curled there upon it, shining in the sun. The word went out, if any were bitten by the fiery serpent, he had only to look at this great brass snake on the pole and suddenly he would be well. I know that doesn't seem to be a proper cure for snakebite, so I can see how some might foolishly doubt it and be hesitant.

Let us imagine a Hebrew man goes to stake out his cow in the grass. There is a shining glimmer at his feet. He feels the sting of the bite in his calf. Oh, he knows he is doomed. His neighbors are dying. Before he can hobble to his tent his leg is severely swollen. He feels faint, his heart beats rapidly. He lays on his cot in despair, in great pain.

Let's imagine here comes his son, twelve years of age. "Hey, Pop!"

"Never mind, Son. Be quiet. I am about to die!"

"But, Pop, listen!" the boy continues in great earnestness. "Listen! I tell you you don't have to die."

"Oh, but I felt the bite of the poisonous snake. I can hardly breathe. My leg is so swollen and my heart is hammering."

"But, Pop, God has made a way so you don't have to die. He told Moses to make a snake out of brass and there it is—a big brass snake shining on a pole right in the midst of the camp. I could see it just down between the tents away."

Let's suppose the man could hardly believe it but his pleading wife gets on one side and insists that he rise. He puts his arm over the shoulders of his boy and hobbling between wife and son he goes to the tent door and then down a few steps, and there it is right before him—the snake on a pole! He looks and—oh, he can hardly believe it! The swelling is gone! The pain is gone! His limb is normal again! The **hammering of his heart which fought the poison has grown**

Snakebitten people were healed by looking to the brass snake on a pole.

normal! He is healed! He is well!

But that doesn't seem like a normal way to cure snakebite. No, this is not normal; this is supernatural, this is an act of God. In mercy He has laid aside customs and rules of nature and healed the man who trusted Him and looked to the snake on the pole.

Jesus preached from the Old Testament. You remember the New Testament was not yet written. One night when Nicodemus, a member of the Sanhedrin, came to inquire of Him, Jesus said, "As Moses lifted up the serpent in the wilderness, even so must the Son of man be lifted up: That whosoever believeth in Him should not perish, but have everlasting life" (John 3:14,15). What did that serpent represent? Why, all the serpents represented sin, of course. When Satan came presumptuously into the Garden of Eden, he entered in the form of a serpent to lead Adam and Eve into sin. And the Scripture speaks of "that old serpent, which is the Devil, and Satan" (Rev. 20:2). Oh, the sad truth is that men everywhere are snakebitten! We are fallen. We are tainted. We have inherited a wicked nature. The fiery serpent spiritually has bitten all of us.

But the serpent on the pole—we thought from what Jesus said to Nicodemus that that serpent pictured Jesus. And so it does. But Jesus never did sin, you may say. Ah, you say it well. He never did. But you see, God was willing to count Jesus a sinner in my place. God made "Him to be sin for us, who knew no sin; that we might be made the righteousness of God in Him" (II Cor. 5:21). God looks down on His Son and says, "All John Rice's sins are on Jesus on the cross. All the sins of every person who ever trusted Him for salvation are laid on Jesus." So God let Jesus suffer as a sinner and Jesus is pictured by the serpent on the pole. I may be counted righteous because Jesus was counted a sinner and suffered for my sins, and yours.

What a gospel sermon Jesus preached from this text! And how did the snakebitten people get healed? Why, they did nothing at all but look! They said in their hearts, "It is true. I don't deserve it, but God says He will heal me if I will look."

And so these guilty people, suffering for their sins, simply believed what God had promised and with one look of faith they were healed!

Dear friend who reads this, all you need to do to get forgiveness and salvation and healing of your poor, sinful soul is just to look to Jesus.

"For God so loved the world, that He gave His only begotten Son, that whosoever believeth in Him should not perish, but have everlasting life."—John 3:16.

The Talking Donkey

As the children of Israel journeyed in the wilderness, they were feared and sometimes hated by the nations near which they passed, or through which they passed. People knew of the awful destruction God had wrought in Egypt. They knew how miraculously God had delivered Israel. King Balak of Moab had, he thought, a wonderful idea. There was a prophet of the true God in his country named Balaam. He would hire Balaam to come and oversee the great encamped host of Israel and pronounce a divine curse on them.

So he sent important men of his government to see Balaam. He would give rooms full of gold and silver if he would come and curse these people who threaten to disrupt all the mideastern countries. Balaam demurred. He could only prophesy what God told him to prophesy. He could only curse people where God cursed them.

At first he refused to go. But upon insistence and alluring bribes offered him, he assayed to go, but protesting he could only speak what God gave him to speak.

But his donkey stopped, seeing something Balaam could not see. An angel stood before him to block the way. Balaam beat the donkey and they passed on until they came to a narrow way with strong walls on each side. Again the angel stood before the donkey. The donkey pressed Balaam's foot against the stone wall, but could not pass. And Balaam beat the donkey unmercifully. Then God gave the donkey a voice which said, "What have I done unto thee, that thou hast smitten me these three times?"

Balaam said, "Would there were a sword in mine hand, for now would I kill thee." Then Balaam saw the angel of God. The angel of God warned him about his greed. The angel allowed him to proceed with the understanding that he could speak only what God gave him to speak.

Balaam came before Balak and instructed the Moabite king to prepare seven altars. On these seven altars he was to offer seven bullocks. Then in a trance, it seemed, Balaam said:

"How shall I curse, whom God hath not cursed? or how shall I defy, whom the Lord hath not defied? For from the top of the rocks I see him, and from the hills I behold him: lo, the people shall dwell alone, and shall not be reckoned among the nations. Who can count the dust of Jacob, and the number of the fourth part of Israel? Let me die the death of the righteous, and let my last end be like his!"— Num. 23:8-10.

Balak was disappointed and angry. Instead of cursing Israel, Balaam had blessed them.

But hopefully Balak selected another place where one could see part of Israel. Again they were to prepare seven altars and offer seven bullocks and without a trance Balaam spoke as a prophet and said:

Balaam's donkey stopped, seeing something Balaam could not see. An angel stood before him to block the way.

"God is not a man, that He should lie; neither the Son of man, that He should repent: hath He said, and shall He not do it? or hath He spoken, and shall He not make it good? Behold, I have received commandment to bless: and He hath blessed; and I cannot reverse it. He hath not beheld iniquity in Jacob, neither hath He seen perverseness in Israel: the Lord his God is with him, and the shout of a king is among them. God brought them out of Egypt; he hath as it were the strength of an unicorn. Surely there is no enchantment against Jacob, neither is there any divination against Israel; according to this time it shall be said of Jacob and of Israel, What hath God wrought! Behold, the people shall rise up as a great lion, and lift up himself as a young lion: he shall not lie down until he eat of the prey, and drink the blood of the slain."—Vss. 19-24.

The same thing happened a third time and Balak, angry and bitter, denounced the prophet who brought him no good.

However, Balaam, who could not as a prophet curse Israel, found another way to curse them. He encouraged some Moabite women to come into the camp of Israel for adultery. Many, many of Israel at Peor were seduced by the Moabite women. And God sent a plague upon them.

But a remarkable priest, Phinehas, found a princess of Moab being led into a tent for adultery by a man of Israel. Angrily and in God's name he went into the tent and thrust them both through the belly and killed them. God was pleased and stopped the plague.

Now it turned out that Israel was compelled to fight the angry Moabites. Many of these Moabites were slain and with them were slain the prophet Balaam whose donkey represented God better than he did.

Goodbye Wilderness:
Israel Enters Canaan

For forty years the children of Israel wandered in the wilderness until at last all those men who doubted God, mature men who had come out of Egypt, had died. Of those men in the first census only Caleb and Joshua remained alive. Moses was not among those who rebelled and doubted, but at the waters of Meribah he had dishonored God by smiting the rock on a second occasion, instead of speaking to it, as God had commanded. That seems a little sin, but no sin is little, particularly with some man so greatly-used of God as was Moses. The more light God gives, the more He holds us accountable. So Moses saw the land from Mount Nebo, and died, and the angels buried him there.

Now the children of Israel camped on the east side of the Jordan River. Joshua sent two men to spy out Jericho, the first big city across the Jordan. They slipped into the city there hiding in the house of Rahab the harlot. When the king of Jericho heard of their coming and sent to find them, Rahab hid them on the roof and covered them with stalks of flax that were drying. She told the king's messengers that the spies had gone away to the river.

Then Rahab talked to these men. She told them she knew all of God's dealings with Israel—the plagues in Egypt, the death of Pharaoh, the manna in the wilderness, and a thousand marvels and signs. She knew that the hearts of the people of Jericho fainted. She knew the true God was with Israel.

Would these men save her father and mother, brothers and sisters alive that they might live with Israel? The spies agreed that if she would keep their mission secret, she could let them down by a scarlet cord or rope from the window, since her house was on the wall. That scarlet cord was to hang there and identify her house when other houses were

The spies escape from Rahab's house.

destroyed. Then when Israel took the city, her house would be spared if she kept her vow.

Now the children of Israel are ready to cross the Jordan. God had instructed that the priests who bore the ark should march boldly into the water of the flooded Jordan. As soon as the feet of the priests touched the water, it receded and fled away. It piled high on the up-river side and flowed away from them on the down-river side.

Now as the priests stood in the river, a clear, dry way was furnished them, and just as Israel had crossed the Red Sea forty years before, they marched triumphantly across the Jordan River. They erected a monument with stones in the riverbed. They carried other great stones to build a monument at Gilgal.

Now they had clear instructions about how they were to take Jericho. Strangely, God Himself would take the city for them. And this is the simple plan God gave. One day they were to all march in a triumphant procession around the whole city, and no one was to lift his sword or bow. Priests with trumpets and carrying the Ark of the Covenant, went before. They returned to camp.

The second day they followed the same procedure exactly, and returned to camp. So it was the third, the fourth, the fifth, and the sixth day. But on the seventh day they were instructed to march seven times around the city, and then when the priests blew loudly on the rams' horns, people were to shout with a great shout. So they did, and suddenly the walls of Jericho fell down flat. Only one small segment of the wall stood securely erect. And that section held the house of Rahab and her family, all saved alive.

There is a sad note in the fall of Jericho. For God had instructed the people that the silver, gold, and treasure of the city were to belong to God. They were to beware to take none of it for themselves. Ah, but Achan, son of Carmi, of the tribe of Judah, took a golden wedge, two hundred shekels of silver, and a rich Babylonish garment. He slipped them out and took them to his tent. We suppose he urged his wife and children to say not a word. And then he buried them in the dirt under his tent. Ah, but God was angry.

When a select army attacked Ai, they were defeated and thirty-six men died. Joshua fell on his face. What would they do now if God had forsaken them? But God urged Joshua to get up and find the answer. God said, "Israel has sinned." So every tribe must stand before God. Where is the guilty party? Finally it came down to the tribe of Judah. At last the household of Carmi, and divine lot showed Achan was guilty. He was stoned, his guilty family was slain. They were cast into a canyon, and burned, along with their possessions. Then great stones were rolled upon them. The people must learn that sin cannot get by unpunished.

But what became of Rahab? She and her family were delivered from destruction. Ah, there is a beautiful ending to the story. In Matthew 1:5 is given us the genealogy, the ancestral line of the Lord Jesus Christ, and it says, "And Salmon begat Booz of Rachab. . . ." Ah! Rahab was a harlot no more. Now she is a godly woman. Salmon, of the tribe of Judah, fell in love with her and married her. Now she bore a son, Boaz. That is the same Boaz who married Ruth, the Moabitess. Boaz, the great grandfather of King David! How wonderful that God should select this Gentile woman, a woman who had been a sinner, a woman with a disgraceful past, but one who put her trust in the Lord God and loved Him and served Him, and so was made one of the ancestresses of the dear Lord Jesus!

Joshua just takes a walk around the walls of Jericho. God had ordered him to take it, and he must.

How many men of the present time would have laughed at Joshua if they had been in Jericho! How much sport they would have made of him! If there had been a Jericho Herald, what articles would have come out! The idea of taking the city in this way! The ark was to come out, and the priests were to blow rams' horns. That was very absurd, wasn't it? Rams' horns!

—D. L. Moody

When the Sun Stood Still
for Joshua

When the children of Israel had crossed over Jordan and destroyed Jericho and Ai, we remember that one great city, desperately afraid, sent messengers to Joshua to make a treaty of peace. These men from the big city of Gibeon pretended that their city was far away. And Joshua and Israel, being deceived, signed a treaty of peace with them.

However, over the whole land of Canaan tales had come forth of the mighty power of God in delivering them from Pharaoh with the plagues of Egypt, the miracles in the wilderness, and now the destruction of Jericho.

So the king of Jerusalem now appealed to other kings of great cities—the king of Hebron, the king of Jarmuth, the king of Lachish, the king of Eglon. These five kings of the Amorites decided they must destroy Gibeon, which had made peace. And as these armies attacked, threatening to destroy Gibeon, the Gibeonites sent word to Joshua calling for help.

But the Lord appeared unto Joshua and told him not to fear, that not one of these kings could stand before him. So Joshua and his army traveled in the night from Gilgal near Jordan and came to the help of Gibeon.

This was an awesome task, but if he could defeat these five kings and their armies, he would have done much to take the land of Canaan.

These heathen armies fled before Joshua and Israel. God

rained great stones from Heaven to kill more of the enemy than were slain by the sword. To chase down and capture so many was a great task. Oh, if they had more time!

So, by faith, Joshua called on the Lord and he said in the sight of Israel, "Sun, stand thou still upon Gibeon; and thou Moon, in the valley of Ajalon." And we are told, "And the sun stood still, and the moon stayed, until the people had avenged themselves upon their enemies. Is not this written in the book of Jasher? So the sun stood still in the midst of heaven, and hasted not to go down about a whole day."

What a wonderful miracle, the only one of its kind, we suppose, in the history of the world. But I doubt not that the God who made the sun and moon and stars and this planet earth, could make them do His will.

Someone says that if the earth had stopped its rotation in relation to the sun that the shock would have thrown down all the buildings and killed all the people. But there is no reason why God could not control the effects as well as the miracle. Today it is not unusual for a fighter plane traveling far faster than the speed of sound, to land and stop within minutes, and that fighter plane goes faster than the thousand miles an hour which the surface of the earth may be turning.

Paul, preaching the resurrection of Christ to Agrippa, said, "Why should it be thought a thing incredible with you, that God should raise the dead?"

If we believe that God created the sun and the earth and chose the normal relationship, why could not God adjust that temporarily any way He wished? Yes, we believe the Bible, so we rejoice in believing that God made the sun to stand still in its relationship to the earth for about a day.

The sun stood still in the midst
of heaven for about a day.

Samson, the Mighty Judge of Israel

JUDGES 13-16

During the time of the judges, one day a young married woman was startled when an angel appeared before her. He announced that she was to have a son and that this son was to be a Nazarite to God from his birth, with God's great power upon him.

She was thrilled and ran to tell her husband Manoah about "the man" who had appeared to her. When the angel appeared again, Manoah asked him, "Art thou the man that spakest unto the woman?" Yes, he was. "How then should we act to rear the child for the Lord?"

Again the angel said that he should drink no wine nor strong drink nor eat anything pertaining to the grape.

When Manoah would offer a sacrifice, the angel said, "Though thou detain me, I will not eat of thy bread: and if thou wilt offer a burnt-offering, thou must offer it unto the Lord." And while the sacrifice was burning, the angel went up in the flame and disappeared. Then Manoah knew it was an angel.

Manoah said, "We shall surely die, because we have seen God." But his wife protested that since God had received their sacrifice, He would not kill them.

With that background, the boy Samson was born and grew up.

A Nazarite was set apart to serve God. In this case, when the Spirit of God came upon Samson from time to time, the

result was tremendous physical strength. Samson was super-
naturally strong, more powerful than any normal man.

God saw the distress of His people who had been conquered and put almost in slavery by the Philistines. One day
Samson went down to Timnath. There he saw a beautiful
Philistine girl. He insisted that his father get the girl for his
wife. Why should Samson want to marry a heathen
Philistine girl? But God was using this infatuation to bring
deliverance for Israel.

The father and mother went with Samson down toward
Timnath. A young lion roared against Samson and he turned
and seized the beast and tore it apart. The father and mother
did not know about the lion.

They made arrangements for a prospective wedding, and
the father and mother came with him down among the

Philistines. On this journey Samson went by to see the carcass of the lion after the bones had been stripped dry and bare. A hive of bees had taken over and there was an abundance of honeycomb and honey. Samson took some of the honey and ate it as he went, and gave some to his father and mother.

Now at the big preliminary celebration were thirty young Philistine men guests. Samson proposed a riddle unto them. Now the riddle was: "Out of the eater came forth meat, and out of the strong came forth sweetness." Samson suggested that in seven days if they could answer his riddle, he would give them thirty sheets and thirty changes of garments. If they could not answer his riddle, they should provide him with thirty sheets and thirty changes of garments.

They pondered and questioned, yet they could not get the answer. Then the young men threatened Samson's bride: She must declare unto them the riddle or they would burn her house down. So she wept before Samson, saying, "You say you love me, but you hate me or you would tell me the riddle."

Samson was a sucker for a woman's tears. So on the seventh day he told her, and she told the riddle to the young men of the Philistines. Ah, they told him, "Now what is sweeter than honey? and what is stronger than a lion?" Samson knew that his bride had betrayed him, and he said, "If ye had not plowed with my heifer, you had not found out my riddle."

Then the Spirit of the Lord came upon him and he went to Ashkelon, a city of the Philistines, and killed thirty men and took their spoil and paid the wages to the Philistine young men.

Disillusioned, Samson went away. He was among enemies. And when he was gone, his wife was given to another man who had been at the feast. Later Samson brought a kid for a gift and came back to see his wife. Seeing that she was given to another, he caught three hundred foxes and tied firebrands between each pair of foxes and turned them loose in the ripened fields of grain of the Philistines. Field after field was set on fire and destroyed. Shocks and standing corn and vineyards and olive trees were burned!

Then the Philistines, seeing that Samson had been wronged and that this was vengeance, burned with fire the woman he had claimed as his wife, and her father.

Now the Philistines came up in Judah and demanded that the men of the tribe bind Samson and deliver him to the Philistines. Samson was on top of a hill when the men of Judah came to him. "Will you deliver me to the Philistines?" Yes, they would. Then Samson said, "Swear unto me, that ye will not fall upon me yourselves." No, they would not.

So Samson allowed himself to be bound and taken down to the encamped Philistines. And when they shouted against Samson, "the Spirit of the Lord came mightily upon him, and the cords that were upon his arms became as flax that was burnt with fire, and his bands loosed from off his hands."

Ah, nearby lay a skeleton of a donkey. Samson seized a jawbone of the ass and with it killed a thousand Philistines. What a slaughter!

Samson, after the fight with such exertion, was desperately thirsty. He prayed and God opened a place in the jawbone of the ass and he drank water abundantly.

Twenty years went by, and Samson judged Israel. Gaza was one of the five principal cities of the Philistines. The others were: Ashdod, Ashkelon, Ekron and Gezer.

Samson went to visit a woman in Gaza. The men of the city learned he was there and planned to take him at daylight. But Samson arose, seized the great gate of the city, tore it out, posts and all, and carried the gate on his shoulders to the top of a hill before Hebron, miles away.

We must remember that God in mercy makes the wrath of men to praise Him. And God uses imperfect men sometimes to do His great will to save others.

Down in the valley of Sorek lived a beautiful young woman named Delilah. She, too, was a Philistine. Samson fell in love with her and went to see her. But she played the traitor. She decided to learn what was the secret of Samson's strength, and then to betray him to her Philistine friends.

She nagged and pleaded. Samson playfully told her to bind him with seven green withs, then he would be weak like others. The lords of the Philistines were hidden in the house, and when she said, "The Philistines be upon thee, Samson," he broke the green withs as if they were thread.

Then he suggested they bind him with new cords, knowing that would not affect his strength. And he broke them from off his arms like a thread while laughing at her.

Now Delilah wept. The Philistines had promised her eleven hundred pieces of silver if she could get Samson helpless.

This time as Delilah pleaded where his might lay, Samson said that if the seven locks of his head were woven with a web of a great loom, he would then be helpless. But when she woke him, he easily pulled away with the pin of the beam and with the web.

Now Delilah really wept. "Samson, how can you say you love me, and mock me so?"

Alas, alas, Samson succumbed to her tears and pleading, because he really loved that poor woman. So "he told her all his heart." He was a Nazarite, committed to serve God all his life. His long hair was a symbol of his perfect surrender to the Lord, from whom his power came. If a razor comes upon his head, he would be powerless.

Perhaps even Samson was not sure. How could he lose this great strength that no other man had? So when Samson went to sleep with his head in Delilah's lap, she called a man to come and shave off those great locks of hair. This time when she screamed, "Samson, the Philistines be upon thee," he awoke, thinking he would go out as at other times, but now his strength was gone! "And Samson wist not that the Lord was departed from him."

How frail is any Christian who compromises, displeases God and loses the power of the Holy Spirit!

Now Samson is a prisoner in the land of the Philistines. They took and gouged out his eyes. They bound him with fetters of brass. They set him in the prison house to pull round and round a great mill, as a donkey would.

What a celebration the Philistines would have! The word

Samson's strength returned, and
a great idol temple was destroyed.

ROSETTA
LENTRICHIA

went out everywhere among the five cities of the Philistines and their villages. Their idol gods had prevailed, and Samson was their prisoner!

Meantime, Samson's hair had begun to grow. There was a tremendous temple of Dagon. And they sent for a boy to lead the blind Samson out for their sport. "And there were upon the roof about three thousand men and women, that beheld while Samson made sport." Now Samson prayed, "Remember me, I pray Thee, and strengthen me only this once, O God, that I may be at once avenged of the Philistines for my two eyes."

The little boy had led him to where he could put his hands on the two great central pillars that upheld the vast crowds on the floor above. Once again God gave Samson strength. He bowed himself mightily and a great idol temple and amphitheater came down, falling upon the lords and the other people that were therein. And those who died at the death of Samson were more than they which he slew in his lifetime.

When Samson died, God raised up other judges to deliver Israel, after they had been delivered into the hands of heathen people for their sins.

Gideon and His
Wonderful 300

JUDGES 7

The book of Judges tells the sad story. Joshua was dead. As long as the elders who made that holy pledge with Joshua in Joshua 24:15—as long as they lived—the nation Israel served the Lord. But the trusted leaders died and for nearly 300 years Israel fell into sin and so was punished by years of slavery or servitude under heathen nations nearby: the Midianites, Philistines and others.

But in these years God again and again raised up some godly men to lead and to deliver Israel. He used two godly women. He used the prophetess, Deborah, who called Barak to assemble an army at Mount Tabor to defeat the Midianites.

Then there was Jael, the wife of Heber, the Kenite, who let Sisera, defeated Midianite captain, fall asleep in her tent and drove a steel tent peg into his head and killed him.

The Midianites were among the most hateful enemies. They brought great flocks of camels and herds to eat up the fields. And Israel was greatly impoverished.

One day Gideon, son of Joash, was threshing wheat by the winepress to hide it from the Midianite oppressors. An angel of the Lord appeared to him and said, "The Lord is with thee, thou mighty man of valour."

"Ah!" said Gideon, "if the Lord is with us, why are we in such distress?" And again he said, "Where be all the miracles our fathers told us about?" And Gideon said, "How

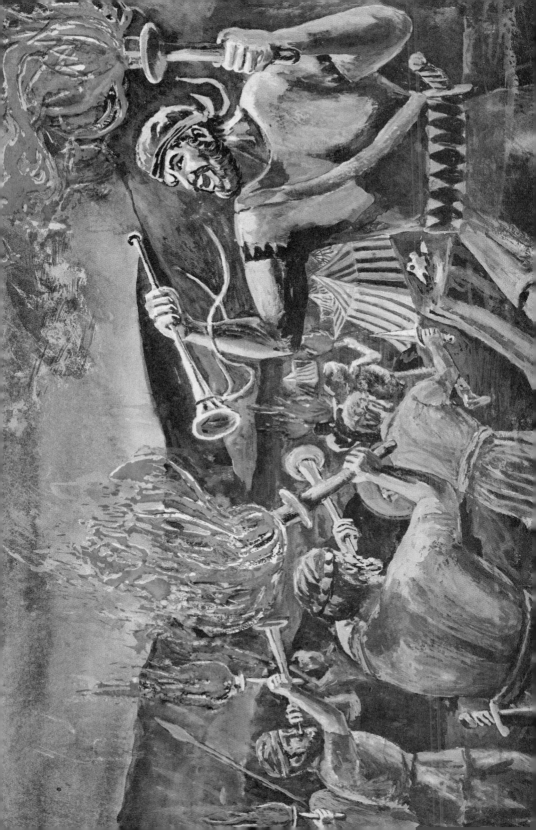

could I deliver Israel?" Gideon felt himself the least of his father's house. His house was not prominent in his tribe.

But the angel insisted, "Go in this thy might, and thou shalt save Israel from the hand of the Midianites: have not I sent thee?"

Gideon offered an offering to God and the angel touched the offering and it was burned up. Then God instructed Gideon that he should cut down the grove that was used for the worship of Baal. He should take his father's second bullock, seven years old, and use it as a sacrifice.

When Gideon and his workers had cut down the grove and Baal's altar was destroyed, the people around came to demand Joash should give up his son Gideon to die because he had destroyed the altar of Baal. But old Joash was proud of his son. He said, "Let Baal defend his own altar if he will and can."

Ah, the enemies of Israel and the enemies of the Lord felt something was happening. So the great host of the Midianites and Amalekites and the children of the east pitched in the valley of Jezreel.

Now boldly Gideon blew the trumpet and called for the people to follow him in driving out these enemies.

As the people gathered, Gideon felt he must have more reassurance. At night he put a fleece before the door and prayed. If this cause was really of God, he asked that there be dew on the fleece and dry all about it. Ah, on the morrow he rung out a bowl full of water from the fleece. But maybe the fleece just attracts the dew. "Lord, would You do it the other way? Let the fleece be dry and all about it be wet with dew." And so it was. God has promised He will give the victory.

My, what a host of Israelites have come to help Gideon deliver Israel! But God said a strange thing. "There are too many, Gideon. Men would want to take the credit. Tell all the people who are afraid to go home." And so the next morning 22,000 returned to their own homes. Now some 10,000 are left.

"There are still too many," God says. "The people would think that by their own might and boldness they have delivered themselves."

Gideon with 300 defeats
the Midianite host.

So Gideon was instructed to take them all down to the brook for water. And those who lapped the water out of their hands quickly to be up and at the battle, he was to set aside; the rest were all sent home.

Now Gideon had a band of only 300 men. Can you imagine the concern of Gideon? I suppose he was plain scared! What chance would he have with a little band of 300 against the tens of thousands of Midianites, and Amalekites and the children of the east? He needs encouragement. So God told him to go with his servant, to slip down to the camp of the enemy and hear them talk. So he and his servant, Phurah, slipped in among those people in the dark.

There were thousands, as thick as grasshoppers. Near a campfire they listened. A man told his dream, that a cake of barley bread had tumbled down the mountain and through this host, striking down tents and men.

His companion answered, "That is the army of Gideon. God has given us into his hand. The hearts of our people are turned to water!"

Ah, now Gideon is encouraged! God can do it.

So they followed God's instructions. Every man was to take a pitcher in one hand, and in the pitcher a burning lamp. In the other hand he was to take a trumpet. The 300 surrounded the great camp of the enemy. At God's word they broke the pitchers. The strange lights suddenly appeared. Gideon's men blew on their trumpets and shouted, "The sword of the Lord and of Gideon!"

What confusion! What dismay on the heathen camp of thousands! They attacked each man his neighbor. They tried to run for their lives.

Now the men of Israel who had returned to their homes came back to the battle and pursued the Midianites and the Amalekites. They took the waters of Jordan and slew all enemies that came. Gideon captured two princes of the Midianites, Oreb and Zeeb. Such a victory! And the men of the tribe of Ephraim felt cheated that they were not called upon to help. They threatened Gideon, but "a soft answer turneth away wrath." He said, "Why, you Ephraimites did more than I. You headed off the fleeing enemies at the River Jordan and gleaned there."

Zebah and Zalmunna, kings of the Midianites, left their defeated armies and fled. And Gideon went after them to complete his victory. His fainthearted men needed food. But the men of Succoth, fearing Zebah and Zalmunna, would not give bread. So solemnly Gideon promised them, "When I return with those kings, I will tear your flesh with briers and thorns." The men of Penuel likewise refused him food. And Gideon promised, "When I return in peace, I will break down this tower."

So Gideon caught the kings of Midian, Zebah and Zalmunna. He came back to punish those cities that refused him bread. Before he killed the kings, he said to them, "What were those men like whom you killed at Tabor?"

"Ah," they said, "they resembled you. They looked like kings."

"They were my brothers," Gideon said. Gideon suggested his young son take his sword to kill these kings but the son was timid, and the kings said, "Gideon, fall upon us yourself." And he killed the Midianite kings. And the land had rest many years.

Ruth, the Beautiful Young Widow, Finds a Godly Husband

Once there was a crop failure and famine in the land of Israel. So one family, Elimelech and his wife, Naomi, and their two sons, went around the Dead Sea and settled in Moab. There the sons married Moabite girls. And then the father and the two sons all died. Naomi and her two daughters-in-law, Orpah and Ruth, were left alone.

But word came to Naomi that God had smiled upon Israel, that crops were good again and that the famine was over. She prepared to go back to her own land. She kissed her daughters-in-law and said, "You stay with your own people. I have no more sons for you to marry. You should marry and have homes."

Orpah kissed her goodbye and went back to her own Moabitish people. But Ruth would not go. She said, "Intreat me not to leave thee, or to return from following after thee: for whither thou goest, I will go; where thou lodgest, I will lodge: thy people shall be my people, and thy God my God." So Ruth and Naomi came back near to Naomi's old home at Bethlehem.

Meantime, they must have food. So Ruth went out, as was the custom, to glean, following laborers in the barley harvest. When a few stalks of grain were left or dropped, or missed in a corner of the field, she gathered it up, and would have grain to take home to Naomi.

The owner of the field came along and inquired as to who this beautiful girl was. Some told him she was Ruth the

Ruth goes with Naomi into Israel,
Orpah turns back.

Moabitess that came with Naomi, the widow of Elimelech, his kinsman. "Oh," he said, "I know about her. I heard how faithfully she serves Naomi, how she has chosen God and His people."

So he spoke to Ruth kindly, saying, "I have instructed the young men not to bother you. You are to come and dip your bread with my maidens at noontime. You are to follow the reapers in my fields until the harvest is past. And may the God of Israel bless thee, under whose wings thou art come to trust."

At last the grain was winnowed, piled up, ready for storage. The laborers have a feast and rejoice in the evening around the winnowed grain. Naomi said to Ruth, "God has a plan to give you rest. Now do as I say. Tonight when the rejoicing and eating and drinking is over, when Boaz, the owner, makes his bed and goes to sleep in the grain pile, then you go softly, uncover his feet and lie down there. He will tell you what to do."

In the night Boaz moved and felt a woman at his feet. Disturbed, he asked, "Who is it?"

Ruth answered as Naomi had instructed her: "Go back to sleep. You are a near kinsman."

Boaz understood that he, as a near kinsman, had some obligation to see that Ruth was married and that the in-

Gleaning in the field of Boaz.

heritance which should come to her must go to her children.

Ere it was light, Boaz arose. He prepared a sack of grain and put it on Ruth's shoulders and sent her on home to Naomi. He said, "Let no one know that a woman was here."

Naomi said, "The man will not rest. He knows his duty."

In the morning Boaz called together certain men, had them sit with him at the gate of the city. One man was closer kin to Elimelech than he, and so Boaz said to him, "Elimelech's sons are dead. Someone should take his inheritance."

The man agreed and said, "I will do it."

But Boaz said, "The one who takes that property must take Ruth the Moabitess as a wife to raise up seed to Elimelech and his son."

"I cannot do it," the other man said, "since that would mar my own inheritance. So you must do it, Boaz."

It was agreed and publicly announced, and Boaz took Ruth to be his wife.

How happy Naomi was! Before, with her husband and both sons dead, she called her name bitterness, but now Ruth bore a lovely son that Grandmother Naomi could hold in her arms and care for. And that son was Obed who later would be the father of Jesse, the father of King David. And Ruth, who came to trust under the wings of the Lord and to know Him and love Him, now had come into the ancestral line of the Lord Jesus, as we see from Matthew 1:5.

How wonderful that Jesus, the Messiah, the Saviour, is not just the Saviour of good people, but the Saviour of foreigners like Rahab and Ruth; the Saviour of harlots and murderers and adulterers. He is the Saviour of kings and paupers. He died for the sins of the whole world.

It is interesting to note that that field of Boaz is thought to be the Shepherds' Field near Bethlehem where the angels announced the Saviour's birth.

Samuel, Given in Answer to Prayer; the Last Judge of Israel

Elkanah lived among the tribe of Ephraim. But every year he went to worship at the Tabernacle of the Lord at Shiloh. Old Eli was the high priest. Elkanah had two wives, and though, as far as we know, both were good women, there was jealousy between them, for Peninnah had children, but Hannah had none. Hannah was the best loved.

As Hannah grieved for a son, Elkanah said, "Am I not more to you than ten sons?" But Hannah's heart was determined. Oh, that God would give her a son!

When they went up to Shiloh to "the house of God," Hannah was greatly burdened. In great distress Hannah stood distracted, unconscious of her surroundings and earnestly prayed. Her lips moved but she did not speak aloud. Old Eli, sitting by the post in the Tabernacle, saw her lips moving but heard no word. Was the woman drunken? He spoke sharply to her, to put away her wine. She replied,

"No, my lord, I am a woman of a sorrowful spirit: I have drunk neither wine nor strong drink, but have poured out my soul before the Lord. Count not thine handmaid for a daughter of Belial: for out of the abundance of my complaint and grief have I spoken hitherto."—I Sam. 1:15.

"Then Eli answered and said, Go in peace: and the God of Israel grant thee thy petition that thou hast asked of Him."—Vs. 17.

**Samuel was brought to the
Tabernacle to live.**

The little family went back to Ramah, and the Lord remembered Hannah. She conceived and now Israel will get a mighty prophet. The child will become the Prophet Samuel.

Hannah had made a vow to the Lord. If God would give her a manchild, "as long as he liveth he shall be lent to the Lord." The next pilgrimage Elkanah made to Shiloh, Hannah stayed at home and cared for the baby Samuel. Some time went by until the child was weaned and thus able to get along without his mother. Perhaps it was five or six years. Then the little baby, with his bundle of clothes made by a mother's loving hands, was brought to the Tabernacle to live. And every year the mother would bring him more clothes. And I am sure that every year she spent hours with him, teaching him about God and right, and insisting that now he must always serve God.

It is strange, perhaps, that in the home of Eli where the old high priest's sons themselves were rebellious and idolatrous and irreverent and unbelieving, Samuel grew up in blameless righteousness. Once in the night the boy heard a cry. "Samuel, Samuel." He thought it was Eli calling and ran to the bed of the old man. "No, I called not. Go back to bed." Twice more he heard a voice, "Samuel, Samuel." When he went to Eli the third time the old man, the high priest, understood that God was calling. So the lad was instructed, If God called again, he was to simply answer, "Here am I, Lord." And that night God told Samuel about the curse that was coming on Eli and his sons because of their wickedness.

Now it soon became evident to all that young Samuel was called of God as a prophet and could speak for God. So after Eli and his wicked sons were dead, Samuel became the high priest as well as judge. He made his circuit with three centers where he would come to meet the people and answer their questions, give his judgment and go to the next center. This he did for many years.

The people, conscious of their recurring backslidings and punishments, felt that they needed a king to guide and control them. Samuel was embarrassed. But God said, "They have not rejected thee [Samuel], but they have rejected Me." So God agreed that they should have a king. And God led Samuel to anoint tall young Saul, son of Kish, head and shoulders above his fellows, to be their king. But Samuel said to the people, "Moreover as for me, God forbid that I should sin against the Lord in ceasing to pray for you: but I will teach you the good and the right way" (I Sam. 12:23).

King Saul did not make a very reliable king. When God sent him to utterly destroy the Amalekites, their families, their oxen and herds and goods, Saul came back leading King Agag behind his chariot with the fattest of the cattle and sheep to be offered as sacrifices. Samuel said, "Has the Lord as great delight in burnt-offerings and sacrifices, as in obeying the voice of the Lord? Behold, to obey is better than sacrifice, and to hearken than the fat of rams. For rebellion is as the sin of witchcraft, and stubbornness is as iniquity and idolatry. Because thou hast rejected the word of the Lord, He hath also rejected thee from being king" (I Sam. 15:22,23).

The boy Samuel tells old Eli of God's voice.

Before this Saul had rather carelessly and presumptuously been unwilling to wait for the coming of Samuel and offered sacrifices. God must get Him another king. So Samuel told Saul, "The Lord hath rent the kingdom of Israel from thee this day, and hath given it to a neighbour of thine, that is better than thou" (I Sam. 15:28).

Samuel killed King Agag the king of the Amalekites, but Samuel went away sadly and came no more to see Saul until the day of his death. Now Samuel was instructed to go and anoint the one the Lord has planned to make future king. He was to go to the house of Jesse of Bethlehem and there among the eight sons of Jesse he was to anoint the one God would point out. Jesse gladly received Samuel. A sacrifice was offered so that King Saul and others would not know the immediate reason for Samuel's coming. Then seven sons of Jesse were lined up. Perhaps this older son Eliab would be the one God chose. "No," God said. Then Abinadab passed before Samuel but God said this was not the one. And so with Shammah. So all the seven sons passed before Samuel but Samuel said unto Jesse, "The Lord hath not chosen these. . .Are here all thy children?" No, there is yet the youngest boy keeping the sheep. And Samuel would not be seated until the lad came. David came in with a ruddy and beautiful countenance. He was a handsome youngster. "And the Lord said, Arise, anoint him: for this is he."

I suppose the lad knelt before Samuel. Samuel poured the anointing oil on his head in the name of the Lord and the Spirit of the Lord came on David from that day forth. David will have many trials before he wears the crown as king, but God will be with him. Samuel loved him and communed with him. And at last the old man Samuel died.

But we should remember this great man was given in answer to the prayers of a good woman who must have a son and who had lent that son to the Lord as long as he would live. She remembered how long Abraham and Sarah had prayed for Isaac. For twenty years Rebekah was barren and her husband Isaac prayed for her and Jacob and Esau were born. Elisabeth and old Zacharias the priest prayed for many years and then in old age Elisabeth bore John the Baptist, the Spirit-filled prophet of God, the forerunner of the Lord Jesus.

And let us remember that God has said, "Lo, children are an heritage of the Lord: and the fruit of the womb is His reward. As arrows are in the hand of a mighty man; so are children of the youth. Happy is the man that hath his quiver full of them."

May more godly women pray, like Hannah, and have more mighty Spirit-filled sons like Samuel.

David, the Shepherd Boy

We can imagine that David's mother was concerned about his keeping those sheep out there in the wilderness alone, a little ways from Bethlehem. I suppose she said to David's father, "But, Jesse, he is just a boy! The neighbors say that upon the plain of Mamre, not far away, one man has lost two sheep already to a lion. You know that a bear would like to seize a lamb if he could, and there are bears in the woods near where David keeps the sheep."

We suppose Jesse answered her: "I saw him making a club out of a limb of a tree. He cut off the little branches and hardened the big end of it in the fire. His brothers laughed at him about it."

But David had told his mother, "I know the Lord is with me. Since Samuel poured the anointing oil on my head and prayed for me, I have known that the Spirit of God is with me. And He will help me."

Then one day while David was out with the sheep, he sat on a stone and played on his homemade harp which looked somewhat like a guitar. Strange how sweet Psalms kept coming to his mind. Suddenly he heard a frantic cry of a mother sheep. David looked and saw a lion had seized a lamb and had started to drag it away.

David immediately seized his club and went after the lion. As the lion turned, he brought the club down on the lion's neck. Pow! The lion was knocked to the earth. Confused and angry, he turned to face David while the lamb scrambled away. Again David raised that club and right over the eyes he hit that lion. The lion was stunned and David hit him again and again and killed the lion.

Ah, we could have warned that lion he was jumping on the wrong person when he chose David, the boy who had put his trust in the Lord.

Another time a bear seized a lamb and David went after that bear with all his energy. Maybe he whispered a prayer: "Lord, help me!" The Lord did. David smote the bear and took the lamb from its paws. Yes, the Lord was again with David.

And one of these days in the future when he goes to meet a giant Philistine who would try to kill him, David will remember that the God who helped him before, will help him once again!

I suppose that when David's older brothers saw the carcasses of the lion and of the bear, they were astonished. They did not know that God had put His hand upon David, filled him with the Spirit, and would be with him from this time forward, to make him king.

David, the Giant Killer

I SAMUEL 17

Israel had war with the Philistines. David's older brothers were in the army with King Saul. Their father, Jesse, sent young David with some food, with gifts for the captain over his sons. When David arrived at the army of Israel, he found a strange, threatening pause in the war. The army of Israel was on one hillside facing a great valley; the Philistine army was opposite them on the other side of the valley. What are they waiting for?

The Israelite army was confused and distressed because every day a giant Philistine came out to challenge Israel.

"Send out a man to fight me! If he kills me, we will be your servants. If I kill him, you remain our servants. I want a man to fight me!"

Does that sound reasonable? But remember, this Philistine, named Goliath, is about ten feet tall. His spear is like a weaver's beam; he must weigh 300 or 400 pounds; he is about twice as big as the average Hebrew soldier. Of course, no one went out to meet him.

But David, ever since the day Samuel poured oil upon his head and anointed him to be the future king of Israel, has had the Spirit of God upon him. And David is indignant that a heathen man, worshiping idol gods, could shame Israel. He spoke up boldly: "Someone ought to go and kill this blaspheming Philistine who mocks at the God of Israel."

David's older brothers are not pleased with David's talk. In the first place, each of them was afraid to go out and fight this infidel giant. In the second place, they thought younger

The giant Goliath will soon topple to the ground.

brothers ought not to talk up so brashly. They said, "David, you just came down to see the battle, didn't you? Now go home to the handful of sheep you shepherd and leave the fighting to men."

"But there is a cause," David said. "Someone ought to go and stop the blasphemy of that man and show that the Lord God is with His people."

Someone suggested, "David, would you go fight the giant yourself?"

His faith flamed up, and David said, "Yes, I will fight the giant. I will kill him and stop his blasphemy, his dishonoring of God."

Someone told King Saul of the lad. Saul had David before him. He protested to David, "Why, that man, a giant, is a man of war all of his life, and you are only a teenager, inexperienced."

"I could not do it by myself," said David, "but God would help me. I kept the sheep and a lion came to steal a lamb. I caught him by the beard and pounded in his head. And another time a bear seized a lamb, but again God helped me. I killed the bear and took the lamb out of his jaws."

King Saul, himself a tall man, head and shoulders above the other soldiers, had no faith to go fight the giant, but he offered David his armor. David tried on the heavy breastplate, the helmet. They were heavy and cumbersome. David did not mean to stand up sword against sword with that giant anyway. So he laid aside Saul's armor.

David took his slingshot, he picked up five smooth stones at the brook and walked out to meet Goliath. The giant was offended. What was wrong with this crazy youngster? "Am I a dog, that thou comest to me with staves?" said Goliath. Goliath was so angry that he took off his helmet.

David put a stone in the sling, whirled it about his head three or four times. My, how it buzzed! He let go one string of the sling in its last circle about his head, and the stone sailed true to its target. It hit the giant in the forehead. He was knocked out completely. Then David ran and took the giant's sword and cut off his head.

When the Philistines saw that their champion was dead and that, like David had said, his body would be eaten by the fowls of the air and prove that the God of Israel was the true God, they fled and were pursued by the Israelites, and many Philistines were slain. David picked up that giant head of the Philistine, carried it by the hair and took it to King Saul.

God had great things in store for this lad. He was filled with the Spirit. He was bold in faith.

David Hides From King Saul

I SAMUEL 21—II SAMUEL 5

King Saul had not pleased God. He had not followed the clear instructions to destroy the Amalekites and their flocks and herds. And more and more he feared David because he knew God was with him.

At last David left King Saul and went into the wilderness to hide and to avoid King Saul, who wanted to kill him.

Other men who were in debt or in trouble came up to be with David, and they formed a band. David fled away. He went to the priest Ahimelech. Ahimelech gave him some of the shewbread which had been removed from off the table of shewbread so David and the group that went with him would have food. And since David had no weapon, they brought him the sword of Goliath, the Philistine giant whom David had killed. And David took that sword with him.

King Saul sent a wicked man to slay the priest and all his family because they had befriended David.

King Saul sent to David's home to seize him there, but David's wife, Michal, and daughter of King Saul, told the messengers that David was sick. Then King Saul sent messengers back to take David and kill him. His wife put a dummy figure in the bed and pretended it was David. But David and his men slipped away and went into the wilderness.

King Saul brought soldiers out to kill David, but David slipped away to the other side of the mountain. Once King Saul stopped and entered into a cave. David and his men where hidden in the same cave. David's friends said, "Now is

the time to kill King Saul." But David said, "I will not put my hand on the Lord's anointed. God has promised me the kingdom, but I will not take it by force, until God gets King Saul out of the way." So he cut off part of the skirt of Saul's garment. Later, when King Saul was going away, David went outside and showed him that he had cut off part of his garment and could have slain him there, but would not.

Saul was conscience-stricken and promised not to bother David any more. But he did not keep that promise. Another time King Saul and his army came out in the wilderness seeking for David. As they all slept in the night, David asked for someone to go with him to King Saul's camp. And God put a deep sleep on all of King Saul's soldiers. David slipped up and took a spear that was in the ground by King Saul's head and the vessel of water. Then he went aside to a hill and called out to King Saul and showed that he had another chance to kill him, but would not.

For a time David joined himself to the Philistine king at Gath, but when they went to battle against Israel, the other princes of the Philistines were afraid to have David along lest he should betray them and fight against them. So God prevented David from fighting against Israel.

At last there came a great battle and Saul and his sons were killed when the Israelites were defeated. Then some men of Judah called on David to come and take the place of king. He was famous among them for the many times he had delivered Israel. God had used David to destroy Philistines and other enemies.

So David became king over the tribe of Judah at Hebron. Some of Saul's friends continued to battle against David and his armies for some time. David reigned seven and a half years. Then he became king over all Israel and moved his headquarters from Hebron to Jerusalem. There the Jebusites had held out long against the Israelites, but David and his men defeated them and there David made his capital Mount Zion, part of the hill facing the valley of Kidron. There he reigned thirty-three years, making forty years of his reign over Judah and Israel.

David's Great Sin

II SAMUEL 11,12

David was God's good man. The Spirit of the Lord had been on him from the day he was anointed by Samuel to be a future king.

There are so many good things about David that pleased God and that rejoice our hearts. He was inspired by God to write many of the sweet devotional Psalms and prayers that have blessed millions and helped them to know God.

But God's men are not perfect. And when good men sin, they must suffer for it.

One night David was up on the palace roof. I imagine he was enjoying meditating as he sat under the night's sky.

"When I consider Thy heavens, the work of Thy fingers, the moon and the stars, which Thou hast ordained; What is man, that Thou art mindful of him? and the son of man, that Thou visitest him?"—Ps. 8:3,4.

He often thought on those things. God inspired him to write:

"The heavens declare the glory of God; and the firmament sheweth His handywork. Day unto day uttereth speech, and night unto night sheweth knowledge. There is no speech nor language, where their voice is not heard. Their line is gone out through all the earth, and their words to the end of the world. In them hath he set a tabernacle for the sun, Which is as a bridegroom coming out of his chamber, and rejoiceth as a strong man to run a race. His going forth is from the end of the heaven, and his circuit

unto the ends of it: and there is nothing hid from the heat thereof."—Ps. 19:1-6.

I am sure that David had not planned to commit adultery that night. But Satan trapped him, as he sometime does us.

Looking down over the parapet he saw in the paved courtyard next door a woman taking a bath. No one could have seen her except someone from the palace roof. And who would expect someone to be there!

She was young and David was attracted by her beauty. Oh, he ought to have turned his eyes away. Instead, he asked a servant, "Who is the lady in the house next door?" He was told she was the wife of his good man, Uriah, the Hittite, a great soldier, who was with Joab now in a war against Ammon. David instructed the servant to bring her unto him.

Bath-sheba was ordered to visit the king. Well, who would resist the command of a king? And who would scorn his advances? She came unto him. David fondled her, then seduced her. Ah, David, how much you and others will suffer because of your sin!

Days went by. Bath-sheba sent word to King David, "I am with child. What shall we do?" Her husband Uriah had been away for months in the war; and now there will be public disgrace. David thought, This sin must be covered.

So he sent word to Joab at Ammon to send home Uriah the Hittite. Of course it was expected that Uriah would go down to his own house. Instead, he slept at the door of the king's house with the servants. That would never do. The next day David kept him and made him drunk; still Uriah did not go home. This great soldier said to David, "Should I sleep in my own bed and enjoy my wife, when Joab and the armies of Israel sleep on the ground and are in constant danger?" No, this loyal man would not go home.

The next morning David wrote a note to Joab. In the attack on Rabbah-Ammon, he should put Uriah the Hittite in the front of the battle. Joab did as commanded and Uriah was killed. Then David took Bath-sheba to the palace as his wife.

Now the Prophet Nathan came to David and told him a

story. A rich man who had flocks and herds and plenty made a feast. Instead of using a lamb from his own flock, he took the one single lamb of a poor man who lived next door. Oh, how this man treasured this little lamb. It slept in his bosom, fed at his table, and now it was destroyed by the rich man. What should David do about that?

Indignantly David answered, "The presumptuous rich man who hath done this thing shall surely die. And he must restore the lamb fourfold."

Then solemnly Nathan the prophet said, "Thou art the man! You have riches, many wives, every luxury, yet you took the one loved wife of Uriah the Hittite to be thy wife." When David confessed his sin, Nathan said, God is merciful, David. Thou shalt not die."

Oh, but David will pay for that sin fourfold. The illegitimate baby was born, but the baby sickened and despite David's fasting and prayer, the little one died. That is one payment, David.

David had a beautiful daughter named Tamar. Her half-brother Amnon fell in love with her and had her come to his apartment, where he seized and raped her. She went away weeping, with dirt upon her head. Another payment, David.

Tamar had a strong, aggressive brother, Absalom. He learned what his wicked brother Amnon had done and vowed vengeance.

Time went by. Absalom had a great party. All the king's sons were invited. Absalom gave strict command to his servants that when Amnon was drunken they should smite him and kill him. They obeyed. Oh, what excitement and confusion as the king's sons rode back to the city. "Amnon only was dead." Payment number three, David.

David was greatly displeased. Absalom retired into the country for safety. But he asked General Joab to intercede for him. David allowed Absalom to come home to Jerusalem. But Absalom was not welcomed to David's heart. So Absalom became bitter and determined to seize the kingdom. He went among the people making friends and saying to any "man that had a controversy. . .Oh, that I were made judge in the land, that every man which hath any suit or cause might come unto me, and I would do him justice!" So he won the hearts of the people, then he rebelled and declared himself king. David and his friends and intimates fled for their lives. David, that is payment number four. But in battle Absalom was killed and David returned to his throne.

How earnestly David grieved over his sin and begged for cleansing, recorded for us in the inspired 51st Psalm. There we have David's penitent prayer:

"Have mercy upon me, O God, according to Thy lovingkindness: according unto the multitude of Thy tender mercies blot out my transgressions. Wash me throughly from mine iniquity, and cleanse me from my sin. For I acknowledge my transgression: and my sin is ever before me. Against Thee, Thee only, have I sinned, and done this evil in Thy sight: that Thou mightest be justified when Thou speakest, and be clear when Thou judgest. Behold, I was shapen in iniquity; and in sin did my mother conceive me. Behold, Thou desirest truth in the inward parts: and in the hidden part Thou shalt make me to know wisdom. Purge me with hyssop, and I shall be clean: wash me, and I shall be whiter than snow. Make me to hear joy and gladness; that the bones which Thou hast broken may rejoice. Hide Thy face from my sins, and blot out all mine iniquities. Create in me a clean heart, O God; and renew a right spirit within me. Cast me not away from Thy presence; and take not Thy holy spirit from me. Restore unto me the joy of Thy salvation; and uphold me with Thy free spirit. Then will I teach transgressors Thy ways; and sinners shall be converted unto Thee. Deliver me from bloodguiltiness, O God, Thou God of my salvation: and my tongue shall sing aloud of Thy righteousness. O Lord, open Thou my lips; and my mouth shall shew forth Thy praise. For Thou desirest not sacrifice; else would I give it: Thou delightest not in burnt-offering."—Vss. 1-16.

Then David added, "A broken and a contrite heart, O God, Thou wilt not despise" (vs. 17).

It is good that we have a record of David's sin and his repentance, for no doubt millions of other disobedient, sinning Christians have made this their own prayer of confession and pleading for forgiveness.

Absalom's Rebellion

II SAMUEL 15-19

We do not know all the reasons that went into Absalom's rebellion against his father David. What an awful thing that a son would be willing to kill his own father and seize the kingdom for himself! However, Absalom must have known David's sin with Bath-sheba. Hence, that would have disillusioned him and broken down his respect for the great king. What a responsibility every father has to live so that his children will know that his sincere professions are followed by faithful, godly living!

Then Absalom was properly indignant over the rape of his sister Tamar. Since King David did not punish Amnon, there was no way for him to be punished unless Absalom took the matter into his own hands. We feel very sympathetic for the wrath of Absalom toward this rapist, Amnon. Absalom took his brokenhearted sister to his home and kept her.

Why didn't David punish Amnon? Surely Absalom would think David careless about that. And King David's forgiveness of Absalom seemed halfhearted. He did not take the son into his loving embrace and sweet fellowship. Bitterness crept into the disillusioned heart of Absalom. All this caused him to decide to seize the kingdom.

Absalom was a handsome man. His pleasing personality, his soft words, his comradeship among the people, won the hearts of thousands. They were ready to follow him. So Absalom gathered together a great army of followers and declared himself king. David and his immediate followers fled for their lives. As they went from Jerusalem around the

Mount of Olives, a wicked man, Shimei, came and cursed David. And he threw stones at him. Others would have slain this man, but David said, "Let him alone. Let him curse me; perhaps God has bidden him to do so."

Back in the city, Absalom had a council of war. Ahithophel, a wise statesman upon whom David had greatly relied, counseled Absalom to take a small band of men, seek out David that night and kill him, and the war would all be won. But David prayed that God would overcome the counsel of Ahithophel. And he had left in the city his friend Hushai. Hushai pretended to be for Absalom. They asked his counsel. He said that since David was a mighty man of war and was probably hidden so they could not find him, they should wait until the great army be gathered from all Israel and then take David.

Hushai then sent David word to escape across the Jordan as soon as possible.

So Absalom gathered an army and they followed David and his army over into the land of Gilead. The armies fought and David's men overwhelmed Absalom's wild volunteers. Absalom fled upon a mule. But his great head of hair got entangled in the branches of an oak. The mule ran away and left him hanging there. He was discovered and Joab came and thrust three darts into him and killed him.

The rebellion was over.

When the men of David had filed out for their battle arrayed against Absalom, David had pleaded, "Deal gently for my sake with the young man, even with Absalom." Now when the victorious filed back into the city where his people had compelled David to stay, they were triumphant. But Joab had sent a runner ahead of the crowd to tell David of the victory. "Oh, but how is it with the young man, Absalom?" cried David. And Cushi answered, "The enemies of my lord the king, and all that rise against thee to do thee hurt, be as that young man is."

David was disconsolate. He turned away from the crowd and went up over the gate to be alone. He cried, "O my son Absalom, my son, my son Absalom! would God I had died for

Copyright in
My Picture Bible Book.
Courtesy Zondervan Publishers

thee, O Absalom, my son, my son!''

The people suddenly felt defeated and sad. They had risked their lives to defend the king; now he wept over the rebellious son who would have killed him. They slunk away like men defeated in battle.

Joab came to David and said, "It seems you would have been contented had all these faithful men who risked their lives for you died and Absalom had lived. If you do not come forth and speak comfortably to thy servants, and appear to them as their joyful, victorious king, the people will forsake us and that will be worse unto thee than all the evil that befell thee before."

So David came forth and sat in the gate and greeted the people and comforted them. He rejoiced with them over their victory. Soon the elders and leaders of the tribe came to escort David back to Jerusalem, and he knew he was again king of Israel.

God Reveals to David the Site
for Solomon's Temple

David was king seven and one-half years at Hebron over Judah and Benjamin. Then the followers of dead King Saul who held onto the northern tribes grew weaker. Finally that group agreed also to have David as king. The Jebusites in Jerusalem were conquered and David set up his capital there and ruled thirty-three and one-half years. Now God had so spread and enlarged David's kingdom that he became proud and gloried in his strength. So David proudly decided to take a census of all men able to bear arms and sent Joab his general to supervise it. Joab saw there was a certain arrogant pride in David that would displease the Lord.

At last the prophet of God, Gad, came to David and said, "Thus saith the Lord, I offer thee three things; choose thee one of them, that I may do it unto thee. . .Shall seven years of famine come unto thee in thy land? or wilt thou flee three months before thine enemies, while they pursue thee? or that there be three days' pestilence in thy land?" (II Sam. 24:12,13).

But David said, "Let us fall now into the hand of the Lord; for His mercies are great: and let me not fall into the hand of man" (vs. 15). A plague killed thousands. Can you imagine David's pain of heart when the angel stretched out his hand upon Jerusalem to destroy it? Ah, but the Lord repented. He said to the angel, "It is enough: stay now thine hand. And the angel. . .was by the threshingfloor of Araunah the

Jebusite." David was instructed to buy the threshingfloor of Araunah the Jebusite. There he was to build an altar and have a sacrifice. And God's judgment would be stayed.

When King David approached Araunah the Jebusite and offered to buy the place for a place of sacrifice, that good man bowed himself before the king with his face to the ground and said,

"Let my lord the king take and offer up what seemeth good unto him: behold, here be oxen for burnt-sacrifice, and threshing instruments and other instruments of the oxen for wood. All these things did Araunah, as a king, give unto the king."—II Sam. 24:22,23.

But David would not have it so. He said, "Nay; but I will surely buy it of thee at a price: neither will I offer burnt-offerings unto the Lord my God of that which doth cost me nothing" (vs. 24).

"So David bought the threshingfloor and the oxen for fifty shekels of silver. And David built there an altar unto the Lord, and offered burnt-offerings and peace-offerings. . .and the plague was stayed." Ah, but God had many things in mind for, behold, that threshingfloor of Araunah the Jebusite was at the same place that Abraham tried to offer Isaac. Second Chronicles 3:1 says later, "Then Solomon began to build the house of the Lord at Jerusalem in mount Moriah, where the Lord appeared unto David his father, in the place that David had prepared in the threshingfloor of Ornan the Jebusite."

It was on Mount Moriah that Abraham offered his son, as we see from Genesis 22:2. Here, then, is the place God had selected centuries before where Solomon will build the Temple on Mount Moriah. And Mount Moriah is a ridge that goes through the old city of Jerusalem. On one end of it was the great Temple square. At the other end of the city Mount Moriah is cut in two by a great gash outside the present city wall. And the scarred face of the cliff looks somewhat like a skull. And that end of Mount Moriah is Calvary where Jesus was crucified.

Solomon Builds the Temple—Jones

You may be sure that in all God's plans for David and Solomon and that reign of kings, it was to end in Jesus our Messiah, our Saviour. "To Him give all the prophets witness, that through His name whosoever believeth in Him shall receive remissions of sins" (Acts 10:43).

Solomon Becomes King

After King David's sin with Bath-sheba, the wife of Uriah the Hittite, one of his greatest soldiers, and after Uriah had died in battle, we know that David and Bath-sheba were grieved over their sin. The baby Bath-sheba bore for David died, and many other troubles followed David. His heartbroken prayer is recorded in Psalm 51.

Then David and Bath-sheba found God was about to give them another baby. His name is Solomon. And God loved him. David knew it was God's will for Solomon to inherit David's throne. So Solomon became king.

David had wanted to build a great temple for God at Jerusalem. He had saved up many, many hundreds of thousands of dollars' worth of gold and silver. But God revealed to David that he was not to build that Temple since he had been a man of war and bloodshed. Rather, Solomon, his son, would build it.

David had made plans. Hiram, king of Tyre and a great friend of David's, had agreed to furnish timber, fine cedars from the forests of Lebanon. Agreement was made that the Israelites would go to help cut the timber and float it in great rafts down to Joppa and, from there, bring the timbers to Jerusalem.

The Temple itself was a magnificent thing! Under the city of Jerusalem was a great stone quarry where, we are told, the stones to build the Temple were cut out and brought to the surface. Of course, cedar beams were used for the roof of the great building and cedar was used to line the stone walls and then they were plated with gold. This Temple was a wonder to all who saw it.

When Solomon became king, God appeared to him in a dream and said, "What shall I do for you, Solomon? Do you want gold? Do you want riches and prosperity?" But Solomon said, "O Lord God, I want wisdom to rule my people, so great a people." He wanted divine wisdom to do right in this great place of responsibility, and God gave him wisdom. And Solomon was wiser than any other man. He ruled his people righteously and people came from far and near to hear his wisdom. Solomon had great income, tribute from the people. His ships brought gold, apes and peacocks from Africa. Foreign kings sent him great gifts. The Queen of Sheba came bringing treasures.

But Solomon made a sad mistake. He had some 700 wives and 300 concubines. God had plainly commanded that kings of Israel were not to multiply wives to themselves, but Solomon did. He married a daughter of Pharaoh and princesses from other heathen countries. And these women led his heart away from God. Solomon built them temples on the "Hill of Scandals," a spur of the Mount of Olives. And there they worshiped their heathen gods, and Solomon went to worship with them. What a sad state for David's great son to become an idolator!

Certainly that was wrong. God warned him that when his son came to reign, the kingdom would be divided. So when Rehoboam came to the throne, the northern tribes of Israel withdrew to make a separate nation. It would now be called Israel or Samaria. But the tribes of Benjamin and Judah stayed together under Rehoboam, and the Levites still ministered in the Temple there.

It was a wonderful thing how God blessed Solomon. But it is sad that this man, so greatly blessed of God, would then be so led of heathen women into idolatry and sin.

Solomon and the
Queen of Sheba

Of all his sons, David had appointed Solomon to be king in his stead. While he was yet alive he insisted Solomon's generals and priests take him to Gihon near the pool of Siloam in the Hebron Valley and there he was to be mounted on David's mule and the people were instructed to cry, "Long live the king." So Solomon entered Jerusalem in triumph and began his reign. We are told that "the Lord loved him." He was the son of David and Bath-sheba.

When he began his reign the Lord appeared unto him in the night and asked him to choose what he would have of the Lord. Long life? Great riches? No, Solomon felt that he was but a child and he pleaded with God that he might have divine wisdom to govern this, so great a people. God granted that request and Solomon was said to be wiser than all the philosophers, perhaps the wisest man that ever lived.

His fame increased and his riches. David's great friend, King Hiram of Tyre, has already agreed to help with the great cedar trees of Lebanon for building the Temple at Jerusalem. Wealth had accumulated, set aside for this purpose. Now Solomon pushed the matter. David would have liked to build the Temple but God had sent a prophet to tell him, no, that was to be the work of his son. David had fought so many wars, shed so much blood, it were better that peaceful Solomon build the Temple.

What a beautiful, rich Temple it was. The whole tribe of Levites were set apart to care for the Temple, to prepare and offer the sacrifices and carry on the service of God for the whole nation.

The Queen of Sheba, queen of a fabulous country, heard of Solomon's wisdom and wealth and the glory of his reign. She heard of his divinely-given wisdom and the blessing of God upon his kingdom. So the Queen of Sheba came to see Solomon.

There have been many legends about the Queen of Sheba. Was she a queen of some little country on the Arabian peninsula? Some thought so. But what country had such riches as the Queen of Sheba manifested? A great scholar, Dr. Immanuel Velikovsky, by diligent research, has found amazing proof that the Queen of Sheba was Queen Hatshepsut of Egypt. He has found evidence in the records of Egypt of her journey to meet Solomon. The Queen of Egypt was enthralled and overcome when she saw the glory of Solomon's court. The Temple itself, the stately ambassadors and

The Queen of Sheba comes to see for herself the wonders of Solomon.

ministers, the beautiful clothing, the processions of priests and Levites, and Solomon's ascent into the Temple to worship—how these impressed the queen! She asked of Solomon every question that occurred to her. She was amazed at his wisdom and could say no more. She said, "I did not believe it, and, behold, the half was not told me."

She presented to Solomon one hundred and twenty talents of gold and beautiful almug trees and precious stones. She brought a great abundance of spices—no such abundance of spices had ever appeared in Israel before. Then the Queen of Sheba took her train of attendants and returned home.

As the Queen of Sheba said about Solomon, so we can say about the Lord Jesus Christ, "The half has never yet been told."

Elijah and Fire From Heaven

Ahab was king of Israel, the northern tribes, with the capital at Samaria. He led Israel to sin more than all the kings before him. He built a great temple for Baal at Samaria and he himself worshiped that heathen god. Added to that, he married Jezebel, daughter of the king of Tyre, who had 450 priests of Baal that ate at her table daily.

Wickedness and idolatry became so widespread that the good prophet Elijah "prayed earnestly that it might not rain: and it rained not on the earth by the space of three years and six months" (Jas. 5:17). He answered that "there shall not be dew nor rain these years, but according to my word" (I Kings 17:1).

What a stir that announcement made! So Elijah hid out. God had him camp by the brook Cherith, and there he drank of the brook and God had ravens to bring him bread and meat daily! Then the brook dried up, since there was no rain. God told him to go to Zarephath near Tyre and Zidon, and there God selected a widow who would feed him.

When Elijah arrived near the town, a widow was outside gathering sticks. Elijah said, "Lady, would you bring me a little water?" She agreed and then he said, "And will you bring me also a morsel of bread when you come?"

The widow looked at the prophet with troubled face. "I must tell you the truth. All I have is a handful of meal, all that is left in the barrel. I came to pick up sticks to cook a cake for my son and me before we die. There is no more meal, no money to buy any."

"Nevertheless," Elijah said, "make a little cake for me first."

She trusted God, and, behold, after Elijah's cake there was more meal in the barrel. When she cooked for herself and her son, there was more still. So for the rest of the famine the barrel of meal never failed. It was like the manna from Heaven which came every day when Israel was in the wilderness. Jesus said in Luke 6:38, "Give, and it shall be given unto you; good measure, pressed down, and shaken together, and running over, shall men give into your bosom. For with the same measure that ye mete withal it shall be measured to you again." How sweet it is to trust God to care for His prophet and to see His constant supply!

When the widow's son died, Elijah prayed and the son was restored to her again. How fortunate to have had Elijah there! I surely would feel safe to have a man like Elijah in my home in time of famine or sickness!

The three and a half years of God's judgment on Israel passed. So Elijah came out of hiding and appeared to King Ahab. "Call all Israel to Mount Carmel," Elijah told him. "Thou and thy fathers' house have afflicted Israel." The land is so distressed. No one argued against Elijah's call.

Here they came. I suppose they gathered on the west side of Mount Carmel near the Mediterranean Sea. (The fine big city of Haifa is built there now.)

Elijah challenged the people: "How long halt ye between two opinions? if the Lord be God, follow him: but if Baal, then follow him." I suppose the people were feeling guilty, yet they hesitated to confess devotion to Jehovah. Ahab served Baal. Queen Jezebel served Baal. Four hundred and fifty priests of Baal who ate at Jezebel's table were present.

Elijah made a proposition. Let the priests of Baal set up an altar, and place upon it wood. Let them kill and dress a bullock and place it on the wood, but no fire. Then let the priests of Baal pray down fire, if they can, to burn the sacrifice. Then he, Elijah, would build an altar, put on wood and a

Elijah on Mount Carmel

bullock, but no fire. Then let the God who answered by fire be God for Israel.

"That is well spoken," the people answered.

The test began. First, the priests of Baal built their altar with wood and a bullock, but no fire. "O Baal, hear us," they cried. But there was no answer. They leaped upon the altar and cut themselves with knives and lancets till the blood gushed out. Of course, the heathen idol god could not show the miracle power Jehovah has.

Elijah mocked them. "Cry a little louder. Maybe Baal is not at home. Maybe he is on a journey. Or sleeping. Keep on praying!" But there was none to answer. That idol god could not send the fire!

The people waited. Did some of them really think Baal would answer? Perhaps. But they were surely shocked now.

Now Elijah, at midafternoon, called the people. They know now that Baal is powerless. Elijah made a new altar of twelve stones. He put wood on the altar, but no fire. Then the bullock was cut in pieces and placed on the wood.

Then Elijah did a surprising thing. He called for four barrels of water to be poured on the sacrifice and wood! Perhaps they lugged it up from the Mediterranean near by. "Four barrels more," he demanded. Then, "Four barrels more!" Then he dug a trench about the altar and filled it with water. When God sends fire miraculously, He can burn wet wood as well as dry wood. Let us learn that. God can save infidels as well as Sunday school boys and girls.

Then Elijah prayed a simple prayer of 63 words.

"Lord God of Abraham, Isaac, and of Israel, let it be known this day that Thou art God in Israel, and that I am Thy servant, and that I have done all these things at Thy word. Hear me, O Lord, hear me, that this people may know that Thou art the Lord God, and that Thou hast turned their heart back again."

Suddenly the fire of God fell and consumed the burnt sacrifice, and the wet wood, and the stones, and the dust, and licked up the water from the trench. What an amazing answer!

The people fell upon their faces and cried out, "The Lord, He is the God; the Lord, He is the God."

Then Elijah had them bring the four hundred and fifty prophets of Baal down by the brook Kishon, and Elijah cut off their heads. Queen Jezebel will not have so many present for dinner tonight!

Do you think Elijah did wrong to kill the prophets of Baal? If you do, then you must remember how many they had led away from God, how many thousands or perhaps millions went to Hell because of them. Remember that in the Flood, God killed millions who would not hear the Gospel. Remember, God Himself announced the death penalty on murder, adultery and idolatry (Exod. 21:12-17; Num. 35; Lev. 20:10). It is God who sends Christ-rejecters to Hell. So Elijah did right to destroy these wicked men who led Israel away from the true God.

But what of the drouth and famine? There was to be neither rain nor dew but at Elijah's word. We might say God gave Elijah the key to the heavens. He who prayed earnestly that it might not rain must pray again for rain. So Elijah went to the mountain top and prayed. Again and again he sent his servant to see if clouds were gathering. After the seventh time of prayer the servant said, "There is a cloud approximately the size of a man's hand." So Elijah knew his prayer was heard. He warned Ahab to enter his chariot and drive to his palace at Jezreel. With God's Spirit on him, Elijah ran before the chariot. And there came a great rain.

How Queen Jezebel hated Elijah! Her prophets of Baal were dead! She was discredited as queen! So she sent word to Elijah she would kill him tomorrow.

The prophet had been through such emotional stress and was so physically worn, he thought he was ready to die. So he slipped away down by Beer-sheba, and requested to die. As he lay and slept, an angel touched him and said, "Arise and eat." Then God told Elijah he must yet anoint Elisha to be

God's prophet, Hazael to be king of Syria, and Jehu to be king of Israel.

But the Mount Carmel experience will always be a lesson that those who seek God with all their hearts can find Him. God honors preachers who are strong against sin and who believe God for His mighty power.

We recall what Longfellow wrote:

> *How beautiful is the rain!*
> *After the dust and heat,*
> *In the blood and fiery street,*
> *In the narrow lane,*
> *How beautiful is the rain!*
> *The sick man from his chamber looks*
> *At the twisted brooks;*
> *He can feel the cool*
> *Breath of each little pool;*
> *His fevered brain*
> *Grows calm again,*
> *And he breathes a blessing on the rain.*

Words cannot express the outward blessings which that rain brought to all the land in Elijah's day, to all—fertile fields, fruitful orchards, golden crops, prosperity, comfort, peace. Abundance of blessings followed the abundance of rain.

—R. G. Lee

Wicked King Ahab and Naboth's Vineyard

I KINGS 21

Ahab was king over the northern tribes of Israel and had his palace at Samaria. Sometimes the country was called Samaria because of its capital. Near the palace was a nice fertile piece of ground belonging to Naboth. In the law of Moses, God had instructed that the land should pass from father to son. So each Israelite treasured his land. But King Ahab wanted that piece of land near the palace for a vegetable garden and offered to buy it or trade another plot for it. But Naboth refused. He dare not trade away the family inheritance.

Ahab went to his bed chamber and lay, like a pouting child, with his face to the wall. Jezebel the queen, who served Baal, was a wicked woman. Why was Ahab so displeased? He wanted Naboth's vineyard and Naboth would not sell or trade. Jezebel was ruthless. She said, "I'll see that you get Naboth's vineyard without paying for it!"

So she wrote to the elders of the city instructing them to call Naboth to trial. Then they were to find wicked men they could bribe to testify that Naboth had blasphemed against God and the king, then convict him and take him out and stone him to death.

The elders carried out the queen's instructions. Was not her letter sealed with the king's seal? It was in effect a royal command. So Naboth was dead. Ahab could now take the vineyard.

King Ahab was pleased. He went down to take possession

of Naboth's vineyard. But, behold, Elijah was there! And he said, "Thus saith the Lord, Hast thou killed, and also taken possession? . . .Thus saith the Lord, In the place where dogs licked the blood of Naboth shall dogs lick thy blood, even thine." What a startling prophecy! Ahab had taken the vineyard, but payday was coming!

"Did you see, Ahab, how the dogs licked the blood of innocent Naboth? Well, the same dogs will lick your blood, Ahab!" And Jezebel? Dogs shall eat Jezebel in Jezreel!

At last it came to pass. Ahab had war with the Syrians. He invited Jehoshaphat, king of Judah, to go with him to the battle. Although he disguised himself, in that battle Ahab was shot with an arrow at a venture, and it went between the joints of his armor.

"Take me out of the battle," said Ahab to the driver of his chariot. And at sundown he died. Word went out to his scattered army to return every man to his house: Ahab was dead.

They took his body back to Samaria. But Ahab's blood had poured out in the chariot. Servants washed out the chariot on the pavement where men had stoned to death innocent Naboth so Ahab could steal his land. There dogs had licked the blood where Naboth died by being beaten to death. Now at the same spot dogs licked the blood washed out of Ahab's chariot.

Retribution! Remember that Jesus promised, "And shall not God avenge His own elect, which cry day and night unto Him?" (Luke 18:7). We read in Galatians 6:7,8, "Be not deceived; God is not mocked: for whatsoever a man soweth, that shall he also reap. For he that soweth to his flesh shall of the flesh reap corruption; but he that soweth to the Spirit shall of the Spirit reap life everlasting."

But will the dogs eat Jezebel? Well, Ahab died, so God anointed Jehu to be king in his stead. He destroyed the house of Baal, when it was filled with the idol worshipers. He destroyed the sons of Ahab who would want to be king.

Now triumphant that his kingdom was established, Jehu drove in his chariot to Jezreel, at the palace. Queen Jezebel dressed her hair, put on her robes and appeared at an up-

Ahab was king over the Northern tribes
of Israel and had his palace in Samaria.

stairs window to
challenge Jehu in
his chariot. Jehu
cried out, "Who is
on my side?" Two
or three servants
appeared at the
windows. Jehu com-
manded, "Throw
her down." So they
threw her down.
Some of her blood
sprinkled on the
wall, and on the
horses. Jehu drove
his chariot over her
broken body. Then
he and his party
went on to a feast.
Jehu said, "Go bury
that wicked woman
for she is a king's
daughter." But the

**Jezebel suggests that Ahab
have Naboth murdered.**

dogs had eaten Jezebel's body, all but the skull and feet
and palms of her hands.

Yes, God's prophecy by Elijah had been fulfilled. The dogs
licked the blood of Ahab where they had licked the blood of
innocent Naboth. And the dogs ate Jezebel in Jezreel.

We find that between his sanctioning Jezebel's having
Naboth murdered and his own death, Ahab had a period of
repentance. That was well and good, but it did not cancel out
the payday promised him for his sins.

The Prophet Elisha
Called and Anointed

II KINGS 2

After that marvelous manifestation of the power of God at Mount Carmel, when a whole nation, in some sense, publicly repudiated the worship of Baal and turned back to God, the exhausted Prophet Elijah thought his work was done. Oh, no! God told him he must first anoint Hazael to be king over Syria. "And Jehu the son of Nimshi shalt thou anoint to be king over Israel: and Elisha the son of Shaphat of Abel-meholah shalt thou anoint to be prophet in thy room" (I Kings 19:16). No, it would not do for Elijah to go to Heaven until God has another anointed prophet to take his place.

Elisha lived on a rather large farm with his father and mother, so large that twelve yoke of oxen were plowing at one time, and Elisha with one yoke. The Prophet Elijah came and with a symbolic flourish, laid his mantle over the shoulders of Elisha. Was some fire of God already burning in the heart of Elisha? We think so. He jumped at the chance to be a prophet of God. And he cried out, "Let me, I pray thee, kiss my father and my mother, and then I will follow thee." Perhaps Elijah was surprised at such an ardent, immediate surrender. "And he said unto him, Go back again: for what have I done to thee?" (I Kings 19:20,21). Now Elisha will be in glad training to be God's prophet. He is known as "Elisha the son of Shaphat, which poured water on the hands of Elijah."

A young preacher may be glad to serve an apprenticeship

by being song leader to an evangelist, or by being an assistant to a good pastor, or by being a Sunday school superintendent, or a bus director, or rescue mission worker; he may learn and grow into a mighty leader. So Elisha humbled himself to be bodyservant to Elijah.

But triumph approached now for Elijah. After the last assignment God had given him, this old warrior, who suffered for God and had faith to stand alone before a wicked king and queen and a backslidden nation, is going to Heaven. He will not die, but in a marvelous miracle, will be taken alive to Heaven. Even as "Enoch walked with God: and he was not; for God took him."

It was an expectancy among all the "sons of the prophets." Elijah was going to Heaven. So Elijah said to Elisha, "Tarry here. . .for the Lord hath sent me to Beth-el."

"Not on your life!" Elisha replied. "As the Lord liveth, and as thy soul liveth, I will not leave thee." What wonderful thing God would do—Elisha is determined to be there. The sons of the prophets gathered around Elisha and said, "Did you know the Lord will take our master Elijah to Heaven today?" Elisha cut them off abruptly: "Yea, I know it; hold your peace."

Then Elijah said to Elisha, "Tarry here, I pray thee; for the Lord hath sent me to Jericho."

Again the determined answer was, "As the Lord liveth, and as thy soul liveth, I will not leave thee." So they went together. At Jericho a group of sons of the prophets gathered around Elisha and said to him, "Knowest thou that the Lord will take away thy master from thy head to day?" Again he said shortly, "Yea, I know it; hold ye your peace."

Then Elijah said unto Elisha, "Tarry, I pray thee, here; for the Lord hath sent me to Jordan." The determined answer still was, "As the Lord liveth, and as thy soul liveth, I will not leave thee." "And they two went on" together.

The other sons of the prophets stood afar off and watched, but Elisha was determined to be present. If he were to be the mighty prophet of God, he must have the prophet's mantle and the prophet's power.

They came to the Jordan River together. Elijah took that precious prophet's mantle of his, wrapped it together and whacked the Jordan water. A wide path opened through the river and they walked through. I think it may be the younger prophet made a note: "That is one of the first things I will do when I get that mantle."

And now Elijah asked solemnly, "You followed me all this way. You are determined about something. I am about to be taken away. What shall I do for you before I leave?"

And Elisha fervently pleaded, "I want a double portion of the Spirit of God that is on thee."

That was a tremendous request. If it were asked lightly, it would be foolish. But, no, this young man who left a large farm to be a servant to Elijah now eagerly wants to pay any price to have the power of God that makes a great prophet. Elijah said, "You have asked a hard thing but if you see me when I am taken up, you shall have it."

Then came a great whirlwind and a chariot of fire and Elijah was saying goodbye to this world. Elisha cried out, "My father, my father, the chariot of Israel, and the horsemen thereof." I imagine he would almost have held on to that chariot until Elijah cast down the prophet's mantle. Now Elisha had inherited the mantle of Elijah.

Did he have the power, too? He marched right back to the Jordan River. He wrapped that mantle together and smote the river and said, "Where is the Lord God of Elijah?" Perhaps if that river could have talked, it would have said, "Behold, another prophet of God!" The river opened a path. Elisha walked back through and began a mighty career of miracles and witness.

Now Elisha had asked for and received a "double portion" of the Spirit that was on Elijah. We do not believe that Elisha was greater than Elijah. But to me there is a wonderful significance in the fact that the Bible records eight major miracles by Elijah and sixteen major miracles, twice as many, by Elisha.

Miracles of Elijah

1. Fed by ravens (I Kings 17:1-6).
2. Widow's meal and oil replenished (I Kings 17:8-16).
3. Raises widow's son (I Kings 17:17-23).
4. Fire comes down from Heaven and consumes his offering (I Kings 18:36-38).
5. Fed by angel (I Kings 19:5-7).
6. Calls fire down from Heaven to consume captain and fifty men (II Kings 1:9-12).
7. Divides waters of Jordan (II Kings 2:8).
8. Elijah went up by whirlwind with chariot of fire into Heaven (II Kings 2:11).

Miracles of Elisha

1. Parts the water and goes over Jordan on dry land (II Kings 2:14).
2. Heals water with salt (II Kings 2:21,22).
3. Bears tear forty-two young people (II Kings 2:23-25)
4. Country is filled with water (II Kings 3:16-20).
5. Increase of widow's oil (II Kings 4:1-7).
6. Birth of son to barren Shunammite woman (II Kings 4:8-17).
7. Restores life to son of Shunammite (II Kings 4:18-37)
8. Heals noxious pottage (II Kings 4:38-41).
9. Feeds one hundred men with twenty loaves (II Kings 4:42-44).
10. Naaman's leprosy miraculously healed (II Kings 5:1-19).
11. Commands leprosy of Naaman to cleave to Gehazi (II Kings 5:20-27).
12. Makes lost ax float (II Kings 6:5-7).

13. Eyes of his servant opened; sees mountain full of horses and chariots of fire around Elisha (II Kings 6:13-17).

14. Brings blindness on Syrians (II Kings 6:18-20).

15. God miraculously scatters Syrians and fulfills Elisha's promise of food (II Kings 7:1-16).

16. Man brought to life by touching Elisha's bones (II Kings 13:20,21).

So Elisha's request was answered. He was now a Spirit-filled prophet.

Naaman the Syrian Healed
of Leprosy

II KINGS 5

For many years the Syrians, with headquarters in Damascus, were enemies of Israel. So raiding parties of Syrian soldiers came often to certain parts of Israel to steal flocks and grain, thinking sometime to kidnap the king of Israel. Once they took captive a little Israelite girl. Naaman, a Syrian commander, took the shy and homesick girl to be maid to his wife. The slave girl fitted into the family, became happy and loved them. Naaman was a great captain and God had allowed him to bring great victory to Syria.

And he was an honorable man, but, sadly, he was a leper. Leprosy was an awful creeping disease, with no known cure, that oftentimes, bit by bit, ate away fingers, toes, nose and ears, until the poor loathsome body died.

The little Hebrew maid was greatly troubled for her master. She said, "If my master were in Israel, there is a prophet of God there and he could be healed."

The Syrians could well believe that God had worked many miracles in Israel. So the word came to the king of Syria and he said, "I will send Naaman to Israel and get him healed." He wrote a letter to the king of Israel and in it put a great gift of money and said, "I am sending my servant Naaman to be healed of leprosy. Please see that he is healed."

The king of Israel was dismayed. Was the king of Syria in asking such a foolish and impossible thing really trying to

Naaman takes the seventh plunge, and comes out. He looks at himself. Behold, his flesh is as that of a little child! He says to his servant, "Why, I never felt so good! I feel better than if I had won a battle! Look! I am cleansed!"

start a war? But the Prophet Elisha heard of the king's request and sent him word, "Send Naaman to me and he shall know that there is a prophet of God in Israel."

So Naaman drove up to the prophet's house. Elisha sent a servant to say simply, "Go dip seven times in the River Jordan and thou shalt be clean."

Naaman was indignant. He had expected Elisha to come ceremoniously to him to pass his hands over the festering sores and say some magic words. He was a chief general of Syria and was indignant that he got no more attention. "Why, we have rivers Abana and Pharpar, far better than this muddy Jordan. I could dip in them."

But his servants reminded him that if the prophet had asked some great thing, he would have done it. Why not obey the simple command and see?

So Naaman drove his chariot down to the river and went into the water. He dipped one time—no change. He dipped twice—no change. Then again and the fourth time and the fifth time and the sixth time—no change. But the seventh time as Naaman rose dripping from the water, behold, the leprosy was gone. He drove again to the prophet's house. He said that he had ten talents and would gladly give the money and many changes of raiment to the prophet. But, no, the prophet made no charge, would not receive the gift. And Naaman would make a joyful journey home.

But first he asked for two mules' burden of earth to make an altar for the Lord from Israelite soil. He would worship the true God, but he explained to Elisha that when he went into the house of Rimmon with the king to worship there, leaning upon his arm, his real allegiance would be to the God of Israel.

And so he drove away.

Elisha's servant, Gehazi, was not satisfied with all that wealth offered, and refused. So he ran after the chariot and stopped it. "Two young prophets had come just now," he said. He asked if Naaman would send back for them each a talent of silver and a change of raiment.

Naaman gave more than asked and Gehazi carried it back

and hid it in the house for himself.

Elisha asked him, "Where have you been?" And the servant answered, "Thy servant went no whither." But Elisha knew. God had revealed it. And he said, "The leprosy therefore of Naaman shall rest on you." And now Gehazi became a leper for his greed.

Is it not remarkable that the little Hebrew girl, though a slave, still loved her troubled master and in that far-off country gave her witness to the God of Israel? Whatever our circumstances we should be true to Christ and witness for Him.

God Delivers Jerusalem From King Sennacherib

II KINGS 18,19

Hezekiah, king of Judah, had a wicked father, but Hezekiah loved the Lord and had a blessed revival in his country and in his capital city, Jerusalem. Judah had been subject to the king of Assyria, but Hezekiah determined to lead Judah to serve the Lord. So he cut off taxes and stopped obedience to the king of Assyria, while he revived the true worship of God in his own country. He also removed the high places of false worship. People had begun to worship the brass serpent which Moses had made as an example of Christ bearing our sins. So Hezekiah broke down the images.

God gave him victory over the Philistines. He defeated them with great victories. These heathen people who lived along the edge of the Mediterranean Sea toward Egypt had troubled Israel from the days of King Saul and King David.

But the best thing about King Hezekiah was, "He trusted in the Lord God of Israel; so that after him was none like him among all the kings of Judah, nor any that were before him" (18:5). Surely he was a believing child of God.

But while King Hezekiah was prospering in leading the southern kingdom, Judah, disaster came to the northern kingdom, called Israel, sometimes called Samaria after the capital city. They had rebelled against Assyria, the great country to the northeast, and King Shalmaneser came with armies to besiege Samaria, and after three years, took it. Then he carried away the mass of the people and had them settled in Assyria. He brought in heathens to repeople Israel's country. These people of mixed blood and religion became the Samaritans of Jesus' day.

About eight years later a new king of Assyria, Sennacherib, determined he would conquer Judah again and control the country. Hezekiah sent him a friendly letter offering gifts, but Sennacherib sent a great host to surround Jerusalem and to besiege it.

But Hezekiah was wise. Outside the walls of Jerusalem was a fine flowing fountain. But why should this water be left to supply the army of Sennacherib? No other springs of water were near. And why should Jerusalem lose this life-saving water for those within the city, when Sennacherib should come?

So Hezekiah had his men dig a tunnel from what is now called the "Virgin's Fountain" under the city for a third of a mile through solid rock to the Pool of Siloam. It was then inside the city wall. The first fountain was closed up to the outside so Jerusalem could have water. Sennacherib moved close by. The tunnel is still there and this water still flows through it to the Pool of Siloam, then overflows down the hill.

But the Assyrian army surrounded Jerusalem, with Rab-shakeh in charge. Three of Hezekiah's men went out to confer with him, Eliakim, Shebna the scribe, and Joah. These suggested, "Speak to us in the Syrian language, not in the Jews' language. Why should the people hear all these threats and your boasting?" But Rab-shakeh insisted it was the people who would suffer and starve to death in a siege.

Rab-shakeh was arrogant. He said, "You are not strong enough to fight all Sennacherib's armies and chariots. And do not depend on Egypt to come to your help." Then he said, "But if ye say unto me, We trust in the Lord our God: is not that He, whose high places and whose altars Hezekiah hath taken away?" Rab-shakeh even boasted that God had sent him to destroy Jerusalem!

When Hezekiah did not yield, Rab-shakeh grew blasphemous. He said:

This tunnel (Hezekiah's) is about 585 yards long and varies in height from 3.5 feet to 12 feet.

*"Neither let Hezekiah make you trust in the Lord
. . .Hath any of the gods of the nations delivered at all his
land out of the hand of the king of Assyria? Where are the
gods of Hamath, and of Arpad? where are the gods of
Sepharvaim, Hena, and Ivah? have they delivered Samaria
out of mine hand? Who are they among all the gods of the
countries, that have delivered their country out of mine
hand, that the Lord should deliver Jerusalem out of mine
hand?"*

The messengers came back to King Hezekiah with clothes
torn, as a sign of their grief and despair. Hezekiah also tore
his clothes, put on sackcloth as a sign of humility and
fasting, and sent messengers with this word to the Prophet
Isaiah. "This day is a day of trouble, and of rebuke, and
blasphemy. . . . It may be the Lord thy God will hear all the
words of Rab-shakeh, whom the king of Assyria his master
hath sent to reproach the living God. . . ."

Isaiah sent word back to King Hezekiah not to be troubled
because God would dispose of Sennacherib. He would die in
his own land.

But Rab-shakeh went to consult the Assyrian king, Sennacherib, at Libnah, and wrote Hezekiah again. He said the
gods of a dozen other nations could not deliver them from the
king of Assyria, so Hezekiah's God was powerless to deliver
Jerusalem from the armies of Assyria surrounding
Jerusalem.

Hezekiah received that blasphemous letter, read it, then
took it to the house of the Lord and read it, then prayed.
Hezekiah reminded God that He was not powerless as were
the idol gods of the heathen cities. He prayed, "Now
therefore, O Lord our God, I beseech Thee, save Thou us out
of his hand, that all the kingdoms of the earth may know
that Thou art the Lord God, even Thou only."

Isaiah the prophet sent word to King Hezekiah that his
prayer was heard. He quoted the Lord as saying:

*"Whom hast thou reproached and blasphemed? and
against whom hast thou exalted thy voice, and lifted up*

*thine eyes on high? even against the Holy One of Israel
. . . .Because thy rage against Me and thy tumult is come
up into Mine ears, therefore I will put My hook in thy nose,
and My bridle in thy lips, and I will turn thee back by the
way by which thou camest."*

God said of the king of Assyria, "He shall not come into
this city, nor shoot an arrow there, nor come before it with
shield, nor cast a bank against it."

So God will prove He is not helpless like the idol gods of
other cities! His anger will punish the arrogant blasphemy of
those who say He can do no more than an idol god. God says,
"I will defend this city, to save it, for Mine own sake, and for
My servant David's sake."

Now read in chapter 19 how God answered the prayer of
Hezekiah and defeated Sennacherib's army:

*"And it came to pass that night, that the angel of the Lord
went out, and smote in the camp of the Assyrians an
hundred fourscore and five thousand: and when they arose
early in the morning, behold, they were all dead corpses.
So Sennacherib king of Assyria departed, and went and
returned, and dwelt at Nineveh. And it came to pass, as he
was worshipping in the house of Nisroch his god, that
Adrammelech and Sharezer his sons smote him with the
sword: and they escaped into the land of Armenia. And
Esarhaddon his son reigned in his stead."*

The wicked king who thought no city could stand against
him had 185,000 dead soldiers. He returned to his country,
and in the temple of his own god his sons killed him!

A Beautiful Jewish Girl Queen in the Media-Persian Empire Who Was Used to Save Her People

ESTHER

About 740 B.C. the Syrians took the northern nation Israel captive, sometimes called Samaria after its capital city. Then later the southern kingdom, Judah, was carried away captive by Nebuchadnezzar, the Babylonian emperor who ruled over the same area claimed of the Assyrians. Then 70 years later Ezra, then Nehemiah, brought a remnant of Jews back to Palestine and rebuilt the Temple and the walls of Jerusalem. Meantime most of the Jews, most of the ten tribes, and many of Judah, stayed in the country of Babylon which later came under the rule of the Medes and Persians.

One of the great kings of the Persians was Xerxes, or called Ahasuerus in the Bible. Once Ahasuerus made a great time of feasting and invited everyone to partake. His governors, counselors and delegates from all over the empire were invited to the great feast.

After some days and when the king's heart was merry, he sent for Queen Vashti. So proud was he of her beauty and dignity and her queenly ornaments that he wanted her to come before his counselors and wise men and deputies. But this beautiful queen refused to come.

Now what should the king do? When he asked his counselors, they advised: "Queen Vashti has not only sinned against the king, but also against all the men of the empire, for now other women will despise their husbands and refuse

to obey them." The counselors advised Ahasuerus that he should put Queen Vashti away and send for the girls throughout the kingdom who had been selected for their beauty and character, and from them choose another queen.

So these beauties came. They were housed in the house of the women and given all the ornaments and cosmetics they required.

One by one they went in to see the king. He fell deeply in love with a Jewish girl, Esther. Her cousin Mordecai had reared her and she had obeyed him like a father. Now Esther replaced Vashti as queen.

Mordecai the Jew, Queen Esther's cousin, sat at the gate. He discovered that two of the king's chamberlains planned to attack the king. He made it known and they were apprehended and the king's life was saved.

King Ahasuerus had a favorite lord whom he liked very much, Haman the Agagite. But Haman hated the Jew Mordecai. Mordecai never rose up to bow before Haman when Haman came to the palace. And Haman came to hate all the Jews.

A wicked plan formed in his mind. If he could have all the Jews killed, he could get rid of that Mordecai who did not do him reverence. So he made a suggestion to King Ahasuerus. "There is a people among you who will do the king great harm. And I will give ten thousand talents to the king's treasury if you will have these people destroyed." That was a strange request. And King Ahasuerus didn't make many inquiries; he just said, "You can sign the order and we will send it out by post to all the provinces and say that on a certain day the people may attack the Jews and murder them."

Now Ahasuerus does not know that his beautiful Queen Esther, or Hadassah, was a Jewess. And she was greatly distressed that the edict had been signed. They told her that Mordecai the Jew was in sackcloth and ashes and refused to eat. She sent garments to wear that he might rejoice, but he would have none of them. Rather, he sent Esther word that she must appeal to the king saying, "Perhaps you have come to the kingdom for such a time as this." Maybe God had allowed her to be queen that she might save her people.

However, she answered back that the king had a rule: anyone who came in to see him to whom he did not hold out the golden sceptre, that person would be killed. She said, "The king has not sent for me for thirty days, and I may get killed."

But Mordecai told her: "If you do not do right about this and see the king, you will be destroyed along with all the other Jews." Esther also told him: "I and my maidens will fast and pray three days, while you fast and pray with the other Jews here at Shushan the palace and we will trust God to deliver us."

So with great concern Queen Esther called her maidens about her. They prayed and fasted three days. Then she put on her beautiful garments and went to see the king. She stood in the outer hall and when he saw her, he reached out the golden sceptre and asked, "What is thy request? I will give it, whatever it is!"

Queen Esther answered, "My request is that you will come to a banquet I have prepared for the king. And bring with you your friend Haman."

King Ahasuerus agreed. They came. A second time Esther

told him, "Come again to the banquet that I am preparing for the king and Haman." And they came.

Now King Ahasuerus knew that some great burden was on Esther's heart and he said, "What is thy request? If it be to the half of my kingdom, I'll give it to you."

She said, "I request that I and my father's house and the Jews will be spared from this murderous rule that has been passed to destroy all my people."

Meantime, as the king was thinking, he was reminded that Mordecai had saved the king's life by revealing that two of his chamberlains would harm him. When he asked, "What has been done to reward Mordecai?" it was told him that no reward had been given, no honor.

About that time Haman came into the palace of the king. The king inquired, "Who is in the outer room?" They told him it was Haman. So King Ahasuerus had Haman come in. He asked Haman, "What shall I do for a man whom the king delights to honor?"

Haman thought, He must mean me. I only am invited to the banquet of Queen Esther with the king. Maybe he wants to honor me especially. So Haman answered, "Let the king's horse, the king's garments, and the king's crown be brought. Let them be put on the man that the king delights to honor. And let some nobleman lead the horse through the city and proclaim to the people, 'Thus it is done to the man whom the king delights to honor.' "

That pleased King Ahasuerus. "Haman, that is right. You take the king's horse and you take my garments and my crown and you put them on Mordecai. You lead him through and everywhere proclaim, "Thus it is done to the man whom the king delights to honor."

Haman, with shame and embarrassment, followed the king's orders. And Mordecai was greatly honored throughout all the city.

Now when they came to the king's banquet, the king asked Esther, "What is thy desire?" She told of the plot to kill all the Jewish people and told him that she was a Jewess. The king said, "What wicked man had planned this?"

She said, "Even this wicked Haman, here."

The king went out in the garden with embarrassment and anger, then he came back and they covered Haman's face. The king learned that Haman had built gallows a hundred feet high and said that they were intended for Mordecai. So Ahasuerus told his workers, "Hang him [Haman] thereon." So yonder, fifty cubits in the air, the body of wicked Haman the Agagite hung.

Then the king gave authority to Mordecai and sent out word through all the empire in the thirty provinces that the Jews should assemble and defend themselves against their enemies for seven days and destroy those who would have hurt them. And so it came to pass. Then they were given seven days more and with great victory the Jews defended their lives and property. And everywhere the Jews had great honor and respect in the kingdom and Mordecai was made sort of a prime minister and grew to great honor and power in the nation.

Now the Jews set aside certain days as the days of Purim, or of a feast once a year, in remembrance of the deliverance God gave to the Jews.

Isn't that a wonderful story about Esther, or Hadassah, the beautiful Jewish girl who became queen and was used to save the lives of the multitude of Jews left after the captivity?

Daniel, Jewish Slave
in Babylon

When Jerusalem was finally subdued by Nebuchadnezzar, and Jehoiakim, king of Judah, was carried captive to Babylon, the Babylonians took also vessels from the house of God to Shinar and Babylon, in the house of Nebuchadnezzar's gods.

And now with the Babylonian kingdom growing and coming to control the whole civilized world, Nebuchadnezzar felt the need of strong young men who could be trained as cabinet members, ambassadors and governors. So he had Ashpenaz to select from the king's seed and princes, young men, good looking, wise, well-trained, suitable to stand in the king's palace, to be taught the learning and the tongue of the Chaldeans.

Among those noble young men were Daniel, Hananiah, Mishael and Azariah. Now these young men, to serve the king, he thought must learn to eat in palaces, must learn to drink wine gracefully, must be fitted to high society in the palace. So it was arranged that every day food was to be brought from the king's table and wine from the king for these young men in training.

"But Daniel purposed in his heart that he would not defile himself with the portion of the king's meat, nor with the wine which he drank: therefore he requested of the prince of the eunuchs that he might not defile himself."—Dan. 1:8.

Now Daniel was a pleasing young man and had gained the favor and friendship of Ashpenaz. But Ashpenaz was shocked. If these young men were not well-cared for, did not stay healthy, did not grow wise, Nebuchadnezzar might cut off Ashpenaz' head. But Daniel suggested that he might have a trial of ten days with vegetable food and without the wine. The Jews' dietary law as given through Moses meant they could not eat pork and some other things that were customary food. And the blood must be drained carefully from all meats. Although he was in Babylon, Daniel felt he must still live by the standards God had set for the Jews. Besides that, Daniel knew the proverb, "Wine is a mocker, strong drink is raging: and whosoever is deceived thereby is not wise" (Prov. 20:1). He knew how wine deceived and "at the last it biteth like a serpent, and stingeth like an adder."

At the end of ten days Ashpenaz was pleased and surprised. The Jewish lads who ate simple, plain food, were not like the pimply-faced young men who ate the fat and drank the wine from the king's table. So Daniel and his fellows were allowed to choose their simple diet as a matter of conscience.

And now we find that God prospered these faithful young Jews for we are told:

"As for these four children, God gave them knowledge and skill in all learning and wisdom: and Daniel had understanding in all visions and dreams. Now at the end of the days that the king had said he should bring them in, then the prince of the eunuchs brought them in before Nebuchadnezzar. And the king communed with them; and among them all was found none like Daniel, Hananiah, Mishael, and Azariah: therefore stood they before the king. And in all matters of wisdom and understanding, that the king enquired of them, he found them ten times better than all the magicians and astrologers that were in his realm. And Daniel continued even unto the first year of king Cyrus."—Dan. 1:17-21.

It is good that Daniel was faithful and had grown in spiritual wisdom, for soon there came a great test. Nebuchadnezzar had a strange dream. Someway he knew that as he was building an empire, the first of all the world empires, God was dealing with him. That dream must have a prophetic meaning. But Nebuchadnezzar could not remember it.

So he called in his wise men, astrologers. They could not tell him the dream. They said, "Tell us the dream and we will interpret it." But no man, they thought, would know what Nebuchadnezzar had seen in a dream which even he did not remember. Nebuchadnezzar was angry. He was convinced there was great importance to that dream. What good were wise men, astrologers, soothsayers, if they could not tell his dream? So Nebuchadnezzar sent word that all the wise men were to be destroyed. When Daniel heard it and when men sought Daniel and his companions to kill them, Daniel spoke boldly to Arioch, the captain of the king's guard, "Why is the decree so hasty from the king?"

So Daniel asked for time and he himself would show the king the interpretation. Now Daniel and Hananiah and Mishael and Azariah all went to prayer that God would reveal the secret and that these Jewish worshipers of the true God would not die with the other wise men of Egypt. Ah, God gave the interpretation to Daniel. He went before Arioch and said, "Destroy not the wise men of Babylon: bring me in before the king, and I will shew unto the king the interpretation."

"Daniel answered in the presence of the king, and said, The secret which the king hath demanded cannot the wise men, the astrologers, the magicians, the soothsayers, shew unto the king; But there is a God in heaven that revealeth secrets, and maketh known to the king Nebuchadnezzar what shall be in the latter days. Thy dream, and the visions of thy head upon thy bed, are these; As for thee, O king, thy thoughts came into thy mind upon thy bed, what should come to pass hereafter: and he that revealeth secrets maketh known to thee what shall come to pass. But as for me, this secret is not revealed to me for any wisdom that I have more than any living, but for their sakes that shall make known the interpretation to the king, and that

thou mightest know the thoughts of thy heart."—Dan. 2:27-30.

Here was Nebuchadnezzar's dream. He had seen a great image of a man. The head was of gold, the arms and his breast were of silver. The belly and his thighs of brass. His legs of iron, his feet part of iron and part of clay. Daniel explained that this pictured four great successive world empires. To Nebuchadnezzar he said, "Thou art this head of gold." After him would come the Media-Persian empire, represented by the silver. Then there would come the Greek empire under Alexander the Great. The Roman empire would follow. It would be divided as pictured by the two legs. And the toes would be ten kingdoms that would come out the dissolving Roman empire. And in the dream a great stone fell upon the feet of the image and the whole image was shattered to dust and was blown away.

Then came the great revelation that the Lord Jesus Christ would come back to reign on the earth and set up His kingdom: The stone pictured the Lord Jesus in the second coming. "And in the days of these kings shall the God of heaven set up a kingdom, which shall never be destroyed: and the kingdom shall not be left to other people, but it shall break in pieces and consume all these kingdoms, and it shall stand for ever."

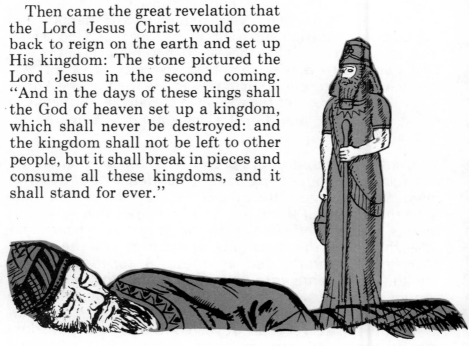

Daniel interprets the strange statue Nebuchadnezzar sees in his dream.

Nebuchadnezzar fell upon his face and said unto Daniel:

"Of a truth it is, that your God is a God of gods, and a Lord of kings, and a revealer of secrets, seeing thou couldest reveal this secret. Then the king made Daniel a great man, and gave him many gifts, and made him ruler over the whole province of Babylon, and the chief of the governors over all the wise men of Babylon."—Dan. 2:47,48.

Three Hebrew Young Men in the Fiery Furnace

We can understand that Nebuchadnezzar, building the first world empire, felt that someway he should solidify his kingdom and get all the different races of people and nationalities to unite as far as possible in the same worship. It would be as much nationalism as religion. So he had built in the Plain of Dura a giant image of gold. It was fifty cubits high (about 90 or 100 feet) and six cubits broad (9 or 10 feet). My, what a lot of gold! King Nebuchadnezzar gave orders and a great multitude assembled before this image. Now the command went out. When the orchestra sounded, everybody was to bow before that image.

"Then an herald cried aloud, To you it is commanded, O people, nations, and languages, That at what time ye hear the sound of the cornet, flute, harp, sackbut, psaltery, dulcimer, and all kinds of musick, ye fall down and worship the golden image that Nebuchadnezzar hath set up: And whoso falleth not down and worshippeth shall the same hour be cast into the midst of a burning fiery furnace."— Dan. 3:4-6.

Here were gathered the princes, the governors, the captains, the judges, the treasurers, the counselors, the sheriffs, and all rulers of the province, with an uncounted multitude of people.

The music sounded and the people fell on their faces before the image.

Somebody reported to the king, "The three Hebrew young men, friends of Daniel, now called Shadrach, Meshach and Abed-nego, have not bowed down to the image."

Nebuchadnezzar's servants insisted they must be put into the fiery furnace and destroyed.

But Nebuchadnezzar decided to give them another chance. They were valuable young men. "Then Nebuchadnezzar spake and said unto them, Is it true, O Shadrach, Meshach, and Abed-nego, do not ye serve my gods, nor worship the golden image which I have set up?" So he offered them another chance. The music would play, and if they did not fall down and worship before the image, that very hour they would be cast into the fiery furnace. And Nebuchadnezzar said, rather arrogantly, "And who is that God that shall deliver you out of my hands?"

That was a bad mistake Nebuchadnezzar made. That made it so God had to stand by these men and prove that He could handle even Nebuchadnezzar.

King Nebuchadnezzar looks into the furnace and is astonished to see Shadrack, Meshach, and Abednego unhurt by the fire.

"Shadrach, Meshach, and Abed-nego answered and said to the king, O Nebuchadnezzar, we are not careful to answer thee in this matter. If it be so, our God whom we serve is able to deliver us from the burning fiery furnace, and He will deliver us out of thine hand, O king. But if not, be it known unto thee, O king, that we will not serve thy gods, nor worship the golden image which thou hast set up."—Dan. 3:16-18.

Oh, how angry was Nebuchadnezzar! "Heat that furnace seven times hotter than before," he commanded. He commanded the strongest soldiers he had to seize Shadrach, Meshach and Abed-nego and cast them into the burning, fiery furnace. So these Jews were seized, were bound up in their clothes, and the raging fire of the furnace was so great that the strong men who put Shadrach, Meshach and Abed-nego into the furnace were burned to death.

And now, wonders of wonders! The fire merely burned off the ropes that bound these three noble young men! They had offered to die, if need be, to be faithful. They believed that God would deliver them, but if He did not, they still would not worship that image!

The startled king looked into the fiery furnace and saw three—no, four people—walking, evidently unharmed, in the fiery furnace. And the fourth was "like the Son of God."

Oh, it is not hard to believe that the Lord Jesus Christ came from Heaven that day and walked in the furnace with Shadrach, Meshach and Abed-nego.

Then Nebuchadnezzar called these men from the fiery furnace and said, "Ye servants of the most high God, come forth, and come hither." How astonished were the princes, the governors, the captains and the king's counselors. The fire had no power over these men of God. But Nebuchadnezzar was greatly impressed with their God. He said,

"Blessed be the God of Shadrach, Meshach, and Abed-nego, who hath sent His angel, and delivered His servants that trusted in Him, and have changed the king's word, and yielded their bodies, that they might not serve nor worship

any god, except their own God. Therefore I make a decree, That every people, nation, and language, which speak any thing amiss against the God of Shadrach, Meshach, and Abed-nego, shall be cut in pieces, and their houses shall be made a dunghill: because there is no other God that can deliver after this sort. Then the king promoted Shadrach, Meshach, and Abed-nego, in the province of Babylon."— Dan. 3:28-30.

Belshazzar's Feast

When Nebuchadnezzar, king of Babylon, died, he was followed by Nabonidus, but King Nabonidus was often away in wars and left his son Belshazzar to rule.

When Daniel was an old man, Belshazzar made a feast for a thousand of his lords. And now with their princes and lords, with their concubines and wives, in a great drunken feast, young Belshazzar, flushed with wine, commanded they should bring out the gold and silver vessels which his grandfather Nebuchadnezzar had taken from the Temple which is in Jerusalem. Wouldn't those vessels make good wine cups! And so they drank from holy vessels and praised the gods of gold, silver, brass, iron and wood.

In the midst of their license and revelry and idolatry, suddenly there appeared on the plastered wall the fingers of a man's hand and wrote. The laughter, the drinking, the idolatry, was suddenly hushed and stopped. Who could this unseen person be? They stared at the miraculous hand that wrote but could not understand the writing.

The miracle had some meaning, but what was it? The words were prophetic and awful, but what did they mean? Wise men and counselors were called but they could not give the meaning of the words.

Then the queen mother addressed Belshazzar and reminded him that his father (literally, his grandfather, Nebuchadnezzar) had called on a Jewish prophet who lived among them and that this Prophet Daniel had divine wisdom, could interpret dreams and solve mysteries. The Babylonian astrologers, Chaldeans and soothsayers could not show the writing and interpretation. "But Daniel," said the queen mother, "is a man in thy kingdom, in whom is the spirit of the holy gods; and in the days of thy father light and understanding and wisdom, like the wisdom of the gods, was found in him: whom the king Nebuchadnezzar thy father, the king, I say, thy father, made master of the magicians, astrologers, Chaldeans, and soothsayers." Now he should call Daniel. So Belshazzar did. When Daniel came in, it seemed Belshazzar had never met him. But he said, "I have heard of thee, that thou canst make interpretations, and dissolve doubts: now if thou canst read the writing, and make known to me the interpretation thereof, thou shalt be clothed with scarlet, and have a chain of gold about thy neck, and shalt be the third ruler in the kingdom."

Daniel was not flattered.

"Then Daniel answered and said before the king, Let thy gifts be to thyself, and give thy rewards to another; yet I will read the writing unto the king, and make known to him the interpretation. O thou king, the most high God gave Nebuchadnezzar thy father a kingdom, and majesty, and glory, and honour: And for the majesty that He gave him, all people, nations, and languages, trembled and feared before him: whom he would he slew; and whom he would he kept alive; and whom he would he set up; and whom he would he put down. But when his heart was lifted up, and his mind hardened in pride, he was deposed from his kingly throne, and they took his glory from him: And he was driven from the sons of men; and his heart was made like the beasts, and his dwelling was with the wild asses: they fed him with grass like oxen, and his body was wet with the dew of heaven; till he knew that the most high God ruled in the kingdom of men, and that He appointeth over it whomsoever He will. And thou his son, O Belshazzar, hast not humbled thine heart, though thou knewest all this; But hast lifted up thyself against the Lord of heaven; and they have brought the vessels of His house before thee, and thou, and

thy lords, thy wives, and thy concubines, have drunk wine in them; and thou hast praised the gods of silver, and gold, of brass, iron, wood, and stone, which see not, nor hear, nor know: and the God in whose hand thy breath is, and whose are all thy ways, hast thou not glorified."—Dan. 5:17-23.

Now the part of a human hand (or an angel's hand) that wrote on the wall, had written, "Mene, Mene, Tekel, Upharsin." And the meaning was, *"Mene;* God hath numbered the kingdom, and finished it. *Tekel;* Thou art weighed in the balances, and art found wanting. *Peres* [a form of the same word, Upharsin]; Thy kingdom is divided, and given to the Medes and Persians."

And now, true to his promise, Belshazzar clothed Daniel with scarlet, put a chain of gold about his neck and proclaimed that he should be the third ruler in the kingdom (Belshazzar was second ruler, subject to his father Nabonidus).

That night Darius the Mede and his army entered the city, Belshazzar was slain, and the Medes and Persians took over the empire.

How foolish was Belshazzar, drunken, idol-worshiping king. His punishment was soon to come!

Daniel in the Lions' Den

We are told that "Daniel continued even unto the first year of king Cyrus." It would appear he was in turn prime minister to Nebuchadnezzar and Darius the Mede and Cyrus the Persian.

Nebuchadnezzar promoted Daniel and so did later kings. Darius had three presidents to help him rule. And Daniel was first. He was preferred above all the presidents and princes, and King Darius planned to set him over the whole realm. We can understand that other presidents and princes would be jealous and envious. They sought some matter about which they could complain against Daniel to the king. But Daniel was so honest and upright, so wise and successful as the ruler, it was hard to find anything against him.

But they had an idea. Daniel was so religious, perhaps they could trap him in his religion and so have him destroyed. They suggested to King Darius that a law be passed that for thirty days no one could pray to any God or authority but to Darius. The law would be like that of the Medes and Persians—it could not be cancelled.

The vain king was pleased. Wouldn't it be nice to have everybody pray to the king and for thirty days not to any other god! So he agreed and signed the decree. The penalty was that anyone found praying to any god but Darius the king for thirty days, he must be cast into the den of lions. Now they craftily set watchers at Daniel's house. And he came now three times daily to the window, praying toward

Jerusalem, just as he was accustomed to do.

Now they rushed back before the king with sworn witnesses that they saw and heard Daniel pray to his God; he must be cast into the lions' den!

King Darius was troubled. He had not planned to lose this man, the best assistant he had, really, a prime minister. He had great respect for Daniel, but his enemies insisted the rules of the Medes and Persians could not be broken, Daniel must be cast into the lions' den.

Sadly, King Darius consented. So Daniel was put in the lions' den. A great stone covered the entrance. What will happen to Daniel!

That night King Darius could not sleep. Early in the morning he rushed to the lions' den and cried out, "O Daniel, was your God able to deliver you?" And, lo, he found Daniel unharmed! An angel of God had locked the jaws of the lions. I can imagine that Daniel pushed the big lion and said, "Here, big boy—lie down. I want you for a pillow, with my face toward Jerusalem." At any rate Daniel was well. And the king gladly received him out of the lions' den.

God delivered Daniel from the mighty lions!

And now these wicked enemies of Daniel were taken by the angry king and thrust in the lions' den along with their families.

It is well for every Christian to remember that God has said, "Let your conversation be without covetousness; and be content with such things as ye have: for he hath said, I will never leave thee, nor forsake thee" (Heb. 13:5).

The God who delivered Daniel in the lions' den can still deliver His own who trust in Him. Jesus said, "And shall not God avenge His own elect which cry day and night unto Him; though He bear long with them?" (Luke 18:7).

Daniel would never have walked amid the bronze lions that adorned the Babylonish throne if he had not first walked amid the real lions of the cave.
—Talmage

Jonah and the Whale

The book of Jonah tells an amazing story. Jonah was a prophet of God but a reluctant one who ran away from duty and got into trouble. But his wonderful experience we know really happened, for Jesus said so; and He said that Jonah, being three days and three nights in the belly of the whale, or great fish, typified the fact that He would be three days and three nights buried and rise again from the dead.

"Now the word of the Lord came unto Jonah the son of Amittai, saying, Arise, go to Nineveh, that great city, and cry against it; for their wickedness is come up before Me."

Nineveh was perhaps the greatest city in the world at that time. She had gone on in her wickedness and idolatry: now God wants someone to go warn the people to repent before terrible judgment comes.

But Jonah hated the people of Nineveh probably because of their sins, and he did not want to go and preach to them. So he thought he would get away from his duty by going to sea.

With pack under his arm, Jonah is on his way to the seaport of Joppa. He perhaps goes and says to the men around the dock, "Which vessel will sail today?"

A sailor may have answered, "There is one going to Tarshish. If you hurry, you may be able to get on board."

Jonah steps on board and asks how much the fare is, and pays it.

Soon after pulling away from the harbor a great storm arose on the sea. The mariners try everything they can to save the lives of those aboard. Now Jonah is down inside the ship fast asleep. The thunder and all the pitching of the ship seems not to have disturbed him at all. But the captain goes down and shakes him out of his sleep. "Wake up and go to praying, if you have a God to go to. Arise, call upon thy God—if so be He will think upon us, that we perish not."

Then Jonah confesses to them that the storm had come because of his running away from God and his disobedience to God. He now tells them that if they would throw him overboard, God will then stop the storm.

The sailors do not want to be guilty of drowning an innocent man, but the storm is so terrible that they bring him to the side of the ship, lift him over and drop him with a loud splash into the raging waves. Perhaps had Jonah been on his knees confessing his sins from the time he went on board, God would have saved him from being thrown overboard.

Now God had prepared a great fish. The King James Version calls it a whale. The word means a great sea monster. It may have been the sperm whale, for we already know that in

a good many cases men in the whaling industry have been swallowed by the sperm whale, then found alive later.

This prepared fish swallowed Jonah. And now, despairing of his life in the belly of the whale, away down at the bottom of the sea, he cries and prays. And God had the great fish vomit up Jonah on dry land, and he went back to Israel.

We know this event is true because of this New Testament Scripture:

". . .there shall no sign be given to it, but the sign of the prophet Jonas: For as Jonas was three days and three nights in the whale's belly; so shall the Son of man be three days and three nights in the heart of the earth."—Matt. 12:39,40.

If God can make a whale and a man, He can make a whale swallow a man.

You say, "But that would be a miracle if he came out alive!" Well, God is a God of miracles. The creation of the world was a miracle. The Flood was a miracle. The virgin birth of Jesus Christ without a human father was a miracle.

Those of us who believe the Bible must believe that God can and did work miracles whenever it suited His pleasure. And from the belly of the whale, Jonah, who cried to God, was delivered.

And Jesus said just as Jonah was three days and three nights in the belly of the whale, so the Son of Man should be three days and three nights in the heart of the earth, that is, in the grave.

Infidels do not like to believe this true Bible story about Jonah and the whale because they do not want to believe that Jesus Christ arose from the dead and that He is really God's own Son, as the Bible declares. But Christians must believe what the Bible says.

Now Jonah is alive and God has spared him. Again the Word of the Lord came to Jonah, the son of Amittai, telling him to arise and go to Nineveh, that great city, "and preach unto it the preaching that I bid thee."

Aren't you glad God gives His servants another chance? God forgave Peter after he had cursed and swore and denied that He was with Jesus and quit the ministry, and God came to tell him again, "Peter, feed My sheep."

We know that John Mark started out as a missionary with Paul and Barnabas but lost his courage and quit the team and went back home. Yet later Paul told Timothy, "Bring John Mark, for he is useful to me for the ministry." I am glad God used Mark again, even if he did play the coward one time and quit on God.

God still loved David after he sinned terribly in killing Uriah the Hittite and causing his wife Bath-sheba to become pregnant, and He forgave David and blessed him after that time.

Now God calls Jonah the second time. Aren't you glad He did?

Jonah went to Nineveh and shouted eight words, "Yet forty days, and Nineveh shall be overthrown." He walked around that great city. People heard, believed and repented. The king heard this warning and was frightened, so he called the people to fasting and prayer. A great time of repentance came to Nineveh and God spared the city.

But Jonah went outside the city to mourn because the city was spared instead of being destroyed. This must surely mean that he did not feel the compassion for sinners he ought to have felt.

God prepared a gourd vine to shade Jonah's head from the sun. Jonah was exceeding glad for this protection. Then God prepared a worm to gnaw the gourd vine so that it withered. And Jonah was grieved, becoming more angry at God. But God told him that he should be rejoicing for the poor lost souls of Nineveh who had been saved because of his preaching there.

Let Jonah be a lesson to us all. No one should rebel at the will of God. Rather, we should thank Him that He gives us another chance if we are honestly penitent and want to do right.

New Testament

The Birth of John
the Baptist

To Daniel the Lord had foretold that some sixty-nine weeks of years (483 years) would transpire from the command to restore Jerusalem, its walls, people and Temple, after the captivity to the coming of the Messiah.

I wonder if Zacharias, the old priest, and his devout wife Elisabeth, were expectant, looking for the Saviour. They may have been. We know that old Simeon in Jerusalem had been told that he would not die before he saw the Lord's Christ.

But Zacharias, as he went one day to his course of the service of the Temple, may have thought of these things. But he had an unceasing burden, a sense of loss. How he and Elisabeth had wanted a son! But the years went by and she remained barren. Now Zacharias could think it was too late to expect a child because Elisabeth was long past the time of childbearing. Why should the old couple pray still for a son?

But as he went about his work in the Temple, suddenly the angel of God stood before him. The angel said, "Fear not, Zacharias: for thy prayer is heard; and thy wife Elisabeth shall bear thee a son. . .he shall be great in the sight of the Lord, and shall drink neither wine nor strong drink; and he shall be filled with the Holy Ghost, even from his mother's womb. And many of the children of Israel shall he turn to the Lord their God" (Luke 1:13-16).

And the angel told him that this son John should be a

John the Baptist is born to Elisabeth in answer to prayer.

forerunner of the Messiah. "And he shall go before Him in the spirit and power of Elias."

What wonderful news! How Elisabeth rejoiced when that old body was made young and fruitful again, as Sarah's had been, and she conceived and rejoiced that her reproach was taken away. So this child was to be the forerunner of the Lord Jesus as promised in Malachi 3:1.

Some six months went by and, behold, Elisabeth's lovely young cousin Mary, a virgin of Nazareth, came to visit Elisabeth. And she told a wonderful tale, that the angel had come to her and said, "Fear not, Mary: for thou hast found favour with God. And, behold, thou shalt conceive in thy womb, and bring forth a son, and shalt call His name Jesus" (Luke 1:30,31).

So at long last the Saviour would come, the Saviour promised to Eve and promised to Abraham and to David. This was to be the Saviour foretold in Isaiah 7:14: "Therefore the Lord Himself shall give you a sign; Behold, a virgin shall conceive, and bear a son, and shall call His name Immanuel." Thus Mary and Elisabeth rejoiced together.

Elisabeth was filled with the Holy Spirit and said, "And whence is this to me, that the mother of my Lord should come to me?" And the baby leaped in her womb.

The months went by and the boy was born to Elisabeth. The angel had said, "His name shall be John." The neighbors and kinspeople who came in to rejoice over this marvelous birth of a son to the old couple suggested they name the child Zacharias for his father. "Won't he rejoice, calling the boy Zacharias," they said! Now all these blessings had been more than Zacharias could believe. How could he expect that an old woman like his wife, long past the time of childbearing, could conceive and bear a child? So to convince him and to punish his unbelief, he had been struck dumb. He could not talk, but vigorously he motioned for them to bring him a tablet, and on it he wrote, "His name is John."

The child grew up in the wilderness. He wore garments of camel's hair. He ate locusts and wild honey.

At last when he was thirty years old, he came out of the

wilderness to preach by the River Jordan. There multitudes were converted as John the Baptist preached, "Repent, for the kingdom of heaven is at hand."

Then one day John saw Jesus. He had known that Jesus was pure and good and a gift of God. He had not known for sure that Jesus was the promised Messiah until He came to be baptized of John in Jordan. John felt unworthy, but Jesus insisted and was baptized. And then praying, the Holy Spirit came visibly in a form like a dove and rested on Jesus. Then John knew that Jesus was indeed the Christ, the Son of the living God. And he announced it to the whole crowd, "Behold the Lamb of God, which taketh away the sin of the world." John the Baptist thus was the forerunner and introducer of the Saviour. He was a great evangelist, winning thousands to trust in Christ.

The Virgin Mother Mary

How Joseph loved Mary! We think Joseph was probably older than Mary, since he died earlier, some time before Jesus was grown. Their romance had blossomed at Nazareth, a village twelve miles west of the little Sea of Galilee. They were both of the house and lineage of David. They expected to be very happy.

But slowly there came to Joseph's attention that Mary was already pregnant. Her form showed it. Yet how could it be? He could hardly believe that Mary, his own dear Mary, could have sinned with some other man and so could have conceived! They were pledged to each other. If he denounced her as having played the harlot, she should be stoned to death! No, he could not do that! He could quietly put her away. How troubling the news! Poor Mary!

But God had an angel come in a dream and comfort Joseph's heart. "Fear not to take unto thee Mary thy wife: for that which is conceived in her is of the Holy Ghost," he said. That wonderful prophecy in Isaiah 7:14 will be fulfilled in her. "Therefore the Lord Himself shall give you a sign; Behold, a virgin shall conceive, and bear a son, and shall call His name Immanuel."

"Do not be ashamed, Joseph," the angel said. "Fear not to take unto thee Mary thy wife."

So Joseph took Mary officially as his wife, and though the marriage was not consummated actually until after Mary brought forth her firstborn son, Jesus.

You see, Mary had not known how to tell Joseph of the

wonderful visit of an angel. Who would believe her? Would even Joseph believe her? But now he believed the angel, and so she told him the story.

She said one day she was alone and the Angel Gabriel appeared unto her and said:

"Fear not, Mary: for thou hast found favour with God. And, behold, thou shalt conceive in thy womb, and bring forth a son, and shalt call His name JESUS. He shall be great, and shall be called the Son of the Highest: and the Lord God shall give unto Him the throne of His father David: And He shall reign over the house of Jacob for ever; and of His kingdom there shall be no end. . .The Holy Ghost shall come upon thee, and the power of the Highest shall overshadow thee: therefore also that holy thing which shall be born of thee shall be called the Son of God."—Luke 1:30-35.

Ah, it had come to pass as the angel said, and she felt the quickening movement of the child within her. She was to bare the long-awaited Messiah, the Saviour.

Now, Mary, pregnant, went to visit her Cousin Elisabeth, wife of the priest, Zacharias. They lived near Jerusalem. And how Elisabeth praised God "that the mother of my Lord should come to me."

So Elisabeth was to bare John the Baptist, to be born some six months before the Baby Jesus.

Mary went back to her home in Nazareth and then there came a decree from Caesar at Rome. Everybody must go back to his ancestral home to be registered for taxation. Both Joseph and Mary are of the house and lineage of David whose home was at Bethlehem. Mary was heavy with child and soon to be delivered, but they must obey the law.

We suppose Mary rode upon a donkey. And they come to Bethlehem of Judaea, some six miles south of Jerusalem.

Joseph and Mary come to Bethlehem.

But David had many sons. There were masses of people of the line of David crowding into Bethlehem. And Joseph and Mary were poor. They could not find a room. At last they found a place to sleep, in a stable "because there was no room for them in the inn." And there the Baby Jesus was born, wrapped in swaddling clothes, and laid in a manger.

Jesus, Baby Jesus, of a virgin mother born,
Laid in manger cradle, wrapped in swaddling clothes and warm.
Birth cry in a darkened stable, in the inn no room.
Jesus, Baby Jesus, Son of God, to share earth's gloom.

Jesus, how the angels with delight the story told,
Told to Mary, Joseph and the shepherds at their fold.
Full of light, the heavens, as they chanted "peace on earth"!
Jesus, Baby Jesus, what glad news, a Saviour's birth!

Wisemen came to see Him, having seen His star afar,
Bro't their gifts of precious gold and frankincense and myrrh.
Herod heard, was troubled, could not kill the holy Child.
Jesus, Baby Jesus, King and Priest, and Saviour mild.

Jesus, Baby Jesus, Son of God and Son of Man.
Tempted, poor and suff'ring, no one knows us as He can!
Holy, righteous, blameless, fitting sacrifice complete.
By His blood atonement, God and sinners in Him meet.

CHORUS:

Jesus, Baby Jesus, There's a cross along the way.
Born to die for sinners, born for crucifixion day!

No room in the Inn.

The Angel's Christmas Message

We know that Jesus was born in a stable and His mother, without midwife or doctor, wrapped the Babe in swaddling clothes and laid Him to rest in a manger. We suppose that Mary and Joseph slept on the straw.

But that sounds as if the birth of Jesus were rather a quiet and commonplace thing. Oh, no. God could not let it seem unimportant. This birth of His Son, this Saviour, He had planned before the world began. He had promised it to Eve in the Garden of Eden. He had promised it to Abraham, to Moses, to Isaiah, and to Jeremiah and Daniel and Zachariah. So God put on a wonderful celebration. We remember that Bethlehem had been the home of King David. We remember that Ruth the Moabitess had come gleaning in the fields nearby, owned by Boaz, an ancestor of David. And now on this holy night, while shepherds kept watch over their flock by night, suddenly they were to see the grandest scene that mortal eyes ever saw.

First, the heavens were full of light, and the angel of God appeared. My, they were scared! But the angel said to them,

"Fear not: for, behold, I bring you good tidings of great joy, which shall be to all people. For unto you is born this day in the city of David a Saviour, which is Christ the Lord. And this shall be a sign unto you; Ye shall find the babe wrapped in swaddling clothes, lying in a manger."—Luke 2:10-12.

Ah, that was the gladdest good news human ears ever

The sky is covered with bright, shining angels, joining in the chant, "Glory to God in the highest, and on earth peace, good will toward men."

heard! A Saviour is born, and will have forgiveness for every sinner who will trust Him.

And now the sky is covered with bright, shining angels. We remember that the Psalm says that when Christ came into the world God commanded, "Let all the angels of God worship Him" (Heb. 1:6). How gladly the angels joined in the chant that filled the sky! "Glory to God in the highest, and on earth peace, good will toward men."

I think it was no trouble after that amazing show of the glory of God for them to believe the angel. Ah, the Baby was right there in Bethlehem. They could see Him for themselves. The angel said He would be wrapped in swaddling clothes and lying in a manger. And now they gladly set out to find the Baby Jesus to bow before Him, and then tell everywhere this good news. At last the Saviour was born! They had seen the Babe with their own eyes and they knew it.

Then they went gladly to tell others of this wonderful good news. A Saviour was born! Yes, and we should be glad to tell it, too!

The Baby Jesus Is Dedicated

LUKE 2

The Lord Jesus was a Jewish Baby. Oh, He was the Son of Adam; He was the Son of man, that is, of all mankind, but in a particular sense He was of the seed of Abraham and of the house of David.

"And this I say, that the covenant, that was confirmed before of God in Christ, the law, which was four hundred and thirty years after, cannot disannul, that it should make the promise of none effect. For if the inheritance be of the law, it is no more of promise: but God gave it to Abraham by promise."—Gal. 3:17,18.

When the Lord Jesus was eight days old, He was circumcised and His name was officially called Jesus, as the angel had announced before He was conceived in the womb.

After the birth of Jesus, Mary was to go through certain days of official purifying, then they would present Jesus to the Lord.

They were to offer a sacrifice of a lamb, but if too poor for that, the law had allowed one to offer two turtledoves or two pigeons (Lev. 12:8). Since Joseph and Mary were very poor, they offered this inexpensive sacrifice. And the Lord Jesus, as a Baby, followed the law.

With the Jews, all these ceremonies pointed to a spiritual truth. When a Jew was circumcised, it spiritually pictured that circumcision of heart when one is born again and so marked for God and for Heaven. The Baby Jesus was only following a good pattern that good Jews were supposed to follow.

We know that many spiritually-minded people were waiting and watching for the coming of the Saviour. John the Baptist sent two of his disciples to Jesus to ask Him, "Art thou He that should come? or look we for another?"

The Wise Men of the East had been waiting long, and they must have known about the prophecies. Then when a star appeared at the appointed time, they knew the Saviour was born.

There are so many prophecies in the Old Testament concerning the coming of Christ, that spiritually-minded people must have longed for Him to come and must have looked forward earnestly to His coming.

One such man was Simeon. The Bible tells us he was

". . .just and devout, waiting for the consolation of Israel: and the Holy Ghost was upon him. And it was revealed unto him by the Holy Ghost, that he should not see death, before he had seen the Lord's Christ."

Now, when the Lord Jesus was presented in the Temple, the Spirit led Simeon also to come. Simeon took the Baby Jesus into his arms and praised God, saying:

"Lord, now lettest Thou Thy servant depart in peace, according to Thy word: For mine eyes have seen Thy salvation, Which Thou hast prepared before the face of all people; A light to lighten the Gentiles, and the glory of Thy people Israel."

What a Spirit-led man was old Simeon! He turned to Mary and said:

"Behold, this child is set for the fall and rising again of many in Israel; and for a sign which shall be spoken against; (Yea, a sword shall pierce through thy own soul also,) that the thoughts of many hearts may be revealed."

Ah, I am sure He referred to the time when Mary would stand by a cross on a little hill shaped like a skull and there she would see the dear Child of her own heart dying on the cross for the sins of men.

Another saint who looked for the coming of the Saviour was Anna, the prophetess Anna, of the tribe of Aser: "she was of a great age, and had lived with an husband seven years from her virginity; and she was a widow of about four-score and four years." She must have been over 100 years old! Oh, she never left the Temple but stayed there with fastings and prayers night and day.

Now, the very moment she came in and saw the Baby Jesus, she "gave thanks likewise unto the Lord, and spake of Him to all them that looked for redemption in Jerusalem."

When John the Baptist was born, his father, Zacharias the priest, was filled with the Spirit and praised God for the promised coming of the Saviour and he said:

"Blessed be the Lord God of Israel; for He hath visited and redeemed His people, And hath raised up an horn of salvation for us in the house of His servant David; As He spake by the mouth of His holy prophets, which have been since the world began: That we should be saved from our enemies, and from the hand of all that hate us; To perform the mercy promised to our fathers, and to remember His holy covenant; The oath which He sware to our father Abraham, That He would grant unto us, that we being delivered out of the hand of our enemies might serve Him without fear, In holiness and righteousness before Him, all the days of our life."—Luke 1:68-75.

Oh, he rejoiced that John the Baptist would go before the face of the Lord Jesus, according to "the tender mercy of our God; whereby the dayspring from on high hath visited us, To give light to them that sit in darkness and in the shadow of death, to guide our feet into the way of peace."

I do not wonder that many people must have felt it was time for Jesus to come. So "when the fulness of the time was come, God sent forth His Son, made of a woman, made under the law." This old wicked world needs a Saviour so badly. The joy that the angels expressed over the Shepherds' Field on the birthday of Jesus must have also been in many, many other hearts when they knew the Saviour was here,

whom they had so long expected and prayed for.
So we gladly sing that sweet hymn,

> Joy to the world! the Lord is come;
> Let earth receive her King;
> Let ev'ry heart prepare Him room,
> And heav'n and nature sing.
>
> Joy to the world! the Saviour reigns;
> Let men their songs employ;
> While fields and floods, rocks, hills and plains
> Repeat the sounding joy.
>
> No more let sins and sorrows grow,
> Nor thorns infest the ground;
> He comes to make His blessings flow
> Far as the curse is found.
>
> He rules the world with truth and grace,
> And makes the nations prove
> The glories of His righteousness,
> And wonders of His love.

Wise Men From the East
Come to Worship Jesus

Some hundreds of miles east of Jerusalem is the country of ancient Babylon. There they learned all the mysteries of nature and philosophy they could. When Daniel came among them, he became the wisest of all because God revealed to him wonderful things that would come to pass. Daniel foretold that after sixty-nine weeks of years, 483 years, from the decree of the king that Jews should go back from their captivity in Babylon and build Jerusalem, its Temple and walls again, that the Messiah the Prince should come. And that part of Daniel's prophecy was written in Chaldaic, not in Hebrew. No doubt wise men, spiritual wise men who revered the memory of the great Daniel, prime minister, kept these prophecies through the years and though Babylon no longer ruled the world there were still wise men in the East, and some of them looked for the coming of this King of the Jews of whom Daniel wrote.

I would think they counted the years so carefully. Then at last they figure that the 483 years are fulfilled about this time. Suddenly a star, a strange, wonderful star appeared in the heavens. They had studied the stars: they know this wonderfully bright new star has some special meaning.

The time is here! Surely the Saviour, the King of the Jews is come. Some of these noble men came together to discuss it. They must go to see this promised "King of the Jews"! With princely camels, decorations, and gifts, they set out to

Jerusalem. They expected to find this Baby King in the palace of Jerusalem, of course.

King Herod received them. "Where is He that is born King of the Jews?" they ask. King Herod was troubled. He knew Jewish Scripture spake of a coming Messiah, "Son of David," to be King of the Jews. When would He be born? The scribes and chief priests would know. He called them.

"Yes," they said, "He is to be born in Bethlehem, the Scriptures say."

Micah 5:2 says:

"But thou, Beth-lehem Ephratah, though thou be little among the thousands of Judah, yet out of thee shall He come forth unto me that is to be ruler in Israel; whose goings forth have been from of old, from everlasting."

Wise men travel from the East, coming to see this promised "King of the Jews." They bring gifts—gold, frankincense and myrrh.

So Herod sent the wise men of the East away six miles or so to Bethlehem. But what house? How shall they inquire? Herod promised if they report to him when they find the Child, he will come, too, and worship Him. Now if they can find the house—.

Ah, there again is the star! The same star they saw in the East. And now it rests over the house where the Baby Jesus is. They had followed the Scripture to Jerusalem. There they learned more Scriptures that told them Christ would be born in Bethlehem and followed it here. Now when they need more light, God gives it. There is the star again!

How happily they went in to see the Baby Jesus and Joseph and Mary! They did not cuddle the Baby, nor say, "Isn't He cute?" Instead, they fell down to worship Him. Then they opened their treasures and brought their gifts to Jesus: gold, frankincense and myrrh.

Maybe there were three kinds of gifts because there were three wise men. We do not know. But we are sure that the gifts had great spiritual meaning and these believing wise men came so far and at such trouble and expense to give them to Jesus.

GOLD would mean tribute for a king. And they called Him King. I think that meant, "Baby Jesus, You are to be King of Israel, but You will always be my King."

FRANKINCENSE was a sweet incense, which pictures, we think, the praise and prayer due to Deity. So surely they knew that Jesus was Son of God, born of a virgin, equal to God the Father, and so they worship Him.

MYRRH was a bitter herb such as was served, perhaps, with the passover lamb, cooked with bitter herbs to picture the sorrows of Jesus. And when Jesus died, it may be those sweet spices with which Joseph of Arimathaea and Nicodemus wrapped the body included myrrh. So these wise men held Jesus to be the suffering, atoning Saviour, so they worshiped Him with these gifts.

Did these wise men report to Herod as he said they should? No, "being warned of God in a dream that they should not return to Herod, they departed into their own country another way." Joseph, also warned of God in a dream, took Mary and the Baby Jesus away quickly and went down to Egypt, for King Herod planned to kill the Lord Jesus. And wasn't it good that Joseph and Mary had the gold, given by the wise men, to live on in those hectic days in Egypt and return?

But Herod hated the idea of another king of the Jews, so he planned to make sure the Baby Jesus was dead. He sent soldiers with strict commands. They were to kill every boy baby in Bethlehem! What a massacre of the innocent! But God had warned Joseph and Mary and they had hurried Jesus away.

Later in Egypt, Joseph heard that Herod the Great is dead and his son ruled in his stead. So he did not bring Mary and Jesus to Bethlehem or Jerusalem, but to Nazareth where they had lived before they married. And there, nearly thirty years, Jesus lived a perfect life, growing in wisdom and in favor with God and men. When He was thirty years of age, He began His marvelous ministry.

Let us learn from these wise men from the East. What holy effort, expense and trouble they took to see and worship Jesus! And they offered their treasures to Him. Oh, Lord Jesus, take all that we have! We would give You all our treasures. Let us, like these wise men, worship Jesus as our coming King, virgin born, God and Son of God, and our atoning Saviour who died for our sins on the cross and forgives every sinner who trusts in Him.

Jesus at Twelve Years of Age

Between the time of Jesus' birth and His baptism at about thirty years of age, there is no record in the Bible about the Lord Jesus except for one incident. We know that Jesus was in a godly Christian home. He went to the synagogue. He observed the Jews' laws and regulations. He went each year, we think, to the feast in Jerusalem, some ninety miles south of His home at Nazareth.

Only one such visit to Jerusalem during Jesus' childhood is recorded. When Jesus was twelve years old, Joseph and Mary took Him with them to Jerusalem. When the feast was over, the great crowd of people who came down from Galilee started the journey home, with the people walking, some having little children, and the women were along, as well as the men. It would take several days to return to the region of Nazareth and the Sea of Galilee.

It is significant that Joseph and Mary felt no concern about the twelve-year-old Boy. He was so wise and so good and so obedient that He had never disobeyed them, nor caused them grief or worry.

So they went a day's journey, thinking that among the many friends and relatives who walked along together, Jesus was somewhere behaving Himself perfectly. When they camped at night, of course, Jesus, they thought, would appear. But, alas, Jesus was not there. They hastened back to Jerusalem.

They remembered how entranced the Boy Jesus was with the scribes and teachers at the Temple. And there they found

Him asking questions about the Law and answering them, His face all aglow with a holy light from His joy in the Word of God.

Mary reproved Him. I expect she rarely or never had reproved Him before, because He was sinless. But now she said, "Son, why hast Thou thus dealt with us? behold, Thy

father and I have sought Thee sorrowing."

Jesus answered, "How is it that ye sought Me? wist ye not that I must be about My Father's business?"

When Mary called Joseph "Thy father," she only meant, of course, that legally Joseph acted as father. He was in the place of a father humanly.

After my mother died, some years later I had a step-mother. I very properly called her "Mamma." But I knew she was not my physical mother, even as Mary understood better than anybody that Joseph was not the father of Jesus.

But there was a little rebuke in the way Jesus answered. He must be about His Father's business, and in this He meant, of course, His Heavenly Father's business.

My, how the doctors of the Law were astonished at Jesus—at the questions He asked, at the answers He Himself gave. What an understanding of the Scriptures! Oh, as a Boy, the Lord Jesus had a holy devotion to the Bible. And He must have studied it a great deal.

But although Jesus was actually God in human form, and living with frail human parents, we learn there was never any rebellion. Jesus returned with them to His home in Nazareth and was subject to them. He "increased in wisdom and stature, and in favour with God and man."

Hallelujah!

The Baptism of Jesus

John was baptizing in the River Jordan and multitudes came to him and confessed their sins and were baptized. Remember John was preaching, "Repent ye: for the kingdom of heaven is at hand." We are told Jesus also preached, "Repent: for the kingdom of heaven is at hand," the same message.

These people who repented of their sins and trusted in the coming Saviour were baptized of John in Jordan.

And here came Jesus to be baptized, too. And John, knowing how pure and sinless Jesus was, was embarrassed to think that he was fit to baptize Jesus, but Jesus insisted and said, ". . .for thus it becometh us to fulfil all righteousness." You see, it becomes Jesus and "us."

When Jesus was baptized, it meant He was looking forward to the time when they would take down that poor abused body from the cross and put it in Joseph's new tomb, that time when death seemed to have conquered and Jesus was put in the grave, but it pictures also His glorious resurrection.

So we should be baptized, too. And it has a double meaning. First it means, of course, that we, too, will be resurrected if we have trusted Jesus Christ as Saviour and are born-again Christians. Then there will come a resurrection time when our bodies will come out of the grave, and we will be gloriously caught up to meet the Lord in the air at His coming. And from then on we will ever be with the Lord. But the second and more important meaning is, when I am baptized I am

Jesus is baptized:
"thus it becometh us to
fulfil all righteousness."

saying to the world, "The old sinner that I was before I was converted, let us count him dead and bury him." Then I am raised up from the watery grave to walk in newness of life. That means I am now to have the power of God upon me, and I should live wholly for Jesus.

I do not mean that I am now sinless or perfect. It is still true that "the flesh lusteth against the Spirit, and the Spirit against the flesh." It is still true that "when I would do good, evil is present with me." I have the old nature, but, thank God, I have a new nature and that new nature should dominate my life always.

So Jesus came to John and was baptized.

It is interesting that every one of the twelve apostles were baptized by John the Baptist. Some people foolishly think that baptism was simply a Jewish rite, an Old Testament matter. No, no. The Gospel of Mark, when it starts to tell about the ministry of John the Baptist, says, "The beginning of the gospel of Jesus Christ." And so baptism is a New Testament practice with a wonderful witness.

It is foolish to make a difference between the baptism of John and the baptism of Jesus. Both of them preached the same kind of sermon: "Repent ye: for the kingdom of heaven is at hand," John said in Matthew 3:2. And again, "Repent: for the kingdom of heaven is at hand" is what Jesus preached in Matthew 4:17. And Christians now, just as in the days of John the Baptist, ought to be baptized as a public profession of their faith.

Baptism doesn't change a black heart, but it is an open testimony that we have trusted Christ and buried the old past and count it dead and set out to live for Christ.

I remember so well when, as a twelve-year-old boy, I was baptized on a cold November day in a little artificial lake or pond in West Texas. I remember I came out of the water with dripping garments and stood at the pool side where Christian people who loved us came by and shook hands with us and said, "God bless you," and all the crowd then joined in singing,

> O happy day that fixed my choice
> On Thee, my Saviour and my God!
> Well may this glowing heart rejoice,
> And tell its raptures all abroad.
>
> He taught me how to watch and pray,
> And live rejoicing every day;
> O happy day, O happy day,
> When Jesus washed my sins away.

I remember that day my heart was so warm I did not feel the need to be wrapped in blankets for the cold drive home. My father knew I might be chilled, and wrapped a quilt about me but my heart was so warmed I was not conscious of the cold. Oh, it is blessed for a Christian to follow Jesus in baptism. For Jesus said, ". . .for thus it becometh us to fulfil all righteousness."

Jesus Tempted at the Beginning
of His Ministry

When Jesus was baptized in the River Jordan, He was officially beginning His ministry. He was filled with the Spirit, and then the Spirit led Him away in the wilderness to be tempted of Satan.

If Jesus is to be my Pattern, and the Pattern of every frail human being who puts his trust in Him, then Jesus must have been tempted like we will be tempted.

Back of Jericho, toward Jerusalem, is a great mountain called The Mount of Temptation. Tradition says that here is the place where Jesus was first tempted. Was there any likelihood or even a possibility that the Lord Jesus would sin, would succumb to Satan's temptation? No, because the Lord Jesus would not consent to sin. He was tempted or tried, and all the allurement that Satan could give, he pressed on Jesus. But a pure and holy Jesus could not consent to sin and did not sin.

The first temptation was that of hunger. Jesus had gone forty days and nights without food, and, oh, what a craving of His body for food. You see, if Jesus is to be tempted, He must be as weak and frail as I will be sometime when I am tempted, or as you may be. So, these forty days went by and the strength of Jesus was ebbing away. But still, when Satan said to Him, "You are hungry, aren't You? Well, why don't You make these stones here into bread and satisfy Yourself?" we remember that the Bible says that Jesus "was in all points tempted like as we are, yet without sin" (Heb. 4:15).

So Jesus knew the pangs of hunger, alone, and with no help except as He depended on His Heavenly Father.

Jesus answered with a quotation from Deuteronomy 8:3, "It is written, Man shall not live by bread alone, but by every word that proceedeth out of the mouth of God."

Here we can see that to Jesus the blessed food of the Spirit, the Word of God, is of far more importance than any bread with which we may satisfy the pangs of hunger.

As the body needs various elements to supply its needs: protein, carbohydrates and vitamins, liquids and solids, so every Christian needs every line in the Bible and the help of every teaching of the Word of God. Men ought to live by the Bible. We ought to feed our souls and strengthen our characters day by day by taking in the blessed Word of God. No wonder the psalmist said, "Thy word have I hid in mine heart, that I might not sin against Thee" (Ps. 119:11).

For the second temptation Satan took Jesus to that pinnacle of the Temple. That is the corner of the city wall of Old Jerusalem with a fall of some seventy feet down to the Valley of Kidron. Here Satan told Jesus, "Cast Thyself down," and Satan quoted Scripture, "He shall give His angels charge concerning thee: and in their hands they shall bear thee up, lest at any time thou dash thy foot against a stone." Ah, but you may be sure when Satan quotes the Scripture he does it for his own bad purposes. And Jesus answered, "It is written again, Thou shalt not tempt the Lord thy God" (Matt. 4:7).

There are some people whom, we think foolishly, believe it would honor God for them to let themselves be bitten by rattlesnakes and thus prove their faith. I think that is a foolish tempting of God. No wonder many have died because of presumption in this matter.

It is true that the Apostle Paul, on the island of Melita, was bitten by a poisonous snake and shook it off into the fire without harm, but he did not do it purposely, nor to be spectacular or to prove to others how great was his faith. We are not to tempt God. We are not to be presumptuous in our prayers.

For the third temptation, Satan took Jesus to the top of a high mountain and showed Him all the kingdoms of the world. He said to Jesus, "All these things will I give Thee, if Thou wilt fall down and worship me."

Satan himself is a fallen angel. Is it strange that he would try to get Jesus likewise to fall into sin? It is true that Satan is now "the god of this world." It is true that now he has the lives and hearts of many, many who follow him and follow

Jesus is tempted to throw Himself from the Temple.

sin. But Jesus wants the heart's love and devotion of all who come to worship Him. He wants it to be a worship in spirit and in truth. He wants it to be a whole-souled devotion and surrender to Christ of everything.

And Jesus is willing to wait for the time when the kingdoms of this world shall be brought to an end. In that great statue of an image representing the world empires, in Daniel 2, we found that a stone is to be cut out of the mountains without hands and smite the image in its feet and destroy it. For the Lord explains that the Lord Jesus Christ will have His kingdom to supercede all the kingdoms of the world. Jesus was willing to wait. He did not need to worship Satan to get the hearts of those who will trust in Him. Christ is coming back to reign over the earth.

Now there are several lessons that we Christians must remember about the temptation of Jesus.

First, Jesus was sinless and perfect and never sinned. No wonder He could face the Pharisees boldly and say, "Which of you convinceth Me of sin?" (John 8:46). No one pretended to find sin in the Lord Jesus. It is said of Him, ". . .who knew no sin" (II Cor. 5:21). The sinless purity and perfection of Jesus proves that He is God in human form. All of us are sinners, but not Jesus.

The second lesson we should learn is that always God has a way out of temptation. "There hath no temptation taken you but such as is common to man: but God is faithful, who will not suffer you to be tempted above that ye are able; but will with the temptation also make a way to escape, that ye may be able to bear it" (I Cor. 10:13). A Christian can have help every day in every need, as he calls on the Lord.

If the Lord Jesus was tempted, then, of course, we may expect to be tempted, too. So we must be prayerful and ready and expect God to help us every day and deliver us from the evil one.

How Jesus, Our Pattern, Was Filled With the Holy Spirit

MATTHEW 3, MARK 1, LUKE 3, JOHN 1

The priests and Levites in the Old Testament were in some sense types and pictures of Jesus. They did not begin their public ministry until they were thirty years old (Num., chapt. 4). Jesus, too, waited until He was about thirty years old to begin His public ministry. He lived in Nazareth, attended a synagogue, studied the Bible, lived a holy and perfect life, but He did not begin His preaching, His miracles, His soul winning, until He was about thirty.

Then He went to the Jordan River where John the Baptist was baptizing. There He insisted that John the Baptist baptize Him.

Then a wonderful thing happened. As Jesus was baptized and as He stood in the River Jordan with water dripping from Him, the Holy Spirit came in visible form like a dove and sat upon Him. John and others saw this image of the Holy Spirit. That meant that that day Jesus was filled, anointed with the Spirit for His public ministry.

You see that Jesus is our Pattern. He is, first of all, our Saviour; then, when one has Christ in his heart, Jesus is the Pattern by which one should live. So when Jesus was baptized He said, "Thus it becometh US to fulfil all righteousness." And we read in I Peter 2:21, "For even hereunto were ye called: because Christ also suffered for us, leaving us an example, that we should follow in His steps."

A born-again Christian should be baptized, then he should set out to live like Jesus.

For that reason Jesus must set a pattern as a Soul Winner. He must be tempted as we are, so He was led into the wilderness and was tempted of Satan in three great temptations. He is not only Son of God, but He is Son of man. He is the pattern Man, a blessed Example.

First, you need a Saviour. Then, when your sins are forgiven and you become a child of God, Jesus is the Pattern. And if Jesus is to be my Pattern, and if He wants me to be a soul winner, then He must be a Soul Winner, too. And if I could not win souls except by being endued with power of the Holy Spirit, so Jesus must for the moment lay aside His power as the Son of God, and all His perfect ministries must be carried on as a Spirit-filled Man. He is still the blessed Son of God, but all His work is done in the power of the Holy Spirit.

Remember that Peter told Cornelius and his family:

"That word, I say, ye know, which was published throughout all Judaea, and began from Galilee, after the baptism which John preached; How God anointed Jesus of Nazareth with the Holy Ghost and with power: who went about doing good, and healing all that were oppressed of the devil; for God was with Him. And we are witnesses of all things which He did both in the land of the Jews, and in Jerusalem; whom they slew and hanged on a tree."—Acts 10:37-39.

Yes, God now will be manifested with Jesus in the power of the Holy Spirit.

When Jesus had been tempted, He went back to Nazareth where He had been brought up and went into the synagogue. Of course they said, "Let's have Jesus read the Scriptures." No one knew as much Scripture as Jesus.

Jesus took the roll of the Prophet Isaiah and turned in it until He came to where it is written in Isaiah 61:1, "The Spirit of the Lord is upon me, because he hath anointed me to preach the gospel to the poor; he hath sent me to heal the brokenhearted, to preach deliverance to the captives, and recovering of sight to the blind, to set at liberty them that are bruised, to preach the acceptable year of the Lord" (Luke 4:18,19).

Then Jesus gave the roll to the servant who put that holy manuscript away safely. And Jesus said to the people in that synagogue at Nazareth, "This day is this scripture fulfilled in your ears."

They marveled as He spake. Jesus had been sinless and perfect all these years He had lived at Nazareth. But now the mighty power of the Spirit of God is upon Him and He is obviously different. You see, Jesus now is our Pattern filled with the Spirit of God. That means we can be filled with the Spirit of God, too.

Then that was the meaning of the golden "candlestick," really the lampstand with seven lamps burning with oil. That pictured Jesus, the Light of the world, burning in the power of the Holy Spirit.

That is why Aaron the high priest must be anointed with oil: Oil was poured upon Aaron's head and it ran down even to the skirt of his garment, for Jesus is our High Priest filled with the Holy Spirit, and Aaron pictured Him.

That is why David was anointed with oil. Samuel took oil and poured it on the head of David, and the Spirit of God was upon him from that time forward. Why? Because David pictured the Messiah, the coming King of the Jews.

Jesus was filled with the Holy Spirit. Every miracle He did, every sermon He preached, every soul He won—these were done always in the power of the Holy Spirit.

Jesus is the sinless and perfect Son of God. I am not. Jesus could do any miracle. He is the Creator of all things, the Sustainer of all things. But that doesn't picture me. And if Jesus is to be a Pattern to me, then He must allow Himself to be filled with the Spirit of God and do His works as God's Spirit-filled Son, the perfect Man, the model Man, our second Adam.

Isn't it encouraging that the Lord Jesus shows us now that we can serve Him, as weak and poor as we are? What we need is simply to be filled with the Spirit of God as was the Lord Jesus; so that what we do, we do by the power of God.

It is not necessarily brains and talent and skill with which we are to serve God; we are to serve Him with whatever little we may have, and whatever we may be, if the Spirit of God comes upon us and gives us power to speak for Jesus and witness for Him and live for Him.

Oh, then, we all need to be filled with the Spirit! We all need to have a special enduement of power, as Jesus told the disciples in Luke 24:46-49.

Andrew Wins His Fisherman
Brother to Christ

Out by the River Jordan where John was baptizing people who came confessing their sins and turning to Christ in heart, a wonderful incident happened. Once when Jesus appeared, John stopped preaching and baptizing. Turning, he faced the Lord Jesus and everybody looked. John shouted, "Behold the Lamb of God, which taketh away the sin of the world." This must have been after Jesus was baptized; John now recognized that Jesus was the Saviour, the Son of God. And how glad John was to announce Him! That was the business of John. He was a forerunner of Jesus. He was to announce and introduce Jesus.

Now in a large crowd, yonder were two who were greatly interested. "Oh, if we could only see Jesus, this Man! If we could only get acquainted with this One whom John says is the Lamb of God which taketh away the sin of the world!" So those two sought out Jesus. One of them was Andrew, Simon Peter's brother. They asked, "Where do you live, Rabbi?" Jesus told them, "Come and see. Go home with Me." They went home with Jesus. The details are not told, but we know that Andrew learned that Jesus was the Saviour and put his trust in Him.

We suppose Andrew was a younger brother of Peter. He was quieter. He was not the great leader that Peter was. But Andrew said to himself, "I must get my big brother to Jesus. Oh, Peter must be saved, too!" So he went to Peter and as the Scripture puts it, "He first findeth his own brother

Simon, and saith unto him, We have found the Messias, which is, being interpreted, the Christ. And he brought him to Jesus."

So Peter came, too, to Jesus, and learned of salvation. Later he will be called an apostle, as will Andrew. Later he will leave his fishing business to follow Jesus. But here in this chapter he put his trust in Jesus and became a Christian.

Those who come in touch with Jesus soon learn that He wants everybody to be a soul winner. So in the same passage we find: "The day following Jesus would go forth into Galilee, and findeth Philip, and saith unto him, Follow Me." Philip was of the city of Bethsaida, the city of Andrew and Peter. Peter and Andrew and Philip all lived at Bethsaida which was a town, we suppose, a little east of Capernaum. It has disappeared now but then was within walking distance. So Jesus found Philip and said to him, "Follow Me." Philip is to be an apostle, too.

We read further, "Philip findeth Nathanael, and saith unto him, We have found Him, of whom Moses in the law, and the prophets, did write, Jesus of Nazareth, the son of Joseph." He was only thought to be the son of Joseph. Joseph was only the official stepfather, but responsible for the family.

Nathanael was at first doubtful. Could anything so good as the Messiah come out of that poor, backward province of Galilee? But that was easy to settle. Philip just said, "Come and see!" Nathanael came and saw for himself and found that Jesus was really the Saviour, the Messiah promised. Jesus is the Saviour that sinners are to trust for salvation.

I am so glad that Andrew won Peter! It may well be that when up in Heaven God wants to reward someone for the blessed revival at Pentecost where Peter preached, an angel may pin an award on Andrew, who won Peter.

It is blessed to win souls!

Jesus' First Miracle

Two people had pledged themselves to each other, hand and heart, and their friends had come in for congratulations. It was at Cana, a little town not far from Nazareth. Jesus and His disciples had received an invitation to the wedding, and with Mary they had walked the four-mile distance.

A wedding was always festive among the Jews and was largely attended. On this occasion there were so many people that it was discovered the supply of wine was inadequate. No doubt Mary was a close friend of the household, or perhaps a relative. So she was told first of the dwindling supply.

Mary, the mother of Jesus, came to Him and said, "They have no wine."

Up to this time Jesus had never worked a miracle, but Mary knew He was the Son of God. She knew His birth was a miracle and His work on earth would be miraculous. And she also knew that Jesus had recently been baptized of John and that a voice from Heaven had said, "This is my beloved Son, in whom I am well pleased." Mary knew the Holy Spirit had come in visible form like a dove and had rested on Jesus. Now wasn't it time for Him to begin His miraculous ministry?

Jesus said to her, when told of the inadequate supply, "Woman, what have I to do with thee? Mine hour is not yet come." Perhaps the hour was not fully come for His public ministry, and certainly not the hour for His crucifixion, yet, by faith, Mary must have known that Jesus would now go into His public ministry.

Before the door of the house stood six large stone jars, filled with water, which were used by the guests for washing their hands and faces, the custom of the Jews, not only as an act of cleanliness but of purification.

Mary said to the servants, "Whatsoever He saith unto you, do it." And the faith of Mary, we think, led Jesus to proceed and work His first miracle.

Jesus instructed that these jars be emptied and filled with fresh water. When this was done, Jesus then commanded the servants to fill a goblet for the governor to taste. When the ruler of the feast had tasted the water that was made wine, he pronounced it super-excellent: "Thou hast kept the good wine until now."

Surely it was not intoxicating wine. In the Bible grape juice is called wine, even called "new wine" when it is first pressed out of the grapes and then when it becomes fermented, it is still wine. But Jesus knew the words of the Old Testament Scriptures, "Wine is a mocker, strong drink is raging: and whosoever is deceived thereby is not wise"

(Prov. 20:1). So nobody could get drunk on the wine Jesus made. It tasted wonderfully good—the best they had ever tasted!

Then the Scripture says, "This beginning of miracles did Jesus in Cana of Galilee, and manifested forth His glory; and His disciples believed on Him."

Wondrous miracle—gallons and gallons of water turned into the purest wine at one word from Jesus! The public ministry of the Lord Jesus thus began with His first miracle.

Jesus Calls Four Fishermen
to Be His Apostles

MATTHEW 4, MARK 1, LUKE 5, JOHN 1

After Jesus was baptized and began His public ministry, we know that He moved to the town of Capernaum on the northwest edge of the Sea of Galilee. There He attended the synagogue, there He healed the man with the withered hand, there He did other wonderful miracles.

Great crowds followed Jesus to hear the wonderful words that fell from His mouth and to see the miracles that He did. One day Jesus came along by the Sea of Galilee and there Peter and Andrew had pulled up their fishing boat to the edge of the water and were washing their nets. Jesus said to them, "May I sit in your boat and preach?" So they launched out a little way so Jesus could be in sight of the multitudes gathered on the bank and so they could hear Him. And He preached the Gospel to them. Then Jesus turned to Peter and said, "Peter, launch out into the deep and let down your nets for a draught."

Peter expostulated, "Why, Jesus, we have fished all night and didn't catch a thing. See, we got our nets so muddy and have been washing our nets because we couldn't catch any fish last night." But he said, "Nevertheless at thy word I will let down the net." So they moved out into that beautiful little Sea of Galilee. It is really a fresh water lake about fifteen miles long and seven and one-half miles wide. And Peter let down one net. Ah, to his surprise, the net was soon filled with fish and was about to break! They called for their partners and friends, James and John and their father Zebedee,

"Come help us quickly," and they filled both ships with the fish that they caught in the net that day!

Peter did not believe he could catch any fish today; he had fished all night. Now suddenly he was amazed at this marvelous miracle. Oh, Jesus is really God's own Son and this was a miracle of God. And Peter felt so weak and helpless and sinful. He said, "Jesus, depart from me; for I am a sinful man." But Jesus encouraged him and said, "Peter, from henceforth thou shalt catch men."

I wonder at the great mass of fishes, the two boatloads they caught that day. Don't you suppose that meant that God intended for Peter to see three thousand people saved at Pentecost and great multitudes in his ministry? I think so.

So Peter and his brother Andrew are called to be apostles and are going to follow Jesus; be His disciples and learn from day to day from Him, and to be fitted as two of His apostles to give witness for Christ after He has been crucified.

But what about James and John? I can imagine how they were awestruck. I can imagine the great joy, the surprise, the wonder in their faces as they looked at this miracle that God has wrought through Jesus.

So Jesus said to Peter and Andrew and James and John, "Follow Me, and I will make you fishers of men." And that day James and John left their father and ship to follow Jesus.

I can imagine that maybe Zebedee said, "But, boys, I need help. Are you going to leave me?"

And maybe James would say, "We must follow Jesus, we must catch men for Christ, so you can have the servants help you with the ship and nets, but we must follow Jesus."

It may be that Zebedee would say, "But, John, your mother, you know, oh, she thinks so much of you. And what will she think, that you leave us now and go to follow Jesus?"

But John would reply, "I must follow Jesus and be a fisher for men."

So now Jesus had four disciples. It may be that God is speaking to someone who reads this today and God is saying, "Follow Me, and I will make you fishers of men." It may be

Jesus calls Peter, Andrew, James and
John to follow Him and fish for men.

that someone today will feel the holy call of God in your heart. God wants you to be a soul winner. God wants you to preach His Gospel. God wants you to give your life as a witness for Jesus Christ. If so, then remember it was well worthwhile for James and John to leave their father and the nets, and for Peter and Andrew to leave their fishing business in order to be soul winners for Jesus.

Jesus Heals Peter's
Mother-in-Law

LUKE 4

The Lord Jesus in His early ministry at Galilee, after John the Baptist had been put to death by Herod, preached all around Nazareth and towns along the Sea of Galilee. After He had called Peter, Andrew, James and John to follow Him and be His disciples, they went into the city of Capernaum and on the Sabbath day they went into the synagogue as was their custom.

Of course Jesus taught the people. How charming were His messages! And how people waited to hear Him! They were astonished because He spoke so boldly and plainly, not as a scribe, but as one who had authority from God the Father.

In the synagogue was a man with an unclean spirit, and this devil in the man cried out, "Let us alone; what have we to do with Thee, Thou Jesus of Nazareth? art Thou come to destroy us? I know Thee who Thou art; the Holy One of God."

We remember that devils often knew Jesus and spoke to Him. But Jesus rebuked the devil and said, "Hold thy peace, and come out of him." And when the devil had thrown him in the midst, he came out of him.

My, what a stir in the synagogue among the people! They said, "What a thing is this? We never saw it like this. Even demons are subject to Him. He has authority over devils and they obey Him."

You can imagine how the fame of this spread through all the country, over across the Jordan, and as far as Tyre and

Sidon toward the seacoast, toward the Mediterranean. The crowds heard about Jesus and the wonderful miracles He did and the strange and amazing teaching that He gave.

After the service in the synagogue and after the casting out of devils, Jesus walked home with Andrew and Peter, who lived at Bethsaida (John 1:44), a little ways east of Capernaum. (Not a trace of the little town is left today.) James and John went along, too, staying with Jesus.

Peter's wife's mother was sick of a fever and no doubt there was a sadness and a distress of spirit in the house. They told Jesus about her illness. He went at once to the bedside, took her by the hand and lifted her up. Immediately the fever left, and she ministered unto them. I can imagine that now, feeling perfectly well, she bustled about the house preparing the meal for Peter and Andrew and the two friends, James and John, and, of course, for the Lord Jesus.

There are several things to remember here. First, Peter and Andrew lived at Bethsaida, not at Capernaum. Again, Peter was married. If anybody thinks that a priest or a preacher ought not marry, then they must remember that Peter was married, and his wife's mother lived in the home with him.

If Peter, Andrew, James and John are to follow Jesus and preach for Him, it is only right that they should expect the power of God in their own homes and among their own families. Oh, one who serves the Lord ought to take all his burdens to the Lord and daily have the help that God can give.

Jesus Tells a Member of the Sanhedrin, "Ye Must Be Born Again"

JOHN 3

"There was a man of the Pharisees, named Nicodemus, a ruler of the Jews: The same came to Jesus by night." I do not know why he came at night. Maybe Jesus was so crowded with visitors that Nicodemus felt he could not talk to Him privately except in the night. Or, it may be that he was a little ashamed for people to know that he, a distinguished member of the Sanhedrin, one of the rulers of the Jews, one of the specially honored religious leaders of the nation, should come to Jesus to ask questions.

We know that the only three times Nicodemus is mentioned in the New Testament, it is to mention that he came to Jesus by night. Then, oh, we can be glad, that after Jesus died on the cross, Nicodemus joined with Joseph of Arimathaea to come and ask for the body of Jesus and to bury it.

Nicodemus came to praise the Lord Jesus. He said, "Rabbi, we know that Thou art a teacher come from God: for no man can do these miracles that Thou doest, except God be with him." Was Jesus pleased with that? I suppose that He was not because He came straight to the great issue of what Nicodemus needed. He told him plainly, "Nicodemus, except a man be born again, he cannot see the kingdom of God."

Nicodemus didn't know about that. He said, "A man as old as I am, can he enter into his mother's womb and be born again?" But Jesus told him He was talking about a spiritual birth. He needed to be made a new creature inside. He needed a new heart.

Ah, Nicodemus, didn't you know that people need to be born again? Don't you remember that the Lord promised us through the Prophet Ezekiel He would take away the stony heart and give a heart of flesh and thus people would be circumcised in heart, not simply in the flesh? And don't you remember that David had prayed, "Lord, create in me a clean heart"? And there is a sweet promise in Psalm 19:7, "The law of the Lord is perfect, converting the soul. . . ." And David promised that if God would restore the joy of His salvation, "Then will I teach transgressors Thy ways: and sinners shall be converted unto Thee." Oh, yes, Nicodemus, it is too bad to be a religious leader and not even know this great fundamental truth. There is only one way to meet God in peace and that is to be born again, born from above!

Well, how can one be born again? All of us are such sinners, we are brought forth with a tainted nature and as soon as we become accountable and know right from wrong, it seems everybody chooses to do wrong. There is nobody in the world but who is a sinner, nobody but needs a new heart. Then how can one have a new heart? We all know, of course, that "the wages of sin is death." We know that the Bible has said, "The soul that sinneth, it shall die." But must God send every poor sinner in the world to Hell?

Oh, no. God loves us so much that He has made a way that a sinner can be forgiven. And so Jesus told Nicodemus that most wonderful verse in the Bible, "For God so loved the world, that He gave His only begotten Son, that whosoever believeth in Him should not perish, but have everlasting life." Ah, Jesus has paid my debt, Jesus has died in my place. As Isaiah 53:6 says, "All we like sheep have gone astray; we have turned every one to his own way; and the Lord hath laid on Him the iniquity of us all." Again and again God says that "He hath made Him to be sin for us, who knew no sin; that we might be made the righteousness of God in Him."

"Nicodemus, except a man be born again,
he cannot see the kingdom of God."—Jesus.

So here God has a way. Now Jesus Christ has suffered in my place and your place. Now one can put his trust in Jesus and thus become a child of God, a born-again Christian.

How the Lord Jesus emphasized that! He said:

"For God sent not His Son into the world to condemn the world; but that the world through Him might be saved. He that believeth on Him is not condemned: but he that believeth not is condemned already, because he hath not believed in the name of the only begotten Son of God."—John 3:17,18.

Thus, many times in the Scriptures we find that one who puts his trust in the Lord Jesus and depends on Him for salvation can have a new heart and everlasting life, can be born again.

I am so glad that Nicodemus at the last seemed to have gotten over his fear of the crowd and so was not ashamed to take down that poor, bruised body of Jesus from the cross and help Joseph bury the body in Joseph's tomb. I believe Nicodemus was really born again and we'll meet him in Heaven.

Jesus and the Samaritan Woman
at Sychar

JOHN 4

We know Jesus had a home in Capernaum on the northwest coast of the little Sea of Galilee, but He went to Jerusalem for the great feasts each year. Once He started back to Capernaum but the Scripture says, "And He must needs go through .Samaria." Instead of turning to the northeast and passing over the common route of travel—down to Jericho and up the Jordan Valley to Galilee—Jesus chose a shorter, though more dangerous road that passed through Samaria, the province which separated Galilee from Judaea. The Samaritans were regarded as hostile by the Jews. But Jesus knew there were people there He should win.

In Samaria, near the city of Sychar, was Jacob's well. Jacob dug this well through rock and soil, perhaps 200 feet deep, centuries before.

Trudging along the dusty road, under a sweltering sun at about the noon hour, Jesus and His disciples came to Jacob's well. All were thirsty and hungry. Being exhausted with heat, hunger and travel, Jesus sat down by the well-side while He sent His disciples on to the village of Sychar to buy food.

Here came a woman down from the city with her pitcher upon her head. She came to draw water from the well, as many other women did. Jesus said to her, "Lady, will you give Me a drink?" Observing at once that He was a Jew, she was astonished and replied, "You, a Jew, ask me for a drink! Me, who am a woman of Samaria!"

Hofmann—Jesus and the Woman of Samaria.

Remember, the Samaritans were a half-breed people. When the nation Israel was carried into captivity, Babylonian settlers were brought in with the heathen religion; so the Samaritans were a mixed people, some with Jewish blood and some with heathen Gentile blood. They were mixed in religion, too. They had no part of the Bible but the Pentateuch. They did not attend worship at Jerusalem. So Jews and Samaritans did not have much, if any, fellowship.

Jesus told her, "If you knew who I am, you would ask Me and I would give you the Water of Life that you need never thirst spiritually again."

She said to Jesus, "Sir, how can You give me water? The well is deep and You don't have a rope and a bucket."

To this inquiry Jesus replied by explaining the difference between the water that quenches the thirst and which she came here to draw, and the Living Water that satisfies the soul and gives life everlasting to him who drinketh. Jesus told her He was not speaking of water from this well but in a spiritual sense how she could have the Gospel and become a child of God. She could drink of spiritual Water and have an artesian well inside in a spiritual sense so that she need never thirst again in spiritual matters.

This answer only served to increase her longing and to excite a curiosity she had never felt before. Now she begged Him to give her of this Water that she might have no reason for coming to draw again.

Seeing she was still unable to comprehend all His meaning Jesus said, "Go call your husband, and I will give you some of this Water."

She answered back, "I have no husband."

Jesus told her what He knew: "You have had five husbands and you are living in sin with a man now to whom you are not married."

The perfect knowledge which Jesus possessed caused the woman to exclaim, "Sir, I perceive that Thou art a prophet." Then she started to argue: "You Jews think the only place to worship God is at Jerusalem, but we think right here on Mount Gerizim is just as good a place to worship." In the eyes of the Samaritans no place on earth was so hallowed as Gerizim.

Jesus had told the woman that the true Temple was in Jerusalem, but knowing the prejudices of Jews and Samaritans Jesus said, 'The hour cometh, and now is when God seeketh people to worship Him, not in Jerusalem, nor in this mountain, but in spirit and in truth. What God wants is a heart worship, heart love.'

The woman was now conscious of her sin. How did that Man know she had been married five times and was now living with another man? And she said, "When the Messiah comes, He will tell us these things."

This was the first time Jesus positively acknowledged His Messiahship. He said unto her, "I am the Messiah."

She could hardly believe it! The Messiah had come! And here she was speaking to the Messiah herself! She put down her pitcher and gathered her skirts and ran back to the city. Then she told the men, "Come, see a Man, which told me everything I ever did. Isn't this the Messiah? Isn't this the Christ?"

And some of those men who must have known they were sinners and must have thought sometimes about the coming Saviour, trusted the Saviour.

The disciples returned bearing provisions and pressed upon Jesus, "Come and eat." But He said, "I have meat to eat that ye know not of." He was not hungry in body. He had had the great joy of winning a soul. And so He did not hunger for food. Then to make His meaning more perfectly understood, He rose up, looked down the valley where the fields were awaiting the reaper and He said to His disciples, "Don't say four months and then there will be a harvest time. Look coming down the hill; see that crowd? The harvest is already white and he that reaps receives wages and gathers fruit to life eternal."

People came to Jesus and besought Him that He would tarry with them. He stayed there two days. Many were saved in that town in Samaria before Jesus and the disciples took leave of their Samaritan friends and journeyed into Galilee.

I tried the broken cisterns, Lord,
But ah! The waters failed.
E'en as I stooped to drink they fled
And mocked me as I wailed.

I came to Jesus and I drank
Of that life-giving stream,
My thirst was quenched, my soul revived,
And now I live in Him.

A Roman Tax Collector Is Called
to Be Christ's Apostle

MARK 2, LUKE 5

Capernaum was something of a trade center. Caravans came down from the northeast by way of Capernaum and on down to Egypt, so the Roman government had a tax agency there in this busy fisherman's town, this town on the caravan route.

The main tax collector here was a man named Levi. His other name is Matthew, and he got to be one of Jesus' disciples and wrote the book of Matthew by divine inspiration.

One day Jesus came along and he was sitting there in his tax position. Maybe he had a little office, or maybe he had a table out by the roadside where those who came by must pay taxes.

The Roman empire had a strange way of collecting taxes. They would assign a certain area to a man and tell him, "Now you collect for us a certain amount of money of taxes in this area for the year, and all you get more than that you keep for yourself." So a tax collector had a good deal of authority and most tax collectors were rich. And, of course, most tax collectors were a little crooked and so were hated and despised by the Jews. But Jesus came by and said to Levi, "Follow me." Ah, his face lighted up. Ah, he was tired of this business of just getting money and serving the Roman government and being despised by the Jews. He was hungry to do more than that. So his heart leaped up with a glad acceptance. He left everything and followed Jesus. I suppose he turned in the amount of taxes he had collected and now he set out to follow Jesus.

Now Levi had grown rich. He said, "I am going to have a great supper, I am going to have all my old-time friends in the tax business, and drunkards and harlots and the other crowd that run with me—I am going to have them for a great dinner at my house."

So Levi (Matthew) had a great dinner and invited Jesus and the disciples to come. And Jesus was at a table with this people, all kinds of people—the kind that a Jew with a bad reputation, a Jew making money of the Roman empire would have. There Jesus met them and talked to them. How these sinful people must have listened eagerly as Jesus preached to them and taught them!

The scribes and Pharisees—how scandalized they were! They told Peter and others, "Why, your Master sat down with publicans and sinners and ate with them."

But when Jesus heard it, He said, "Oh, they ought to

Jesus was walking in Capernaum, by the lake of Galilee. He saw a Customs Officer sitting at his desk. Jesus said to him, "Follow Me." This man was Matthew.

remember that God has said back in the Old Testament, I will have mercy and not sacrifice." Oh, the one thing God wants is for sinners to hear the Gospel. And so when Levi had the big dinner and gave Jesus the chance to meet these sinners and preach to them and try to win them, he did what was right. And what all of us ought to remember is the Lord Jesus wants every poor sinner in the world to hear the Gospel.

I know we are not to be like those who get drunk, those who commit adultery, I know we are not to tie in with them as our best friends and curse when they curse and drink when they drink and so be like them. We are not to be yoked up with them as our best friends. A Christian is not to marry that kind of person, yet we are surely to love sinners everywhere and try our best to win them. We should remember Jesus said, "I will have mercy, and not sacrifice."

So now Levi is one of the disciples of Jesus and he is called Matthew. He will write the Gospel According to Matthew, by the inspiration of God.

The Blesseds: Jesus Tells Eight Ways to Be Happy and Fortunate

The multitude followed Jesus so He went away up into a mountain and there, with great multitudes of people spread around where they could hear Him, Jesus gave what we call The Beatitudes. They are so precious I want you to read them for yourself in Matthew 5:1-12. You will do well to memorize this Scripture.

"And seeing the multitudes, He went up into a mountain: and when He was set, His disciples came unto Him: And He opened His mouth, and taught them, saying, Blessed are the poor in spirit: for their's is the kingdom of heaven. Blessed are they that mourn: for they shall be comforted. Blessed are the meek: for they shall inherit the earth. Blessed are they which do hunger and thirst after righteousness: for they shall be filled. Blessed are the merciful: for they shall obtain mercy. Blessed are the pure in heart: for they shall see God. Blessed are the peacemakers: for they shall be called the children of God. Blessed are they which are persecuted for righteousness' sake: for their's is the kingdom of heaven. Blessed are ye, when men shall revile you, and persecute you, and shall say all manner of evil against you falsely, for my sake. Rejoice, and be exceeding glad: for great is your reward in heaven: for so persecuted they the prophets which were before you."— Matt. 5:1-12.

"Blessed are the poor in spirit," Jesus said. As this message is quoted in Luke 6:20, it is, "Blessed be ye poor." Ah, it is blessed to be poor. It is especially blessed if in your heart you feel your poverty.

A man might have a million dollars but feel there is no one to love him, or, if he had poor health, or if he had no work that was worthwhile, he could feel very poor, and ought to feel poor. In the first place, that means that money is not so important, but a certain heart attitude is important. The simple truth is that rich people are usually not as happy as poor people who are upright in heart. Some one said that John D. Rockefeller, who founded a family of millionaires, could have money to buy all the food he wanted, but his stomach was so weak that he could only have milk and crackers for his supper! And he was not so rich as somebody else, was he? A rich man might find that he had a wife who didn't love him and who made his life miserable. A poor man with a good, loving wife would be better off, wouldn't he?

So poverty may mean work. That is good for us. Blessed is the man that works.

And here the Scripture says, And what will be the result of this blessedness in poverty? Ah, "Their's is the kingdom of God." One day those who have nothing now will be heirs of God and joint heirs with Christ. "All things are yours," Paul said, "and how rich you will be then." So, "Blessed are the poor in spirit."

Again Jesus said, "Blessed are they that mourn: for they shall be comforted." That sounds like a contradiction, doesn't it? But it is really true that there is a great blessing in mourning. Sometimes when trouble comes we find friends we didn't know we had. Sometimes when there is great sorrow and trouble, we find the Lord Jesus such a comfort, and He is nearer than ever before, it seems. You know the Scripture says, "The Lord is nigh unto them that are of a broken heart; and saveth such as be of a contrite spirit" (Ps. 34:18). Does one's father and mother forsake him? Ah, then God has promised the Lord will lift him up.

And the great blessing of mourning is that "they shall be

comforted." It is said that someday the Lord Jesus "will wipe away all tears from their eyes." Oh, when the Lord Jesus takes His weeping followers, those who love and trust Him, in His arms to wipe away their tears, I want to be among those who have tears wiped away. I want the comfort of God that comes to those in trouble.

I sat with a Roman Catholic archbishop of the Solomon Islands on a plane. He loved his work. I said to him, "Well, in that far-off heathen country the Lord can be just as near as in the homeland."

He said, "He is even nearer there—you need Him more."

So, "Blessed are they that mourn." Oh, then don't be afraid of trouble. Don't be afraid of the valley of the shadow of death for God's loving comfort and God's powerful protection are yours. No wonder that Paul called God "the Father of mercies, and the God of all comfort."

I can say, as did the psalmist, "This poor man cried, and the Lord heard him, and saved him out of all his troubles" (Ps. 34:6).

"Blessed are the meek," Jesus said, "for they shall inherit the earth." Did you think that the strong and arrogant and mighty are the ones who inherit the earth? No, Kaiser Wilhelm tried it. It ended up with him defeated and without a kingdom in lonely exile in a foreign country.

Adolph Hitler tried it, and when all his great nation with

his armies and planes and tanks collapsed, he committed suicide and his body was burned in a bunker in Germany in the hour of his defeat and ruin. You may know the meek shall inherit the earth.

That is a blessed truth, then, that one may be content with what he has, content with the place that God has put him and rejoice that in due season he, with the other saints of God, will inherit the earth. And day by day he carries on with security and blessings around him.

"Blessed are they which do hunger and thirst after righteousness," Jesus said, "for they shall be filled." Oh, the Scripture does not say, "Blessed are the righteous." The righteous are blessed, but the best righteousness is that heart hunger, that holy desire, that concern that all I do may please God. I should want the Lord Jesus to have His kingdom and to reign in every heart. You may say, as every Christian must say, "I have failed so often." But, praise God, if your heart hungers for righteousness and hungers for God, then that is acceptable and blessed in His sight. Ah, happy the Christian who wants to do right and in his heart chooses righteousness, for he will be filled, he will become righteous. And how glad it will be when we awake in the likeness of Jesus and all our sins are gone and we attain that which we could not yet attain here.

"Blessed are the merciful: for they shall obtain mercy."

My father reminded me once in the ranch country in West Texas, of something close to that, "The merciful man will be merciful to his beast." It is good, then, to be a merciful man. It is good that we should be quick to forgive others. It is good that no man try to avenge himself but rather we are to forgive others as we want God to forgive us. So we are taught to pray, "Forgive us our trespasses, for we forgive those who trespass against us." How sweet it is that God is glad to forgive and forgiveness in any great measure is ours if we have a forgiving heart for others; then we have a right to claim God's forgiveness, too.

"Blessed are the pure in heart: for they shall see God," Jesus said. I suppose my heart has more often cried to God for this blessedness than for any other. Well, one day I'll receive it. But how eagerly we ought to obey the command, "Keep thy heart with all diligence: for out of it are the issues of life." How we ought to pray with the psalmist:

"*. . .cleanse Thou me from secret faults. Keep back Thy servant also from presumptuous sins; let them not have dominion over me: then shall I be upright, and I shall be innocent from the great transgression. Let the words of my mouth, and the meditation of my heart, be acceptable in Thy sight, O Lord, my strength, and my redeemer.*"—Ps. 19:12-14.

And, oh, one day, thank God, all impurity and stain and sin will be taken away and we will awaken in Christ's presence to go with Him at the rapture.

"Blessed are the peacemakers," said Jesus, "for they shall be called the children of God."

Jesus is the Prince of peace, He is the One only begotten Son, the only Son God has physically begotten. And if Jesus is the Prince of peace and the great Peacemaker, then those of us who, like Him, try to have peace, long for peace, are blessed as sons of God. We might try to make peace between others who are estranged, try to make peace with those who are angry with us, then we, too, can be called the children of God in truth. For Jesus said, "By this shall all men know that ye are My disciples, if ye have love one to another" (John 13:35).

And the crowning happiness—how strange it seems—the crowning happiness and blessedness is here announced for those who are persecuted. Great is the reward in Heaven for those who are persecuted. The Lord Jesus said that if men hate us they hated Him first and the servant is not better than his Lord. And there is the clear promise of the Scriptures that those who live godly in Christ Jesus shall suffer persecution. It may be that of all the blessedness, of all the happiness, the greatest reward is for those who are persecuted for Jesus' sake. Not for our sins, but because we are true to Christ and love Him. Then, in His dear name, let us be willing to suffer some shame, some reproach, and so be in the line of the prophets and apostles who were persecuted for Jesus' sake and will be rewarded in Heaven.

Oh, how sweet are these blesseds, these Beatitudes of Jesus.

The Palsied Man Had Four
Friends Who Brought
Him to Jesus

MATTHEW 9, MARK 2, LUKE 5

After Jesus had healed Peter's wife's mother, He went on a preaching tour throughout the little province of Galilee. Then He returned to His home which now was in Capernaum. But He didn't quit preaching and so everywhere He went crowds gathered to hear Him. He was in a home in Capernaum preaching and people had gathered so that rooms were filled and the dooryard was filled. Jesus preached the Gospel to them.

But here came a strange procession. Why, there are four men who are carrying—what is it? Why, they are carrying a stretcher, or a bed of some kind. And a man is upon it! They come to the front of the house and, my, the dooryard is filled with people and they can't get through. They go, perhaps, to a side door, but again they can't get in the house; it is full. What will they do?

But one of these men may have said to his friends, "We have to get this man to Jesus so he can be healed and so he can be saved. He wants to get to Jesus and have his sins forgiven. What will we do?"

I can imagine another man said, "We'll get him up on top of the house and let him down. There may be [there sometimes were] steps down from the roof into the house. But if not, we'll make a way."

So with boosting from the bottom and pulling from the

Four men carry the palsied man to the top of the roof, the tiles are removed, an opening is made and the man is lowered to the floor.

top, they raised that man to the top of the house. I can imagine the critics stood by and said, "You'll drop that man; you'll kill him that way." And somebody else would say, "You can't get in; there is no room; the house is full." I can guess somebody would say, "You mustn't interrupt the sermon. Jesus is preaching to the people now and you will disturb." But these four men were determined that this poor palsied man, so sick, and conscious of his sins, needed to be forgiven and saved. And so they get to the top of the house.

It was a nice house. It had tiles for roofing, but they began to systematically tear away the tile roofing and make a hole in the roof. My, what consternation! Down below I can imagine that chips began to fall and dust from the roof. The people are astonished and maybe they are indignant. I think maybe there was a gleam in the eye of Jesus, a gleam of pleasure, for He knew what was going on. They tore up enough roof to make a way for the bed of the man. And by the four corners they let it down into the room in front of Jesus as He stood speaking.

Jesus looked up into those faces of the men on the rooftop. They looked down happily, earnestly, believing that Jesus would forgive the man's sins and save him, hoping that Jesus would heal his body. "And when He saw their faith, He said unto him, Man, thy sins are forgiven thee."

What a stir that caused among the scribes and Pharisees! Why, they said among the scribes who were present, "Why does this Man speak blasphemies? You ought to know that nobody can forgive sins but God only." But Jesus knew their hearts and He boldly answered their questionings and their criticisms. He said, "Why reason ye these things in your hearts? Whether is it easier to say to the sick of the palsy, Thy sins be forgiven thee; or to say, Arise, and take up thy bed, and walk?" He paused and then said, "But that ye may know that the Son of man hath power on earth to forgive sins, (he saith to the sick of the palsy,) I say unto thee, Arise, and take up thy bed, and go thy way into thine house."

The man on the bed, oh, how his face lighted up! He raised himself up. He had been deathly sick and paralyzed, but now he stood alone with gratitude and praise and Jesus said, "Take up your bed and take it home with you now." And so the man rolled up the bed and carried it back home to tell his wife he had been forgiven and saved. I guess the four men who brought him went gladly along, praising the Lord that they had been able to bring a man to Jesus to get forgiveness and to get healing.

Ah, people wondered and commented and were amazed. They said, "We never saw such a miracle as that before." Now they must believe that Jesus had the right to forgive sins because He had the power to heal the poor, paralyzed man.

Aren't we glad that poor, paralyzed man had friends who were willing to go to the trouble to bring him to Jesus, who were willing to be criticised and misunderstood? Yes, and maybe they had to pay for the roof of that man's house they tore up, too. But they were good friends. You know, sometimes one cannot win a soul alone, but Christians can work together and get people saved. And Christians ought to go to a good deal of trouble to love people and help people and get them to Jesus for salvation.

At the House of a Pharisee, Jesus Meets and Saves a Sinful Woman

LUKE 7

Among the Jews, the most influential people in the time of Christ were the Pharisees. They had very strict standards, trying seriously to keep every little jot and tittle of the law and, in addition, the rules they had made. Nicodemus was a Pharisee and, like most of the Pharisees, he was unsaved until he came to Jesus.

While the Pharisees had very strict standards, they were often hypocrites, as you see from Matthew 23 where Jesus said again and again, "Woe unto you, scribes and Pharisees, hypocrites!"

The Pharisees were not friendly to Jesus, yet Jesus was so prominent and so many people crowded to hear Him that they were glad to have this famous Man come to their houses, even though they did not love Him and did not follow Him.

Once a Pharisee had Jesus at his house for dinner. It was a great meal. We imagine it was on a patio. It is likely that the Pharisee had as his guests many rich friends. The custom then was to lie on couches facing the table, not to sit in chairs. As Jesus reclined at the table, a poor woman, widely known as a sinner and probably a prostitute, slipped in and came to the feet of Jesus and knelt. What a shock to the Pharisees! They would have nothing to do with such a woman! Perhaps they thought it very presumptuous for her

The woman anoints the feet of Jesus and wipes them with her hair.

to crowd in uninvited to that great dinner. The host said within himself, "Now, if Jesus were a prophet of God, He would not have let that woman touch Him, for she is a sinner."

Meantime, the woman began to weep and her tears dripped upon the very feet of the Saviour, dusty from walking on the unpaved streets. (When Jesus came in to the home of the Pharisee, this man had not shown the usual courtesy of having a servant wash His feet.) Then the woman took down her long hair and wiped the wet feet of Jesus after her tears had washed them.

Of course, the Pharisee was scandalized. But Jesus knew his thoughts and said to him, "Simon, I have something to say unto you!"

He said, "Master, say on!"

Jesus said, "There was a certain creditor which had two debtors: the one owed five hundred pence, and the other fifty. And when they had nothing to pay, he frankly forgave them both. Tell me therefore, which of them will love him most?"

Simon answered, "I suppose that he, to whom he forgave most."

Jesus said unto Simon, "Thou hast rightly judged." Then he turned to this poor woman weeping at His feet and said, "Simon, seest thou this woman? When I entered your house, you gave Me no water to wash My feet—an ordinary courtesy—but this woman washed My feet with tears, and wiped them with the hair of her head. Simon, when I came in, you didn't give Me a kiss on the cheek, a courtesy of respect and affection. But this woman has not ceased to kiss my feet. Oh, her sins were many, but they are forgiven. That is why she loves me."

And He said to this woman, "Thy sins are forgiven."

Oh, surely her tears stopped. She came for forgiveness, I am sure.

Well, the Pharisee and his critical guests did not like that. They said within themselves, "What right has He to forgive sins?" But Jesus said to the woman, "Thy faith hath saved thee; go in peace." And with a glad heart, that poor sinful woman went away forgiven to live for the Lord and to meet us all in Heaven.

Isn't it wonderful that the Lord Jesus loves sinful people and is willing to forgive us and save us, just like He did that sinful woman?

Jesus Raises the Daughter of Jairus From the Dead and Heals a Persistent Woman Who Intervenes

MATTHEW 9, MARK 5, LUKE 8

Jesus was back on the west side of the Sea of Galilee near Capernaum. One of the rulers of the synagogue named Jairus came to see Jesus. Oh, he was deeply distressed. He fell down at the feet of Jesus. He must have something serious to beg Jesus to do.

Yes, he said, "My little daughter lieth at the point of death: I pray Thee, come and lay Thy hands on her, that she may be healed; and she shall live." So Jesus started out with Jairus to go to the home where the little daughter lay at the point of death. I can imagine how earnestly the father urged, "Let's hurry! Jesus, we don't want to wait till she dies. Let's hurry so You can heal her."

Everywhere Jesus went a crowd followed Him. They wanted to hear everything He had to say. They wanted to see every wonderful thing He did. Now there was somebody behind who touches Him. So Jesus knew that virtue had gone out of Him. He knew power had gone out from Him. He said, "Who touched My clothes?"

Peter and the others answered, "Why, Jesus, a crowd is around You all the time and, of course, people touch Your clothes."

But Jesus said, "No; I mean healing virtue is gone out of Me. Find who touched Me." I think He knew who it was. And there is a poor woman with pale face. She had an issue of blood twelve years. She spent all her money with the doctors. She had taken all the treatments and the medicine they could recommend and day by day her life strength was flowing away.

But she saw Jesus and knew what He had done for others. She said, "If I could only touch the hem of His garment, I believe I would be healed." So with trembling finger, she reached out to touch the garment of Jesus. And Jesus knew her need and He knew the healing power that went out from Him, and suddenly the woman was healed.

But Jesus said, "Who touched Me?" That doesn't mean that Jesus didn't know. I think He knew all right, but He wanted that woman to make it public. When people are blessed, He wants them to give Him the credit. Remember Jesus had said, "Whosoever therefore shall confess Me before men, him will I confess also before My Father which is in heaven" (Matt. 10:32). So now Jesus insisted and the woman very timidly stood up and said, "I touched You. I have had

"Who touched Me?"

this issue of blood these long twelve years and no doctor could help me, and I knew if I could but touch Your garment, I would be healed, and I was healed."

Then Jesus said to the woman, "Daughter, thy faith hath made thee whole; go in peace, and be whole of thy plague."

But what about Jairus' little daughter whom he loved so much? Here came certain people from the house of Jairus and said to him, sadly, "Thy daughter is dead: why troublest thou the Master any further?"

Oh, poor Jairus. He must have been greatly distressed to hear that. But Jesus heard that and said to the ruler of the synagogue, "Be not afraid, only believe." And so He went into the house of Jairus. He said to Peter, James and John, "You come with Me." And nobody else.

He came to the house of the ruler of the synagogue and a great tumult and multitude were there, people wailing over the dead girl. He said, "My, why do you make this to-do and weep? The damsel is not dead, but sleepeth." Ah, they

One who is dead is only asleep if Jesus is there!

laughed a bitter laughter. They knew she was dead. Ah, but one who is dead is only asleep if Jesus is there.

So He put them all out but the father and mother of the damsel and Peter, James and John with Him, and entered in where the body of the little girl lay. "And He took the damsel by the hand, and said unto her, Talitha cumi; which is, being interpreted, Damsel, I say unto thee, arise. And straightway the damsel arose, and walked; for she was of the age of twelve years. And they were astonished with a great astonishment" at this great deliverance. He said, "Give the child something to eat," and warned them not to tell it. He knew that wicked men wanted to kill Him already. He worked this miracle out of His loving compassion but knew it would cause enemies to hate Him more.

The Feeding of Five Thousand
With One Boy's Lunch

MATTHEW 14, MARK 6, LUKE 9, JOHN 6

The crowds that followed Jesus pressed upon Him day and night. So after a tour of Galilee with the apostles, Jesus said to them, "Come ye yourselves apart into a desert place, and rest a while: for there were many coming and going, and they had no leisure so much as to eat" (Mark 6:31). So they went into a desert place, literally, it was a country place away from the crowded and inhabited cities, not desert in the sense of sand and bare ground, but into a country place away from the towns.

They went by ship and then turned in down the coast a ways and then into a country place. But the people saw them departing and a great many followed on foot from the cities. So the great crowd came where Jesus had drawn apart for a little quiet rest and leisure. Oh, how the heart of Jesus "was moved with compassion toward them, because they were as sheep not having a shepherd: and He began to teach them many things." How they hung upon His words out there on that hillside not far from the Sea of Galilee.

The day drew toward a close. The people had come out without preparation and as night came on they had had nothing to eat. Some had followed so long and had rushed after Him until they had been as much as a day, I suppose, without food.

The disciples had pity on the people, so frantic to hear the Lord Jesus they had come away from home without lunches;

now the evening drew on, and they had no food. They suggested to Jesus, "Jesus, send them into the towns and villages nearby so they can buy food. They will be fainting with hunger here."

Jesus said to Philip as they looked on the great multitude of people, "Philip, where will we buy bread to feed this multitude?"

Philip said, "Two hundred pennyworth of bread is not sufficient for them, that every one of them may take a little." We think he meant two hundred denarii, that is two hundred days' wages.

But Jesus said, "They don't need to go away to the cities and villages. You disciples give them food to eat."

Then Andrew, Peter's brother, said, "There is a lad here, which hath five barley loaves, and two small fishes: but what are they among so many?" Ah, the disciples did not have the faith to expect that the Lord Jesus would multiply those little loaves and fishes, one little boy's lunch, enough to feed five thousand men besides the women and children!

He told them to do it, but since they had no faith to try, Jesus Himself had the people seated by fifties and by hundreds, then He took that little boy's lunch of five barley loaves and two small fishes and began to break them and break them and fill a basket and Peter took that; then another basket full and James took that; and another basket full and Andrew took that; and another basket full and John took that—and so they kept on going and there kept being some more fish and some more bread in the hands of Jesus and He broke them until the twelve were passing out fish sandwiches to everybody and they got all they could eat! And when they got through they had twelve baskets full left! I have sometimes thought Jesus fed those five thousand men besides the women and children and what they ate was for them. But the twelve baskets full left were for others. That meant there is plenty when Jesus provides for His own.

Jesus had prayed and blessed the bread and the fishes and they were plenty.

I imagine that little boy, who brought his lunch that day

"They need not depart; give ye them to eat." So five barley loaves and two small fishes feed five thousand!

and came out to hear Jesus, had plenty to take home with him, too, so he wouldn't be hungry.

Somebody says, "But that would be a miracle. How could Jesus make enough out of that one little lunch to feed the five thousand besides the women and children?"

Well, you remember the Lord Jesus is the Creator. The Scripture says, "All things were made by Him; and without Him was not any thing made that was made" (John 1:3). And if the Lord Jesus could make the world and everything in it, He surely could make a little more bread and let it multiply under His hands and make the fishes multiply to feed the crowd there. Oh, don't ever think there is anything too hard for the Lord Jesus. We must take the Bible at face value, for what the Bible says, is true, and what the Bible says happened, really happened.

Don't you remember in the wilderness the Lord brought manna from Heaven every day for forty years to feed the millions of Israel encamped in the wilderness? To create bread for the hungry is not hard for God. It is a miracle, but Jesus is a miracle-working Saviour.

Some of the people who saw that fish and bread multiplied to feed thousands of people and satisfy everybody, said, "This is of a truth that prophet that should come into the world." They meant that back in the Old Testament, in Deuteronomy 18:15, Moses said, "The Lord thy God will raise up unto thee a Prophet from the midst of thee. . .like unto me. . . ." Yes, this is the prophesied Saviour.

When the people saw the marvelous miracle, thousands of people fed miraculously, they thought, Oh, wouldn't it be wonderful to have Jesus as King and He could feed everybody and we wouldn't have to work or be hungry and nobody would be so poor? They knew that the Messiah was promised one day to be a King. God had promised David that of his descendents One should sit on the throne. And even Mary, when the angel told her that she should bear the Saviour, was told, ". . .and the Lord God shall give unto Him the throne of His father David: And He shall reign over the house of Jacob for ever." Of course, those promises are about Jesus at His second coming, but the people didn't have a very good idea of it and they wanted a king like that who could make bread from nothing!

So Jesus slipped away into the mountains and His disciples got in a boat and started rowing back toward Capernaum on the little Sea of Galilee. And Jesus stayed apart to pray. Then in the middle of the night as they rowed hard against the wind, the Lord Jesus came walking upon the water to them. "Oh, it is a ghost, it is a spirit," some of them said. But Jesus said, "No, it is I; be not afraid." Ah, walking on the water, what a wonderful thing! So Peter spoke up and said, "Lord, if it is You, let me come to You walking on the water, too." So Jesus gave permission and Peter stepped out of the boat on the water and started walking toward Jesus.

But then he suddenly thought, What a strange thing is this? Why, one can't walk on the water, and he began to sink. And he cried out, "Lord, save me." And Jesus took him by the hand and said, "O Peter, why did you doubt!" Then they both got in the boat and soon they were at Capernaum. What a wonderful day it had been! And Jesus had shown that He is not only the Creator of all things, but He controls the wind and the waves of the sea, too.

Jesus Walks on the Water: Tells Peter to Come to Him

MATTHEW 14:27; MARK 6:50; JOHN 6:20

After Jesus fed the 5,000 men, besides women and children, with the multiplying of five barley loaves and two small fishes, the lunch brought by a boy, and after they had collected and saved the twelve basketsful of fish and bread sandwiches, the Lord told the disciples they should take their boat and row back north on the Sea of Galilee to Capernaum. Jesus stayed behind and went into a mountain to pray.

The disciples pulled away from shore. But a furious storm arose. So great was the storm that though Capernaum was only four miles from Bethsaida, after nearly eight hours of toilsome rowing the apostles were still not at their destination. Then in the night they saw an object moving over the tossing waves. They were frightened. "It is a spirit, a ghost!" one of them said. But Jesus called to them and said, "It is I; be not afraid." What a wonderful thing it was to see Jesus walking boldly on the water, as if it were dry land.

In loving enthusiasm Peter called out, "Lord, if it be Thou, bid me come to Thee on the water." And Jesus told him, "Come."

Peter leaped out of the boat onto a solid wave that bore him up! For a moment it seemed he would make it, but he looked down at the dashing, angry waves and his faith began to fade. I am sure he thought, Oh, I am about to go under! In despair he called to Jesus, "Lord, save me." So Jesus

Reaching out a helping
hand, Jesus lifts Peter
above the waves.

reached His hand to Peter and held him up and said by way of rebuke, "O thou of little faith, wherefore didst thou doubt?" The Lord had given Peter power to walk on the water, but he did not believe it much, did he?

When they were come into the boat the wind ceased, the waves were stilled and soon the ship was at the home shore.

Let us remember that all storms are easily controlled by the Lord Jesus. As the psalmist has said, "The earth is the Lord's, and the fulness thereof; the world, and they that dwell therein" (Ps. 24:1). And whatever Jesus permits us to do, we can do *by His power.*

Wasn't it a wonderful thing that Peter could sometimes tell of that event: "Yes, I walked on the water, right on the top of the waves!"

The Home of Mary and Martha
at Bethany

LUKE 10:38-42

Bethany was a little village on the eastern slopes of the Mount of Olives. There lived Mary and Martha and their older brother, Lazarus.

They were up early and Mary said, "It is a feast day! Martha, don't you think Jesus will come today with the twelve disciples? He nearly always comes to Jerusalem on a feast day. I heard that the last time He was in Jerusalem He slept the night on the ground in the Garden of Gethsemane! Oh, I want to see Him! Don't you think He will come?"

Martha smiled and said, "Yes, I think so. I certainly hope He will. And now we must get ready a nice dinner for Him and for the twelve. I am sure that ofttimes Jesus goes hungry. And I am so glad He comes to see us. We will look for Him today."

Sure enough, Jesus came and with Him all the twelve He had selected as apostles to go with Him and to learn His message and be a witness of His life and of His future resurrection from the dead.

How Martha planned for that dinner! She was the older one and some way she took the heavy responsibility of the house and the meals. I imagine she said, "Mary, Jesus will like the curried lamb with rice. And we must have some figs and dates to go along with the meal. Now hurry, Mary. Help me get it ready!"

But when Jesus came, Mary sat at His feet and asked

questions. She no doubt asked Jesus to tell her about that poor fallen woman who came to the house of Simon and wept over His feet and how Jesus forgave her and she went away happy. Jesus explained how the Pharisee had thought that He wouldn't even speak to the poor prostitute woman, and was astonished when He loved her and forgave her. He told Mary how penitent the sinful woman was as she knelt at His feet and kissed them as tears ran down to wash those dusty feet and how she took her long hair and wiped His feet.

But Martha was working hard to get a big dinner ready for the big crowd—Jesus and His twelve disciples, Mary and Martha and Lazarus. Martha was impatient because it seemed Mary had forgotten to help and just kept sitting at the feet of Jesus.

But Mary asked other questions, for her heart was hungry

Mary has chosen
the best part.

to know more about Jesus. Jesus must have told her how He would die and rise from the dead again. Yes, Lazarus had told her a little about His teaching on this, that He would rise from the dead. As they talked, Mary must have said in her heart, "Oh, that dear body to be crucified and laid in the tomb! I wish some way I could comfort His heart!" She thought that one day she too would take an alabaster box of ointment—very precious, sweet-smelling perfume—that she had saved for it at great expense. And if she could follow the example of that poor fallen woman, she would pour that ointment on the head of Jesus and show her faith that He was to be anointed as His poor dead body would be laid in the tomb before His resurrection.

But Martha came in and said, "Jesus, tell Mary to come and help me. I am so glad You and the disciples are with us, but she has left me to serve alone. Bid her help me."

But Jesus said, "Martha, you are cumbered about much serving. You want to feed our bodies, and that is very kind. But that is not the main thing. Mary wants to know about spiritual things, so she sits here at My feet and listens. She has chosen the best part, which shall not be taken away from her."

I have no doubt that Mary was even then thinking that one day perhaps she could do better than the poor fallen woman, and pour sweet incense on the head of Jesus, anointing Him for His burial.

Wouldn't you like to have been a visitor, along with Jesus, in that home at Bethany? Wouldn't you like to have known Mary and Martha and Lazarus and seen how they loved and entertained and waited on the Lord Jesus and the disciples?

We, too, must choose the better part; i.e., sitting at Jesus' feet and learning more of Him!

Jesus Tells the Story of the Prodigal Son

LUKE 15

When Jesus spoke, people crowded around Him, and the Pharisees and scribes complained because publicans and sinners crowded in to hear Jesus. Jesus explained that God loves sinful people, and He spoke three parables to illustrate that.

First was the parable of the lost sheep. If a man had a hundred sheep and lost one, he would go into the mountains and seek that one lost sheep. And when he found it, he would lay it on his shoulder rejoicing and come home and tell his friends and neighbors that he had found his lost sheep. That is how God feels about sinners.

He told about a woman with ten pieces of silver who lost a piece. She lighted a candle in that house with no windows and swept it because the coin might be in a crack in the stone floor. She searched diligently until she found it, and then she called her friends and neighbors and said to them, "Rejoice with me; for I have found the piece which I had lost." Jesus says that in Heaven there is joy over one sinner who repenteth.

Then Jesus told the famous story of the prodigal son. A certain wealthy man had two sons. The younger son, tired of parental dependence, came one day to his father and said, "Father, give me the portion of goods that falleth to me." Whatever he was to get from his father's property, he wanted it now! That was thoughtless and wrong. This indulgent father made a division of his property. After a little while the younger gathered his all together and took a journey into a far country to establish himself. I am sure he went in style, because he had money. Maybe he had horses and a coach. Having considerable wealth, he soon made many friends who were glad to help him spend it. In the far country he wasted his substance with riotous living. The young man and his money soon parted. There is no money left with which to meet his heavy expenses. Besides that, the crops had failed, and there arose a mighty famine in that country. There always comes a famine when people play the fool and waste their money and opportunities in sin. And he was hungry, so he went to join himself to a citizen of that country. And that man sent him into his fields to feed the swine. The poor fellow was so hungry he wanted to eat the husks that he fed to the hogs!

Eats now what swine eat.

What a contrast! From riches to rags! Money all gone, deserted by friends, so hungry that he will gladly eat what swine eat!

Then he came to his senses. He saw how foolish he had been, and he said, "Just think! Back home tonight all the hired people have plenty to eat and a safe place to sleep. Here I am, the younger son and favorite—I have wasted my substance and am starving. Oh, for a scrap from Father's table!" So dejected, half starved and full of remorse he said, "I am going home. I'll say to my father, 'Father, I have sinned against heaven, and before thee, and am no more worthy to be called thy son.'"

And so he arose and came home to his father.

The father had loved his son, had longed over him and wished to see him return. The son expected a chilling reception, but when yet some distance away, dressed like a beggar and looking like a tramp, the father saw him. Now all the finery is gone. Now he is walking instead of riding. But the father, with a glad shout, rushed to meet him and fell into the arms of his son and kissed him in love. "My son! My boy!"

The wayward son began to apologize. "Father, I have sinned against heaven, and before thee, and am no more worthy to be called thy son." He intended to ask to be just like a hired servant, but the father shut him up and called for somebody to bring a robe for him, and shoes for his feet, and a ring. He shouted to the servants, "Go kill that fat calf we have been saving. We are going to have a feast, a banquet, now." And I think he told the servant to go to all the neighbors and tell them to come and share this joyful day. My, what a time of rejoicing! The house is full of congratulators. The boy has come home and the father said, "My boy was lost and is now found; he was dead and is alive again!" Oh, what a time of merriment they had!

The older son was in the fields, and as he drew near the house he heard music and dancing. He called a servant and asked about it and the servant said, "Your brother has come! Your father has killed the fatted calf for him and is rejoicing!"

The older son felt bad. He sulks in a corner. One would think that on hearing a younger brother had come back he would have gone into the house and rejoiced. No. Not him. "I stayed at home and worked on the farm. You never made a party for me. But this vagabond goes off in fine clothes and comes back not fit to be seen, and how you make over him! He breaks your heart, and you pay him for it! He deserves a whipping instead of a banquet. Veal is too good for him!"

That night, as the younger son tells his father about his adventures, and asking what has happened at home in his absence, the senior brother goes to bed disgusted. Friends, that senior brother still lives today!

That is the way the Pharisees were about the publicans and sinners coming to hear Jesus. They didn't like that. They didn't want publicans and sinners to be saved. But Jesus was explaining how God feels about poor sinners and how we ought to be glad to see them saved.

Many a poor sinner, no doubt, has heard that story of the prodigal son and saw that as the father was waiting so eagerly to greet the lost boy when he came home, so God in Heaven loves sinners and is anxious for them to return to Him with repentance and faith.

If you in your heart feel you have been a prodigal and wandered away from God, I hope today you will say, "Father, I have sinned and I am coming home."

Jesus Heals the Maniac of Gadara

After Jesus had spoken some wonderful parables to great crowds in Galilee and not far from Capernaum, He said to His disciples, "Let us pass over unto the other side."

So He sent away the multitude that had been following Him, and He and the disciples got in the boat to sail across the Sea of Galilee, that little lake seven and one-half miles across.

Other little ships followed, but a great storm arose. The wind whipped the waves so they were high and the water washed over the sides of the boat until it was about to be full.

Jesus had had such a heavy, heavy schedule preaching to the multitudes; so He was asleep on a pillow in the hinder part of the ship during the storm. The disciples became afraid and woke Jesus up. "Master, don't You care if we perish?" Jesus arose and rebuked the wind. He said unto the sea, "Peace, be still." And marvel of marvels, the wind suddenly stopped, there was a great calm, and the tempestuous sea was smooth. "And He said unto them, Why are ye so fearful? how is it that ye have no faith? And they feared exceedingly, and said one to another, What manner of man is this, that even the wind and the sea obey Him?"

Oh, if we would only learn that "The earth is the Lord's, and the fulness thereof; the world, and they that dwell therein" (Ps. 24:1). He is the Master of all nature; the Master of the wind and waves and the sea; the Master of kings and princes, as well as common men.

Well, they got safely over to the east side of Jordan, to the country of the Gadarenes, now called the Golan Heights. There they came upon a strange man, a devil-possessed man. I think there were two of them, but the story deals principally with only one. When Jesus asked him his name, this man said, "My name is Legion." He meant he had a whole army of devils in him, a legion of devils. So dangerous was this poor, devil-possessed man that everybody was afraid of him.

They tried to put him in jail; he would break out. They tried to chain him; he would break the chains. He ran around naked. He slept in the caves where they buried the dead. He cut himself with stones and cried in the night. Everybody was frightened by him; nobody could control him.

But Jesus said to the demons in this man, "Come out of him." They protested. "And all the devils besought him, saying, Send us into the swine, that we may enter into them." There was a great herd of swine feeding there close to the mountain. And Jesus gave them permission: "And the unclean spirits went out, and entered into the swine: and the herd ran violently down a steep place into the sea, (they were about two thousand;) and were choked in the sea."

Oh, the herders of the pigs ran to tell their bosses that "those two thousand hogs are all dead, drowned in the Sea of Galilee. Jesus let the devils from the wild man go into the hogs; and now see what happened!" The owners of the hogs were not concerned about that poor, demon-possessed man.

When they came out, they found this once-wretched man sitting at the feet of Jesus, clothed and in his right mind.

Remember, when people get right with God, they cover their nakedness and clothe themselves, as did this man. He sat there learning.

These men who owned the swine had gone to the city and had told everything. So the Scripture says the whole city came out to meet Jesus and demanded that He leave their country. "See how much damage You have done! And think of all those nice hams we could have had, and all the bacon, and all the money we could have made out of those hogs! Now see what You have done! We want You to leave this country."

Jesus prepared to go. But what about the poor, devil-possessed man who had been cleansed and healed? He said, "Jesus, let me go with You." I think he knew now these people didn't care about him at all, only about the money they had lost with their pigs. (Jews were not supposed to eat pork. Then why should they be raising pigs for other people to eat?) This man now wanted to go with Jesus and leave that country where people thought more of hogs than humans.

But Jesus said, "No. Go back to your father's house, go back to your own city and tell them how great things the Lord has done for you and been merciful to you."

He obeyed His Lord. He went back to tell his loved ones what a marvelous deliverance and salvation Jesus had given him.

Isn't it wonderful that Jesus can cure the vilest sinner! can make drunkards sober! can make harlots pure! can make infidels into saints of God! Oh, we ought to trust Him daily to help us win all those who are in trouble with sin, all those who are devil-possessed. We ought to have compassion on souls as Jesus did. We ought to rejoice when we can find them clothed and in their right mind sitting at the feet of Jesus.

Getting devils cast out and lost men saved is much more important than making money, isn't it?

Wicked King Herod Has John the Baptist Beheaded

MATTHEW 14, MARK 6

John the Baptist was the forerunner of the Lord Jesus. But when great crowds came to hear Jesus preach and Jesus had many more people baptized than John, John the Baptist rejoiced and said, "He must increase, but I must decrease." Afterward, John the Baptist was put in prison because he preached so plainly. King Herod was angry because he preached that it was wrong for King Herod to take his brother's wife and live in adultery. But John, in prison, got to wondering. Oh, was Jesus really the Messiah? Then why didn't He finish the work and take His place? Was Jesus not to be the prophesied King of the Jews? So John sent people to Jesus to say, "Art thou He that should come? or look we for another?" Jesus told John's messengers to see all the wonderful healings and the preaching of the Gospel to the poor and fulfillment of all the promises about the Saviour. And they went back and comforted John with the sweet assurance that, yes, Jesus was really the Messiah.

And Jesus said about John, "Among them that are born of women there hath not risen a great than John the Baptist."

But plain preaching brings opposition and so King Herod had put John in prison. And one day King Herod had a great party and his wife's daughter Salome came and danced before him. We do not know all the details of this dancing, but she pleased Herod very much and he made a foolish promise. He said, "Ask of me whatsoever thou wilt. . .I will give it thee, unto the half of my kingdom." It was Herod's birthday and many lords and ladies were there and they heard his promise to her. Salome went at once to her mother and said, "Whatsoever I ask, King Herod will give it to me, even to the half of his kingdom."

Her mother Herodias hated John the Baptist. He had preached so plainly about her adultery when she left her husband to live with King Herod. Now was her opportunity for vengeance. So she said, "Go ask for the head of John the Baptist." So Salome came back to talk to King Herod and said, "What I want is the head of John the Baptist here on a big platter." Herod was amazed and perhaps troubled. He hadn't thought of anything like this and he didn't like to kill John the Baptist, but he had made an oath and the other officers there had heard it and he felt he must keep his word.

So he sent to the prison where John the Baptist was and had him beheaded. And they brought the head on a platter and presented that gory spectacle to the girl and she took it to show her mother that John the Baptist had died.

Later the conscience of Herod troubled him and when he heard about the wonderful miracles of Jesus he said, "This is John the Baptist risen from the dead." Poor, wicked Herod. His conscience did not give him peace and he must account to God for the murder of a good man, John the Baptist, the forerunner of Jesus.

And let us remember that those who preach plainly against sin, as John the Baptist did, may expect persecution and hate from those who do not repent.

Jesus Heals the Devil-Possessed
Daughter of a Woman of Canaan

MATTHEW 15

The Lord Jesus lived at Capernaum during the days of His ministry. He went, perhaps, two or three times a year to Jerusalem, but most of His ministry was in the province of Galilee. However here the crowds came from so far. So Jesus covered a wide area in His travels. We find He went over into the country of Tyre and Sidon, in what is now Phoenicia or Lebanon. And there came a Canaanite woman crying out to Him for help. She was a Greek, we suppose, by her blood and language, but lived in the land of Canaan. So she cried out to Jesus, "Lord, have mercy upon me, have mercy upon me!"

"Why, what is wrong?" Jesus asked her.

And she answered, "My daughter is grievously vexed with a devil. Oh, have mercy on me!"

I am sure Jesus decided just then that He would teach His disciples a lesson. Yes, and He would teach us a lesson, too, for He wants us to know how His heart is open to the cry of anybody, whether he be a Jew or Gentile. Remember the Bible tells how Ruth, the Moabitess, came into the land of Israel and married Boaz and became the ancestress of the Lord Jesus. Remember Rahab the harlot of Jericho who married Salmon, and so was a woman in the ancestral line of Jesus. So Jesus was kind to Samaritans and to crooked tax collectors and to various kinds of sinners and people in trouble and people who were looked down upon.

Now let's watch what He does as the woman cries to Him,

"Lord, have mercy on me. . .my daughter is grievously vexed with a devil."

What did He do? He did nothing at all for a moment. He waited for His disciples to complain. They were vexed in the first place because the woman was not a Jewess and they didn't think Jesus ought to pay her any attention. And they were vexed also because she kept crying out to Jesus for help. So the disciples came and drew Him aside and said, "Send her away; for she crieth after us. She makes us uncomfortable and nervous." So He turned to the woman and said, "I am not sent but unto the lost sheep of the house of Israel."

Ah, she knew better than that. Of course, you and I know better than that, too. Yes, He came not only for Jews but for

Gentiles. But here He pretended for a moment that He didn't come to help anybody but Jews. And I am sure the disciples thought so, too. Remember, later, when God called Peter to go preach to Cornelius and his Gentile soldiers at Caesarea, Peter didn't want to go and wouldn't go until God let down a vision from Heaven three times and insisted that he go. Well, the disciples thought that was right, Jesus didn't come to anybody but the Jews.

But that poor, troubled woman knew better than that, so she kept on pleading. She fell down before Him and said, "Lord, help me." And again He said a strange thing. He acted as if the Jews were the only real children of God and the Gentile people were no better than dogs! He said, "It is not meet to take the children's bread, and cast it to dogs."

Oh, but she was not going to be discouraged. She knew someway, in her heart, that this Saviour will answer her prayer. And she kept on pleading. She said, "Truth, Lord: yet the dogs eat of the crumbs which fall from their masters' table." Ah, Jesus was pleased. I can imagine that later He would refer to this to the disciples and remind them how they didn't believe He would love and answer and bless a Gentile woman. He said to her, "O woman, great is thy faith: be it unto thee even as thou wilt. And her daughter was made whole from that very hour," we are told (Matt. 15:28).

There is a wonderful lesson for us. The dear Lord Jesus is close to every troubled heart. He is anxious to hear the cry of anybody who is in need. It is not just good people, but troubled people, sinful people who are encouraged to cry to Jesus for help. So if sometimes you do not deserve God's help, then let that Syrophenician woman be a good reminder that God has a tender heart and the Saviour loves people in trouble and is always able to help. So Jesus said, "Ask, and it shall be given you; seek, and ye shall find; knock, and it shall be opened unto you: For every one that asketh receiveth; and he that seeketh findeth; and to him that knocketh it shall be opened" (Matt. 7:7,8).

Peter's Great Confession
at Caesarea Philippi

There were two Caesareas in the Holy Land in Bible times. One is on the eastern shore of the Mediterranean Sea, as we go north from Joppa and what is now Tel Aviv, toward Haifa. This Caesarea was built as a great city.

But there was another Caesarea, that is, Caesarea Philippi, away up north of the Sea of Galilee, near the foot of Mount Hermon. All that country was densely populated in New Testament times. And Jesus went up to that country, too, preaching from town to town.

At Caesarea Philippi three important things came to pass. One, Jesus asked the disciples, "Who do men say that I am?"

Some said He was John the Baptist risen from the dead. Some said He was Elijah the prophet. Others said He was some other of the prophets.

Then Jesus said to them plainly, "But whom say ye that I am?"

Peter answered boldly, "Thou art the Christ, the Son of the living God." Oh, how that pleased Jesus!

He said, "Blessed art thou, Simon Bar-jona: for flesh and blood hath not revealed it unto thee, but My Father which is in heaven."

Yes, and all of us can now say with Simon Peter, "Thou art the Christ, the Son of the living God." Jesus is the only begotten Son of God, i.e., the only Child of God physically begotten of God. He is the promised Messiah, the Saviour.

Another thing that happened there was that Jesus foretold some of His sufferings and the crucifixion. He told that the Son of Man would be arrested, tried and abused, then He would be crucified and slain.

How indignant Peter was! He knew Jesus was the Saviour, yet some way he did not understand what had been so often foretold in the Old Testament, that Jesus must die for sinners. So Peter protested. It should not be! They could not kill Jesus.

Jesus said to him sternly, "Get thee behind Me, Satan: thou art an offence unto Me: for thou savourest not the things that be of God, but those that be of men."

Oh, we must remember this: Jesus coming into the world is not enough. He must die for the sins of the world. In my song, "Jesus, Baby Jesus," read the chorus:

> **Jesus, Baby Jesus,**
> **There's a cross along the way.**
> **Born to die for sinners,**
> **Born for crucifixion day!**

Had Peter understood the 53rd chapter of Isaiah, he would have known that Jesus must die for our sins.

Will you notice that Jesus called him "Satan," because the suggestion was from Satan. Before, God had helped Peter to understand that Jesus was the Christ, the Son of the living God. Now Satan had him unwittingly opposing the crucifixion. So that advice from Peter was from Satan.

There would be no salvation if Jesus did not die for sinners. The Gospel is "how that Christ died for our sins according to the scriptures; And that He was buried, and that He rose again the third day according to the scriptures" (I Cor. 15:3,4).

But another teaching comes to light there. Jesus said to Simon Peter, after he had confessed that Jesus is the Christ, the Son of God, "That thou art Peter, and upon this rock I will build My church; and the gates of hell shall not prevail against it."

Some people have thought that the church would be built

upon Peter. Now the word Peter means a stone. Peter was a stone, a movable stone. But Jesus said, ". . .upon this rock [Himself] I will build My church," i.e., on the bedrock of Jesus Christ Himself.

First Corinthians 3:11 says, "For other foundation can no man lay than that is laid, which is Jesus Christ." Salvation doesn't depend on Peter, nor upon any successor of Peter, nor on any preachers. It depends on Christ Himself. The church is built on Jesus. It is that body of Christians who have trusted Christ, those who will be gathered together in the great gathering at the time of the rapture, at Christ's second coming. Then the dead in Christ shall rise first, and we that are alive and remain shall be caught up together with them to meet the Lord in the air. That church, or that body, of all the Christians in the world is built on Jesus Christ Himself.

Remember, Jesus said in John 14:6, "I am the way, the truth, and the life: no man cometh unto the Father, but by Me."

And so I Peter 2:5 tells us that all who have trusted in Jesus and are born again are put in like living stones into the building which the Lord is building. That is another illustration of the body of Christ, the church of Christ, and all who put their trust in Christ become part of that group that will be called out when Jesus comes, and who will meet Him in the air.

Oh, how wonderful that that great company of all the saved will be kept for the Lord and for our gathering to meet Him when He comes again!

Jesus Transfigured to Appear as
He Will at His Second Coming

MATTHEW 17, MARK 9, LUKE 9

One day Jesus said to His disciples, "Verily I say unto you, There be some standing here, which shall not taste of death, till they see the Son of man coming in His kingdom" (Matt. 16:28). What did He mean?

He meant that He was soon going up to the Mount of Transfiguration. There He would be transformed. His garments would be white as the light, and He would appear even as He will when He comes in His glory at His second coming.

Some of these disciples did see Him, in that appearance. Now a few days after, Jesus took Peter, James and John and brought them up to a high mountain, probably Mount Tabor, a beautiful mountain rounded like a big bowl turned upside down. Jesus, Peter, James and John went up on that mountain to pray.

Behold, there on the mountaintop two wonderful creatures appeared. They were Moses and Elijah who came down from Heaven. Elijah went to Heaven without dying, so his transformed, physical body is in Heaven. Although Moses died and was buried, we suppose he now has a heavenly body. Now these both appeared, and Peter, James and John recognized them.

These three were astonished and overwhelmed. So greatly impressed was Peter that he spoke out: "Lord, it is good for us to be here: and let us make three tabernacles; one for Thee, and one for Moses, and one for Elias." He was so ex-

The Transfiguration

cited, he hardly knew what he said, but Peter thought they should set up some tents and stay there on the mountain— tents for Moses, Elijah and Jesus; he and James and John could sleep on the ground, without a tent.

But it was a mistake to rate Moses and Elijah along with the Lord Jesus. Suddenly a bright cloud overshadowed them and a voice out of the cloud said, "THIS is My beloved Son: hear Him." Oh, Moses and Elijah are but servants, created beings. They are saved, and are prophets; but Jesus is the Creator, God in human form. No one is ever to rate any other as equal with Jesus Christ. It is true that all the Bible is true, and it all fits in with what Jesus would say, but the authority is in Jesus Himself. He is the One who said, "All power is given unto Me in heaven and in earth." He is the One who said, "I am the way, the truth, and the life: no man cometh unto the Father, but by Me."

Then when the cloud disappeared, there was no one there but Jesus, Peter, James and John. But they had seen Jesus so transformed. His face was shining like the sun. His garments were as white as the light. Oh, they saw Jesus as He will be in His resurrected, glorified state when He comes back to reign on the earth.

Peter would never forget that time. He was inspired to write of it:

"For we have not followed cunningly devised fables, when we made known unto you the power and coming of our Lord Jesus Christ, but were eyewitnesses of His majesty. For He received from God the Father honour and glory, when there came such a voice to Him from the excellent glory, This is My beloved Son, in whom I am well pleased. And this voice which came from heaven we heard, when we were with Him in the holy mount."—II Pet. 1:16-18.

There could be no doubt that Jesus is the Son of God, and all He claimed to be. But Peter said, "We have even better witness than that wonderful spectacle. We have the Word of God itself."

Those of us who have not yet seen the Lord Jesus in the body have the sure Word of prophecy that tells us He is the

Saviour whom we have trusted, the One who is coming again one day to take us to Himself, and, then, to return and set up His kingdom on the earth.

The Rich Young Ruler Who Wanted to Be Saved by Good Works

MARK 10

There was a rich young ruler who once came to Jesus in deep humility and bowed himself and said, "Good Master [or Rabbi], what good thing shall I do, that I may have eternal life?" Jesus answered him, "Why callest thou Me good? there is none good but one, that is, God."

The young man had called Jesus "Master" or "Rabbi" but if Jesus is no more than a Rabbi, if He is not God in human form, then He would not be good, for all men have sinned. One who comes to Christ must come to Him as the Saviour, the Son of God who died and paid for our sins on the cross.

This rich young ruler made another mistake. He wanted to get saved by doing good things. Jesus turned to him and said, "If you want to be saved, then keep the commandments." Of course, you and I know that people are not saved by keeping the commandments. But remember that the Scripture says that "the law was our schoolmaster to bring us unto Christ." So the more one realizes that he cannot keep all the commands of God but that he has sinned, has failed, that much more he feels a need of the Saviour. Jesus named to him the commandments to do toward mankind. One is not to kill, not to commit adultery, not to lie, not to steal, not to covet.

Ah, the rich young ruler proudly said, "Master, all these commands I have kept from my youth."

Poor man! He was not conscious of failure and sin, and

that is too bad. The only people who ever get saved are self-confessed sinners! So Jesus said to him, "Go and sell all you have, and give to the poor, then you come and follow Me."

The simple truth is, this man loved his possessions. He had not from his heart kept the commandments about honoring father and mother, had not had no hatred, which is equal to murder. Of course he could not declare that he had no adultery nor lust, which is equal to adultery; and no covetousness, which is a part of the thieving mind! Oh, he had not really put God first; had not sought God with all his heart. He held on to his money and his position, this rich young ruler.

And the young man turned and went away lost, for he had great possessions. But Jesus loved him and looked after him longingly.

Oh, let us learn that no one can come to Jesus aright unless he accepts Him as the Saviour, as God's own Son, born of a virgin, who lived a sinless life and died for our sins. And no one can be saved by keeping commandments. The commandments only show us how far we fail to do the will of God, and how we need a Saviour.

Zacchaeus Who Climbed a Tree
to See Jesus

LUKE 19

Jesus was going to Jerusalem for the last time. That week in Jerusalem will close with His crucifixion. He came down the Jordan River Valley to Jericho. People turned out en masse to see Him.

One well-dressed man eagerly wanted to see Jesus, but he was short in stature and could not see over the people's heads. His name was Zacchaeus, a publican, a chief tax collector, and a rich man. How could he see Jesus closely?

It may be he had heard that Matthew of Capernaum, also a publican or tax collector, had been saved and was now one of Jesus' disciples. But he had heard of many people healed by this Man, Jesus. He had heard of the wonderful things Jesus had been telling the people. Now he felt he must see Jesus personally.

He thought of a way. He went ahead and climbed into a sycamore tree that was on the road leading from Jericho toward Jerusalem. Jesus would pass just below him. There he could look Jesus in the face.

People are crowding around. But the Saviour looks up at the little man in the tree and says, 'Zacchaeus, come down. Today I must abide at thy house.'

Zacchaeus slid down that tree and was converted before he came to the ground. He showed evidence of deep repentance. As a tax collector, he had often wronged people, no doubt, by charging them too much. This was an honest calling, but the

opportunity for stealing was so great that it was too much for him. A tax collector was allowed to keep all the extra he could get from people, so they generally took advantage of people.

Now Zacchaeus said, "If I have wronged any man, I will restore him fourfold. And I am going to give half of my goods to the poor!"

Jesus said, "This day is salvation come to this house. . . . For the Son of man is come to seek and to save that which was lost."

But the people murmured while Jesus went home with Zacchaeus. They said, "He is gone to eat bread with a man who is a sinner!" Of course, all men everywhere are sinners, but in Bible times they especially counted those guilty of drunkenness and adultery, those who obviously scorned the strict laws of God, as known sinners.

But Zacchaeus was saved, and Jesus died for sinners like Zacchaeus and like you and me.

Aren't you glad that anybody who wants to know Jesus can come to know Him?

Lazarus Raised From the Dead

On the eastern side of the Mount of Olives was the little village of Bethany. There, in the home of Mary, Martha and Lazarus, Jesus loved to visit. There Martha had been so eager to prepare lovely meals for Jesus and the disciples. And there Mary had sat at the feet of Jesus and learned all she could about His work and about His coming death for the sins of the world. We suppose Lazarus was an older brother, at least he was now the head of the household.

One day Lazarus becomes ill. The sisters are concerned. With Father and Mother gone, they feel very nervous lest they lose their brother. "Oh, if Jesus were only here, He would save our brother!" So Mary and Martha sent Him word, "He whom Thou lovest is sick!" They knew how Jesus loved Lazarus. Oh, then, Jesus must come quickly to heal him or Lazarus would die. There is no response to their message. Lazarus grows weaker. Not much sleep about that house now. But why was Jesus not there, as He so often had been?

When Jesus heard that Lazarus was deathly sick, He waited still in the same place. He said, "This sickness is not unto death, but for the glory of God." And He knew the very moment when Lazarus died, for He told the disciples, "Lazarus sleepeth." A Christian who dies in the Lord is counted as sleeping, and Jesus knew what He would do here. He knew He would raise Lazarus from the dead.

He went on preaching for some days. At last Jesus said to His disciples, "Let us go into Judaea again." Some of the disciples were afraid to come to Jerusalem, near the Mount of Olives, because many there had threatened to kill Jesus. Jesus said, "Our friend Lazarus sleepeth; but I go, that I may awake him out of sleep."

Can you imagine how anxiously Mary and Martha waited for Jesus? Lazarus had died and they had buried him in a cave nearby. On their near approach to Bethany, the disciples and Jesus met Martha. She, with fresh grief, told Jesus Lazarus had lain in the grave four days and exclaimed, "Lord, if Thou hadst been here, my brother had not died." Then Martha told Mary, when she came, "The Master is come, and calleth for thee." And weeping she went to see the Saviour. She, too, said to Him, "O Jesus, if You had been here Lazarus would have lived."

But Jesus told Mary and Martha that Lazarus would rise again. Martha answered, "I know that he shall rise again in the resurrection at the last day." But Jesus replied, "I am the resurrection, and the life." Jesus could have a resurrection any time He wished. He asked them to show Him where they had laid Lazarus. The two sorrowing sisters led Jesus to the grave, accompanied by a curious crowd.

There was a stone over the mouth of it. Jesus told them to roll the stone away.

Martha protested and said, "Lord, he has been dead already so long—four days—that now the body stinks."

Jesus was troubled because of the grief of Mary and Martha. He groaned in spirit and as others wept there before the grave, Jesus wept also. And the people said, "Behold how He loved him!"

Some of the people said, "Could not this man, which opened the eyes of the blind, have kept this man from dying?"

Jesus commanded them to roll away the stone from the door and then He cried with a loud voice, "Lazarus, come forth!" And Lazarus came out of the grave bound with the grave clothes hand and foot. And Jesus said to them, "Loose him, and let him go." So they took off those grave clothes from Lazarus. And what a happy, rejoicing reunion they had!

Lazarus went home with his two sisters and they had a great feast in a neighbor's big home, and Martha helped serve. And Mary took a very expensive pound of ointment and as Jesus lay on a couch facing the table, she anointed His feet and wiped them with her hair and the odor of the sweet perfume filled the house.

What a wonderful testimony it was to Jesus that Lazarus was raised from the dead! There he sat and everybody could see him. Wicked Pharisees and scribes who hated Jesus even plotted to kill Lazarus because Lazarus was such a testimony of the power and authority of Jesus!

Can't you imagine how happy was that little home of two sisters and a brother now restored from the dead!

Jesus Makes Triumphant Entry
Into Jerusalem

MATTHEW 21, JOHN 12

The Old Testament had plainly foretold that the Lord Jesus should sit on David's throne. Even the angel who announced to Mary that she would bear the Saviour, foretold her, "The Lord God shall give unto Him the throne of His father David: And He shall reign over the house of Jacob for ever; and of His kingdom there shall be no end." And so people sometimes forgot that the Lord had clearly prophesied that the Messiah, the Saviour, should first suffer for the sins of the world and that He should take upon Himself all our sins and trouble and pay our debt on the cross before His reign. They forgot, I suppose, that it was written in Isaiah 53, "All we like sheep have gone astray: we have turned every one to his own way; and the Lord hath laid on Him the iniquity of us all."

But it was still prophesied that Jesus would one day ride into Jerusalem on the colt, a foal of an ass. So back in Zechariah 9:9 the Old Testament had said, "Rejoice greatly, O daughter of Zion; shout, O daughter of Jerusalem: behold, thy King cometh unto thee: He is just, and having salvation; lowly, and riding upon an ass, and upon a colt the foal of an ass." So now the Lord Jesus is ready to fulfill that prophecy.

He has come to Jerusalem for the last week of His life before the crucifixion. I suppose He had come down the Jordan Valley to Jericho and now from Jericho up to Jerusalem. So He came round the Mount of Olives and there

are two villages, Bethpage and Bethany. He sent two of His disciples and told them, "Go into the village near you and you will find a donkey with her colt. Untie them and bring them to Me."

And what if somebody should object? Then tell the man, "The Lord hath need of them; and straightway he will send them." You see, Jesus surely must have known about the man and about the donkey. So they brought the donkey and the colt and put their garments upon them so Jesus could sit on the donkey colt. And a great multitude spread their garments in the way. They know the prophecy. They want Jesus to be publicly proclaimed as King.

They cast palm branches in the way, and now the little procession goes down across the vale of Kidron and into the city of Jerusalem near the Temple. My, what shouting and rejoicing as the people cry out, "Hosanna to the Son of David: Blessed is He that cometh in the name of the Lord; Hosanna in the highest!" And some of the little children cried out and joined in the chorus of shouts and praises.

Some of the scribes and Pharisees didn't like that. Some of the Pharisees insisted to Jesus, "Master, rebuke Thy disciples." And Jesus answered that if these should hold their peace in this wonderful fulfillment of the prophecy announcing His future kingdom, He said, "the stones would immediately cry out."

You see, God has so arranged it that even nature is someway conscious of the Saviour. When Christ returns we are told that the desert will "blossom as a rose. . .and all the trees of the field shall clap their hands." What a glorious time it would be, as may be when Christ returns and enters Jerusalem to reign. Let the stones cry out! There are so many stones in Jerusalem that there would never be such a chorus of rejoicing and praises if all those stones begin to cry out to glorify God!

So Jesus entered Jerusalem riding upon a donkey. He was lowly. He came the first time as a Saviour so He made Himself of no reputation, took on Himself the form of a servant. But one day, when He comes back to reign, the Lord

When they brought the little animal to where Jesus was, the disciples put their colored garments on the colt, and Jesus made His triumphant entry into Jerusalem.

Jesus coming riding a white horse and crowned with many crowns, all the armies of Heaven will follow Him on white horses. Then all the enemies of the Lord Jesus will be put down and Christ will reign over the whole earth.

The Ten Virgins: Bridesmaids for the Marriage

Jesus told about a marriage where ten virgins went out to meet the bridegroom as he tarried. I suppose we could call them "bridesmaids." But five of them were wise and five were foolish. The wise took vessels with oil. They could dip their wicks or torches down into the oil and the lamps would burn brightly. The foolish took only wicks or torches, dry and without oil. These soon burned out.

At midnight there was a cry, "Behold, the bridegroom cometh. Go ye out too meet him." The foolish said to the wise, "Give us of your oil; for our lamps are gone out."

But the wise virgins answered, "No, lest there be not enough for us all. You must buy for yourselves."

And the wise virgins trimmed their lamps and the others were left outside. And when they came to knock at the door and say, "Open to us," at midnight, the answer came, "We know you not, who you are."

The Lord Jesus was illustrating that the only way to come to the heavenly Bridegroom and the marriage of the Lamb is to trust Jesus and let the blessed Holy Spirit come in to live in your body. He is represented by the oil here. Those who carried the vessels of oil with them with their lamps are like Christians who have the blessed Holy Spirit living in their bodies. When Jesus comes for us and there comes the cry, "Behold, the Bridegroom comes," all of God's saved people will be caught up to meet Him in the air.

But the lesson is that everyone must have the oil of salvation and be regenerated in order to be at the great wedding in Heaven.

Are you sure that you have the oil of salvation? Have you been born again?

The King's Wonderful Marriage Feast for His Son

LUKE 14

I think the most beautiful, illustrative stories ever told are the parables of Jesus. They were not only interesting stories, but each one was teaching some great truth.

Jesus said there was a king who made a marriage supper for his son and invited many, many people. I think Jesus meant to remind us that one of these days up in Heaven God's children will have a wonderful feast at the marriage supper of the Lamb. The King is God, Jesus is the Son, and in this case all Christians will be there. But God wants many, many more to be saved and to be ready to be called out at the rapture and meet for the wonderful wedding feast in Heaven.

Now a wedding is always a time of joy. Our hearts are touched with the love of the young bride and bridegroom. All the guests are delighted at the happiness of the bride. And what joy the King will have when His Son, Jesus Christ, is honored as He ought to be by the millions who will love Him!

We will have a real feast and eat real food in glorified, resurrection bodies, as we gather around and meet with Jesus and all the saints of the ages. God will have a wonderful wedding supper for His Son.

Jesus tells another parable. In the parable of the ten virgins in Matthew 25, Christians are pictured as bridesmaids at the wedding. In this parable of the King's wedding feast for His Son, Christians picture the guests at

the wedding. Elsewhere the husband is commanded to love
his wife as Christ loved the church. So in that sense Christians picture the bride. But here Christians are to be the
guests at the heavenly wedding. Oh, God wants everybody
saved and to be at the wedding.

The king sent out invitations to many. The time for the
wedding comes and the king sends messengers out to all
those who have been invited. He tells them, "Behold, I have
prepared my dinner: my oxen and my fatlings are killed, and
all things are ready: come unto the marriage."

Here is a strange, sad thing. Those who were invited did
not come. Some made light of it and ignored the invitation.
What do they care about the bridegroom and the great
meeting? So like many lost people who ignore the invitation
of the Gospel to come and be saved.

They went about their business, ignoring the invitation.
Others mistreated the servants and even killed some of his
messengers. Sadly, sometimes wicked people have killed
God's preachers and prophets, just as Cain killed Abel. They
hate the king and the Lord Jesus His Son and do not want to
attend that heavenly feast. How sad, sad!

Do people not want to accept God's sweet invitation? Do
they not want to go to Heaven? Do they not want to honor
Jesus Christ as the great Bridegroom?

The king was properly angry. Such people who would kill
even the king's servants who invite them to a free wedding
feast! So the king sent his armies and destroyed those
murderers and burned up their cities.

But the king still wants a great feast to honor his son. And
God still wants everybody saved who will be. So the king said

to his servants, "The wedding is ready,
but they which were bidden were not
worthy. Go ye therefore into the
highways, and as many as ye shall find,
bid to the marriage." They did as they
were told. They went out into the
highways and "gathered together all as

many as they found, both bad and good." So the wedding was furnished with guests.

God is not willing that anybody should go to Hell. He invites "whosoever will, let him take the water of life freely." Oh, even the vilest sinners may come, for He said, "Come now, and let us reason together, saith the Lord: though your sins be as scarlet, they shall be as white as snow; though they be red like crimson, they shall be as wool" (Isa. 1:18). Don't let anybody tell you there are some people God does not want to save. God wants the bad and the good. The good He will make better, and the bad He will make right if they will come to Him for salvation.

Now the great crowd is gathered for the wedding. Oh, what a gathering that will be!

The king has made a happy arrangement. The poor cannot all dress well, so he has provided a garment for all who come.

That is like us poor mortals. If God does not provide us a robe of righteousness, we could never be righteous. But God lets Jesus pay for our sin and then He takes the white garment of Christ's righteousness and wraps it about us.

So the king had provided a wedding garment for all who came to the wedding.

But, lo, here comes in a man who doesn't have on the wedding garment! The king accosts him: "Friend, how camest thou in hither not having a wedding garment?"

He was speechless. Many people will be, then. They argue now, and they make fine excuses as to why they are not Christians; but one day when they face God Himself, they will be speechless. Sadly, the man who wanted to come pictures one who would like to go to Heaven without being born again, one who wants to go to Heaven without trusting Jesus Christ as Saviour.

The king had him bound hand and foot and cast outside where there is wailing and gnashing of teeth. Nobody can come to that wonderful wedding feast except he has on the garment of Christ's righteousness covering his poor sinful nature. We can be taken into God's family only if Jesus

Christ has paid out debt and only if God changes our heart and makes us fit to go.

I beg you, make sure you too have on the wedding garment. Have you trusted Christ to cover your sins and pay your debt and make you a Christian? You are invited to the wedding supper, but you must have on the wedding garment; you must trust Jesus Christ to forgive you and save you.

Mary of Bethany Anoints
the Saviour

A marvelous miracle has happened at Bethany, near Jerusalem. Lazarus has been raised from the dead! My! Everyone wanted to see him! So they made Jesus a great feast at Bethany and had Lazarus there in a prominent place at the supper, for all to see.

Mary had learned a great deal about Jesus. It may be she had more understanding than others did—of what was coming—His crucifixion and resurrection. We do know that she had talked with Jesus and sat at His feet. I am sure she had heard about that sinful woman who had wept over the feet of Jesus and kissed them and went away forgiven.

Now she had put away an expensive, very precious alabaster box of ointment. Perhaps inspired by the example of the sinful woman, she brought that ointment of spikenard and anointed the feet of Jesus and wiped them with her hair. The whole house was filled with the odor of that incense.

Judas Iscariot, the one who would later betray Jesus, said, "This is a waste! This ointment might have been sold for three hundred pence (perhaps three hundred denarii) and given to the poor; but now it is wasted!" Judas sounded very pious, but the truth was, he carried the money for the disciples and took out of it what he wanted for himself. In other words, he was a thief. He was covetous and wanted that ointment sold for money so he could use some of it for himself.

But Jesus turned and said, "Let her alone. She hath done this anointing against the day of My burying. She kept this ointment for this time. Do you want to give to the poor? You have poor people always, but you will not always have Me with you."

The Pharisees and those who hated Jesus were there to see Lazarus, whom He had raised from the dead. Some of them wanted to kill Lazarus because he was such a testimony to the miraculous work of Christ. But Mary had given her sweet testimony in a way that everybody would remember. And as the Bible is spread, her sweet story of her love for Jesus and trust in His atoning death, and burial and resurrection, would be told.

It is better to serve Jesus even than to give to the poor.

Jesus Eats the Last Supper
With the Disciples

MATTHEW 26, MARK 14, LUKE 22

We know that the passover lamb in the Old Testament was a picture and type of the Lord Jesus. In I Corinthians 5:7 the Scripture says, "For even Christ our passover is sacrificed for us." So Jesus knew, of course, that the death of the passover lamb pictured His coming death and He was preparing for that. Remember that He had given Himself up to die. Nobody could take away His life unless He consented. Jesus came to die for sinners.

So as the passover season approaches, Jesus sends Peter and John and says, "Go prepare a place for the passover." Jesus would not be there through all the passover season, but the disciples would. And Jesus would there eat a preliminary meal with them. But where would they find a place? He told Peter and John to go into the city and, "Watch now," He said, "and you will see a man carrying a pitcher of water. Just follow that man and go into the house that he enters, and there you may ask the master of the house, 'Where is the guest-chamber, where I shall eat the passover with My disciples?' " So they followed the man and he led them and gave them an upper chamber where they would meet together, where they prepared for the passover.

But Jesus understood, of course, that He would not be here to eat the passover supper, for at the very time of the afternoon when the passover lambs were being killed the Lord Jesus would die on the cross.

And God had a rule that they should have no leavened bread in the house when they had the passover supper, so Jesus will eat a preliminary meal with the disciples. I do not suppose they had a lamb. They did have bread and grape juice or sour wine, and they ate together.

Can you imagine the tension, the concern of the disciples as they all realized that soon Jesus was to be taken away? For He told them plainly that He was to die. In that Upper Room Jesus washed the disciples' feet and taught them that each one should help to spiritually wash the feet of other Christians, for all of us walk in a dirty world. We are clean, but we need daily cleansing, too. And Jesus reminded them, "By this shall all men know that ye are My disciples, if ye have love one to another."

Jesus loved His disciples and was so pleased to meet with them this last time. He said, "With desire I have desired to eat this passover with you. . . ." Well, they had this preliminary meal of the Last Supper and Jesus told all the disciples that one of them would betray Him. How they were

By Warner Sallman

smitten in heart! Peter said, "Lord, is it I?" John must have said, "Lord, is it I?" So did all the disciples. And John the apostle had felt especially close to Jesus. Now he seemed to have had his cot pulled over beside that of Jesus and he leaned his head on Jesus' breast. And they motioned for John to ask Him, so John asked Him who it would be that would betray Him. And He said, "Watch now, for he that dips with Me in the sop is the one who shall betray Me."

And they watched and saw when Jesus dipped His bread into the grape juice or sour wine that Judas Iscariot dipped at the same time. Judas would betray Him! And then Jesus had something to say to Peter, too. He said, "Simon, this night thou shalt betray Me. Before the rooster crows you will deny Me three times."

"Oh," Peter protested, "no, I will never deny Thee. If I should die with You, I would not deny You." I am sure he meant it, but he didn't know what awful temptation would come later when he sat by the fire in the high priest's house and when the soldiers were around him who would crucify the Saviour. And so his courage would be gone and he would deny the Saviour. It was foretold there.

Finally Jesus said to Judas, "That thou doest, do quickly." Judas had made an arrangement with the high priest that he would betray Jesus. He had said, "I know where He goes so often to be alone in the Garden of Gethsemane, for many a night He spent there when He had no other bed but the ground. I can lead you to Him."

And they had promised him thirty pieces of silver if he would lead them to the Saviour somewhere where the crowd would be absent and they could arrest Him and take Him to be tried and slain. Judas went out and made his bargain with the chief priests.

That was a holy time there in the Upper Room. There the Lord Jesus gave the great teaching in John, chapters 14, 15 and 16. Then Jesus had the high priestly prayer, chapter 17, and they sang a hymn and went out. Jesus went to Gethsemane where He would be betrayed. You should now read John chapters 13 to 17 and see all that was done in the Upper Room.

Judas, the Disciple Who Was a Traitor

MATTHEW 26-28, MARK 14, LUKE 22, JOHN 18

Judas was one of the twelve disciples picked out to follow Jesus. We suppose that he, with all the apostles together, was empowered to cast out devils. He was not saved, and Jesus knew that. He plainly said one time, "Have not I chosen you twelve, and one of you is a devil?" referring to Judas Iscariot.

It may be that Judas was allowed to be one of the twelve disciples because, again and again, in the Christian world, we will find people who pretend to be Christians who are not, people who are false prophets, people who are sometimes demon-possessed, people who join the church but are unconverted, people who are in the pulpit but do not believe in the Bible, are not Christians at all in heart or in doctrine.

We find that Judas was money-minded. When Mary offered a beautiful alabaster box of ointment worth, it was said, three hundred denarii, Judas protested and said it ought to have been sold and given to the poor. But the Scripture tells us that he said this because he was a thief and he carried the money that was given to take care of the expenses of the apostles and the things they would give to the poor. Ah, Judas, the poor thief, wanted the money for himself.

Maybe that is one of the reasons he was never saved. He loved sin. He was not willing to give it up. He wanted things for himself, even by crooked means.

I do not think he was at first the enemy of Jesus that he

came to be. You see, one who goes on in sin, rejects the Saviour, does not take Him as one's Lord and Master and Saviour, tends to get further and further away from God and hardened more in heart.

I suppose that as Judas saw that enemies of Jesus were more and more and that Jesus would eventually be arrested and tried and, as Jesus Himself plainly foretold, would be crucified, Judas felt there was no prospect of any great success in following Jesus. He did not feel he would get to be great in this world if he followed the rejected Saviour. And so in his heart he schemed; he could make some money out of this.

So when they were assembled in that Upper Room in the preliminary meal of the passover, the last supper Jesus had with them, Jesus foretold, "One of you shall betray Me." All the disciples were surprized. I suppose none of them knew, as Jesus knew the wicked heart of Judas, that he would betray Jesus. But Jesus said, "One of you shall betray Me."

Oh, with what startled looks they gazed at Jesus. "Lord, is it I?" one said and then another. And Jesus told them it would be the one who dipped in the sop with Him. It was Judas.

Then Jesus said to Judas, "That thou doest, do quickly," and the Devil entered into Judas and he went out and made a trade with the chief priests.

"I know where He often goes in the night, when He has no home in which to sleep. I can lead you to the very place where there is no crowd around. How much will you pay me?"

And they offered him thirty pieces of silver. I don't suppose they remembered that this was foretold back in the Old Testament.

So Judas, after he had made his deal with the chief priests who hated Jesus, waited until they had that last sweet time of fellowship in the Upper Room after He had washed the disciples' feet and when Jesus had given the wonderful promises and teachings of John (chapters 14 and 15 and 16). Then Jesus spent a time in prayer. We call it the high priestly prayer, as it is recorded in John 17, and then they went to the Garden of Gethsemane.

We know how Jesus stayed there in earnest prayer; how Peter and John went to sleep, when they were supposed to pray with Jesus. And Jesus was in such distress that the blood was about to break from His body and He sweat a bloody sweat and He said, "My soul is exceeding sorrowful, even unto death" (Matt. 26:38). But He prayed and God sent an angel to comfort and relieve Him. And that cup of death was passed on to the next day when, according to prophecy, Jesus must die at the time the passover lambs would die, and must die on the cross and fulfill the Scriptures.

Then here came a crowd. Judas was coming. The high priest had his soldiers, and there was a mob of people along with sticks and staves. And they came into the garden where Jesus and the other disciples were. And Judas had given them a sign. He said, "I will go up and greet Him and kiss Him on the cheek, and you must seize Him then and bind His hands behind Him. That will be the One."

So Judas came and said, "Hail, Master." And Jesus answered him, "Friend, wherefore art thou come?"

Is it strange He would call Judas "friend"? Oh, He was a friend of Judas, though Judas was His enemy. But I think that Jesus meant He had come to die for sinners and that Judas was a part of the plan. And even though it meant betrayal by a friend, yet it was meant the way to the cross and Jesus is going to die for the sins of the world. And so He called Judas, "Friend."

Jesus turned to that mob that was standing rather abashed, I suppose, and said to them, "Whom seek ye?"

And they said, "Jesus of Nazareth."

And Jesus said, "I am He."

But these men, in the presence of the majesty of Jesus, were awed, and they fell backward to the ground. Again Jesus said, "Whom do you seek?"

And they answered, "Jesus of Nazareth."

And Jesus said to them, then, "I have told you that I am He. If you want Me, then let these others go their way."

Simon Peter had a sword and with it he sliced angrily at one of the men in the lead and cut off his ear. But Jesus told Peter to put up his sword and He touched the man's ear and it was suddenly attached whole again! And they led Jesus away to the house of the high priest.

But what about Judas? Did he have no conscience? Oh, yes, he did! I do not know what all happened immediately. But in a little bit Judas Iscariot went back to the chief priests and said to them, "I want to give you back your money. I want you to release Jesus. I have betrayed the innocent blood!" He meant, of course, that Jesus is the only truly pure innocent One in the world of men. But these hardhearted Pharisees and chief priests simply said, "That is your business, you see about that."

Judas throws down
the 30 pieces of silver.

And Judas Iscariot, now, with the money burning his pocket and the sin burning in his soul, threw the money on the pavement and went out and hanged himself. He hung himself, I suppose, over a bluff in the valley of Gehenna, or from a tree, and there his body swung until the rope frazzled and broke and his body fell and burst open. Poor, poor Judas!

Judas was never saved. He could have been saved. Jesus died for him and loved him. Oh, let us beware of what sin will do to the human heart if we give way to sin, as Judas did.

And Judas is always now the worldwide type of a dishonest traitor who betrayed the Saviour. Oh, Judas, you could have been one of the apostles who won many souls! You could have been one of those who will sit on the twelve thrones of the twelve tribes of Israel with the other apostles judging Israel! But instead you rejected the Saviour and you went to Hell. For when the apostles would elect another man to take his place as a witness they said that Judas had "gone to his own place."

Oh, let Judas be a warning to all. One may be religious, may be a church member, even a preacher, but never be saved, and be a traitor to Jesus!

🍀🍀🍀🍀

JUDAS ISCARIOT! The very name is anathema! Souls shudder at its awesome sound. The hiss of its pronunciation makes for loathsomeness of spirit. It is the synonym of all trickery and cupidity. What a name to conjure with! We sometimes feel that he is only a black symbol, not a reality. But, Judas was a man—remember that!
　　　　　　　　　　　　　　　　　　　　—Ayer.

There is a familiar saying: *"Every man has his own price."* Ahab had his, and he sold himself for a garden. Judas sold himself for thirty pieces of silver. And Esau, for a mess of pottage.
　　　　　　　　　　　　　　　　D. L. Moody.

Jesus Sweats Bloody Sweat
in Gethsemane

MATTHEW 26, MARK 14, LUKE 22

After Jesus had met with the disciples in the Upper Room, had had the preliminary passover meal, had announced that Judas would betray Him and had foretold that Peter would deny Him, then He gave sweet teaching for all of us and went out to the Garden of Gethsemane to pray. I suppose He had prayed there many times. He said to Peter, James and John, "Will you come and watch with Me?" And they went along further with Him than the others, yet strangely, they were weary and sad. I suppose they were so discouraged and depressed, so as they waited, instead of praying earnestly, they fell asleep.

But Jesus prayed and was in great stress. He said to Peter and the others, "What, could ye not watch with Me one hour?" He said, "My soul is exceeding sorrowful, even unto death. . . ."

What did He mean? He meant, of course, that He was about to die in Gethsemane and already the blood was about to burst from His capillaries and He was sweating a bloody sweat—the dear Lord Jesus, alone in the Garden and about to die.

And He prayed. Don't misunderstand His prayer. He prayed, "O My Father, if it be possible, let this cup pass from Me: nevertheless not as I will, but as Thou wilt." So many people have listened to that part and have copied that part of the prayer, ". . .not My will, but Thine, be done."

It was alone my Saviour prayed in dark Gethsemane.

And that is good, but do not get the idea the Lord Jesus is praying to avoid Calvary, to avoid dying on the cross. No, no. What He is praying for is in the will of God, not against the will of God, for He knows that if He dies in the Garden of Gethsemane, it will be a failure.

You see, it is already foretold in the Old Testament that Jesus would die on the cross and it is already foretold, "They pierced My hands and My feet." He has already foretold in the 22nd Psalm that on the cross He would cry out, "My God, My God, why hast Thou forsaken Me?" He has already foretold that the soldiers would take His garments when He was nailed to the cross and cast lots for them.

You see, the Gospel is, ". . .how that Christ died for our sins according to the scriptures; And that He was buried, and that He rose again the third day according to the scriptures" (I Cor. 15:3,4). If Jesus should die here in the Garden of Gethsemane and not on the cross, if Jesus should die tonight instead of tomorrow, the day when the passover lambs were supposed to die, then that would nullify the Gospel for He would not have died "according to the scriptures." So what Jesus is praying for is, "My Father, pass the cup on till tomorrow, the right time and place, and let Me die as prophesied to die, let Me fulfill the Scriptures." He was praying not against the will of God, but in the will of God. Don't you remember Jesus said to His Father one time, "I know that Thou hearest Me always"? So He was praying in the will of God and got His prayer answered.

And what is the answer? That He would be spared that night to go to the cross tomorrow and that He would die according to the Scriptures. And we know that Hebrews 5:7 tells us about Jesus, "Who in the days of His flesh, when He had offered up prayers and supplications with strong crying and tears unto Him that was able to save Him from death, and was heard in that He feared." Ah, so in Gethsemane that night the dear Lord Jesus prayed and God heard Him and sent an angel to comfort and strengthen Him so He would have the strength to go on to the cross tomorrow and die in the way God had foretold so He could be our Saviour. He died according to the Scriptures.

Jesus met every requirement, fulfilled every prophecy about His atoning death. Thank God He is able to save all who come to trust in Him!

How Shocking That Simon Peter Should Deny Jesus and Curse and Quit the Ministry!

JOHN 19, 21

Judas was a lost sinner who betrayed Jesus. But Peter was an apostle. He was the first named in every list of apostles. Peter was the one who boldly said to Jesus, "Thou art the Christ, the Son of the living God." Peter is the one to whom Jesus said, "I will give unto thee the keys of the kingdom of heaven." Perhaps that meant he would be the first one to preach to the great crowd at Pentecost and then the first one to preach to Cornelius and the Gentiles. But at any rate, Peter was a spokesman, greatly loved of the Saviour and the most prominent of all.

I suppose Peter must have been greatly distressed when at the Last Supper Jesus said, "This night, before the cock crow, thou shalt deny Me thrice." Oh, Peter insisted, "I would never deny Thee! I would die before I would do that!" And I am sure Peter meant it, too, for he loved the Saviour truly.

But in the Garden of Gethsemane, when Peter would have used his sword to fight to deliver Jesus, Jesus told him to put the sword up. And there was frustration there. No doubt they are going to kill Jesus. They are taking Him to the judgment, to the hall of Caiaphas the high priest, and there the Sanhedrin will condemn Him to death.

Peter followed afar off, I suppose, across the valley of Kidron and up to the high priest's house. Peter followed that mob and the soldiers of the high priest who had Jesus with them, hands bound behind Him. Peter went in and sat on the stone floor, we suppose, in the basement. He sat there with the same wicked soldiers who are going to beat Jesus and who will nail Him to the cross. An hour or so he sat there, and in that bad company his courage was soon all gone. And when someone said to him, "Aren't you one of His disciples? You have the accent of Galileans and all the disciples came from Galilee; you must be one of His disciples."

But Peter said, "No, I'm not. I don't even know the Man."

A relative of the man whose ear Peter had cut off in the Garden of Gethsemane came and said, "You must be His disciple." But again he denied it. And when a maid, the third time, came to say to him, "Are you not one of His disciples?" he cursed and swore and denied and said, "I don't even know the Man." Ah, poor Peter. You sat there with the Devil's crowd until your courage was gone. You didn't pray as you ought, for Jesus had told you about this, "Watch and pray, that ye enter not into temptation: the spirit indeed is willing, but the flesh is weak." So Peter cursed and swore and denied Jesus.

Poor Simon Peter. He loved the Lord, but, oh, how he has

"Peter, this night, before the cock crows, thou shalt deny me thrice."—Jesus.

HOW SHOCKING ... SIMON PETER ... !

fallen into sin. Christians do, you know. If you are shocked at Peter, cursing and swearing and denying Jesus, you must remember that Noah got drunk. You must remember that Moses, the meekest man who ever lived, lost his temper and hit the rock instead of speaking to it when God told him to speak. Remember that David committed adultery and murder. Remember that Solomon fell into sin and worshiped idols with his heathen wives. Oh, what a sad story it is of Christian men and women who have fallen into sin! So Peter had fallen into sin.

In the first place, all of us like Peter have an old carnal nature, and we have to watch it because the flesh lusts against the Spirit. And it was a time of special temptation when Satan had desired to tempt Peter and was given permission. And Peter had not prayed as he ought. Peter sat down with the wrong crowd, and so now he has fallen into terrible sin.

Peter was at the cross, though he was not close by, because you don't find him mentioned as being at the crucifixion in Matthew, Mark, Luke and John, but in I Peter 5:1 Peter says, "The elders which are among you I exhort, who am also an elder, and a witness of the sufferings of Christ." So Peter was there at the cross, somewhere in the crowd, brokenhearted and ashamed, no doubt.

What would Peter do now?

I can understand how he felt. Peter thought, "Who will want to listen to an old cussing preacher? I am washed out. I'm no good." And so Peter said, "I'm going back to the fishing business." So up in Galilee he went again, and some of the others went with him. And he got a boat and started out to fish. He fished all night, but he couldn't catch any fish. Fishing is a bad business when you ought to be preaching. So in the early morning, they had fished all night, and yonder is Jesus on the shore. They didn't know it was Jesus at first. He is resurrected from the dead. He said to them, "Let the net down on the other side of the boat." And they did. And surprise, the net was filled with 153 great fishes! Ah, what a shocking thing! And John, the more spiritually-minded, maybe, said, "Peter, that is bound to be Jesus. Don't you remember when He called us to preach and He said to launch out in the deep and let down the nets and we got two boatloads of fish? That is Jesus."

Simon Peter was so hungry-hearted, so guilty feeling he couldn't wait. So he put on his fisher's coat and jumped in the sea and swam to the shore. I can imagine they said, "But, Peter, help us pull in the fish." But he said, "Never mind the fish, I have to get to Jesus!"

And Jesus said, "Bring Me of the fish you have caught."

And Peter pulled that old net to the shore and began to clean fish, and Jesus broiled them over a campfire. Then He called them to come and dine and they gathered around that fire by the Sea of Galilee, the resurrected Saviour and some of His apostles, and poor old brokenhearted Peter. And Jesus loved Peter still and told him, "If you love Me, feed My sheep," and, "If you love Me, feed My lambs."

Poor old Peter was called back into the service again and started out to be a great soul-winning preacher.

Aren't you glad God gives people another chance to serve Him? He called Jonah back, when Jonah had run away from the call. He calls Peter again now. Peter started back in the ministry.

Let us remember this; poor and weak as we are, God loves His children and is always willing to help us start over and do better.

Jesus Condemned to Die

When Jesus was arrested in the Garden of Gethsemane, He was taken to the house of Caiaphas the high priest. There the Sanhedrin met and put Jesus on trial. They "sought false witness against Jesus, to put him to death." Many people were willing to witness some lie about Jesus, to make some accusation against Him, but none of that was effective. Finally two men came who had heard Jesus say, "Destroy this temple, and in three days I will raise it up." He had said that referring to His body. He would be buried for three days and after three days would rise from the dead.

But they said He applied that to the Temple of God. The high priest and the Sanhedrin were frustrated. Finally the high priest said to Him, "I adjure Thee by the living God, that Thou tell us whether Thou be the Christ, the Son of God." Ah, now here is a real question. "Jesus saith unto him, Thou hast said: nevertheless I say unto you, Hereafter shall ye see the Son of man sitting on the right hand of power, and coming in the clouds of heaven." Jesus has plainly said it. He is the Son of God. He said it often before in one way or another. Now He is publicly committed. He claims to be the Son of God. He claims He will be returning in power and glory to judge the world.

The high priest tore his clothes in pretended indignation. He said about Jesus, "He hath spoken blasphemy; what further need have we of witnesses? behold, now ye have heard His blasphemy." And then they voted that He was guilty. He should be put to death.

This was no honest seeking of the truth. There was no honest investigation of Jesus. This was the hate and spite of Christ-rejecters. So now they spit in His face, they hit Him with their hands and sometimes they would say, as one would hit Him from the side with his hand, "Prophesy, who was it hit You that time?"

Jesus, we suppose, spent the rest of the night at the high priest's house. In what we suppose are the remains of the high priest's home, there is evidence there were cells where people were confined. And the high priest had the right to have people fined or beaten. Jesus was kept in some such cell the rest of the night. Tomorrow morning He would be brought before Pilate.

Early in the morning they brought Jesus from the high priest's house. They sent word to Pilate and got him out early. And the trial, we think, was on "the pavement," that is, the basement floor of the Fortress of Antonia, which still remains.

Some had brought foolish charges against Jesus. They said

He was taken first to Annas, father-in-law of Caiaphas the high priest, where He was questioned. Then they bound Him and sent Him to the palace of Caiaphas for trial.

He had refused to pay taxes to Caesar. They said He was against the government, that He was a troublemaker. They said He had blasphemed, claiming to be the Son of God.

Pilate said to Jesus, "Art Thou the King of the Jews?" Jesus plainly admitted He was the One who would one day be King of the Jews. But when the scribes and Pharisees accused Him of various things, He answered nothing.

Pilate said, "Didn't You know I have power to release You or power to put You to death?" And Jesus said, "You would have no power over Me at all except God gave it to you."

Pilate was not impressed with the chief priest's complaints about Jesus. When he saw that the charges were from envy and hate, he hoped to save Jesus from the cross. He said, "I find no fault in this man." Pilate had been waked early and urged to come to the Judgment Hall by these Jewish leaders. Now there comes a message from his wife, who had slept later and was troubled by a dream about Jesus. "Pilate, have nothing to do with the condemnation of Jesus," she said.

"Ever since Jesus came down from Galilee, He has caused division and strife," the elders said.

"Oh," Pilate said, "if He is from Galilee, King Herod is over that province. And he is visiting Jerusalem today. We will let Herod judge."

So Jesus was sent to Herod. Herod had heard much of Jesus. "Work me a miracle," he demanded. Jesus would not display His power to Herod, so Herod turned Him over to his soldiers who crowned Him with thorns, clothed Him with a scarlet robe and mocked Him saying, "Hail, King of the Jews!" So Herod sent Jesus back to Pilate.

It was the custom each passover season to release some prisoner to please the people. Pilate thought he might release Jesus. "Shall I release Jesus or Barabbas?" he asked the people. Barabbas was a thief and a murderer. But the people, at the insistence of the chief priests, cried, "Give us Barabbas."

"What shall I do then with Jesus which is called Christ?" Pilate asked. They replied, "Crucify Him, crucify Him."

Pilate offered to scourge Jesus and release Him, but the

"And they cried, Crucify Him! Crucify Him!"

leading Jews and chief priests insisted Jesus must be crucified.

Pilate called for water and washed His hands saying, "I am innocent of the blood of this just person." Then he had Jesus scourged and the Jews led Him away to crucify Him.

Jesus was so near collapse in the Garden of Gethsemane the night before. We suppose He had little opportunity to rest in the short hours between His arrest and trial before the Sanhedrin and the early morning trial before Pilate. Now He went forth bearing His cross. However, we suppose He fainted under the burden or could not carry it far, so they "laid hold upon one Simon, a Cyrenian, coming out of the country, and on him they laid the cross, that he might bear it after Jesus."

The little procession went outside the city to a hill shaped like a skull, Golgotha, where Jesus was crucified and two thieves with Him, one on either side.

❧ ❧ ❧ ❧

Poor Pilate! His conscience was after him. He knew the blood stain would never be washed from the right hand or the left hand; that, until the day of his death, though he might wash in all the lavers of the Roman Empire, there would be still eight fingers and two thumbs red at the tips.—Talmage.

The Crucifixion of the Lord Jesus

God had made many plans ahead of time, and He had given many prophecies about the time and place and way Jesus would die.

For 1500 years the passover lamb had been sacrificed by each family of Israel at midafternoon on the 14th of Nisan each year, and the roasted lamb eaten after sundown as the law commanded. So Jesus did not die the night before, as we think Satan wanted. It was foretold, "He made His grave with the wicked, and with the rich in His death." So Jesus will die between two thieves, counted a criminal, but buried in the grave of a rich man, Joseph of Arimathaea. Nailed to the cross there are wounds in His hands and feet, as had been prophesied.

About 9:00 (the third hour) in the morning it was when they stretched Jesus out on the cross. A soldier put a knee on His wrist, I think, and nailed the hand there; one, then the other. Big spikes were driven through His feet. Then the cross was lifted and dropped in the hole in the ground prepared for it.

Jesus cried out, "My God, My God, why hast Thou forsaken Me?" Did not Jesus know why? He came into the world to die for sinners. But it was foretold in Psalm 22 that He would cry these words. God meant we should hear them, see them, and so realize that God turned His face away so Jesus could die for our sins.

It was outside the city walls at a public place, and a great crowd assembled there. Hanging there Jesus prayed, "Father, forgive them; for they know not what they do." John the beloved and his mother and Christ's mother Mary were standing nearby and Jesus said, "Woman, behold thy son!" and, "Behold thy mother!" And John would take Mary home with him now and care for her until she died at Ephesus some years later.

"Come down from the cross and we will believe You, then," mocked some of the bystanders. And one of the wicked thieves crucified with Him cried out, "If Thou be Christ, save Thyself and us."

Oh, no, the Lord Jesus could not, must not, come down from the cross. For if Jesus does not die there and pay for my sins and for the sins of my poor sinning race, then there would be no salvation, there could be no Heaven, for the sins of the world were laid on Jesus. "All we like sheep have gone astray; we have turned every one to his own way; and the Lord hath laid on Him the iniquity of us all." No, Satan would like to have brought Jesus down from the cross and ruin the crucifixion and thwart the atonement which His blood would make. No, Jesus could not come down from the cross. He cried out, "I thirst."

We understand that dying men on the battlefield, with the blood draining away, often cry out for water. I think this meant the body of Jesus was somewhat tormented with thirst. Yes, and there was a holy thirst in His heart also. Oh, that salvation for sinners could be completed.

The one thief beside Him had railed and cursed at Him, but the other rebuked him saying, "Dost not thou fear God, seeing thou art in the same condemnation? And we indeed justly; for we receive the due reward of our deeds: but this man hath done nothing amiss." And with penitent heart he cried to Jesus, "Lord Jesus, over Your head it is written, The King of the Jews. When You come to that kingdom, will You remember me?" Oh, the thief knew he had ruined his life and wasted the years, now he wanted forgiveness.

That was not a very intelligent prayer, perhaps, but a

prayer need not be intelligent to reach the Lord Jesus. For the promise is that "whosoever shall call upon the name of the Lord shall be saved." He called and the dear Lord Jesus said, "I will not wait for the kingdom. To day shalt thou be with Me in Paradise." And that day peace entered into the heart of the thief, and Jesus met him in Paradise.

The sun has beaten down pitilessly on those three hanged on the crosses on a hill shaped like a skull. But at noontime there was a sudden change. Darkness covered the earth and the sun refused to shine. A great Christian man said that the sun looked down and saw her Creator in such distress and so hated of men and the sun refused to shine upon such a scene. Then the earth trembled and quaked. Someone came running to say, "The Temple! The veil of the Temple is torn from the top to the bottom!" Ah, that great veil torn not by the hand of men but by the hand of God, from the top to the bottom. For God is showing that although in all the Old Testament times the way was partly shown, now the way into the Holy of Holies and the way to Heaven is made abundantly manifest. The dear Lord Jesus has opened Heaven's doors. Those who trusted in Him in the past and those who trust Him now—all may enter in for Jesus has made the atonement.

On the cross the Lord Jesus at last cried out, "It is finished." Not only the suffering is finished, not only has man finished the most awful thing human hands ever did when they turned to kill the Saviour, the God-Man, God in human form, but the price of salvation is paid, the atone--

ment is completed. It is finished, praise God!

Then Jesus said, "Father, into Thy hands I commend My spirit." And with a loud cry He gave up the ghost.

The chief priests who paid the thirty pieces of silver to have Judas betray the Saviour and who took Him in the Garden of Gethsemane, now have pressed and forced through the condemnation by the Sanhedrin and by Pilate—now they want the event closed. At sundown tonight begins the day of the passover and the beginning of the feast of unleavened bread. It was a high Sabbath, that is, an annual Sabbath, a day that every year was set apart without any labor, a holy convocation when they have the passover lambs and the feast of unleavened bread. These bodies must not remain on the cross until sundown when that holy, high Sabbath day begins! So they give the orders. They are to break the legs of each of these on the cross and take them down. Their vengeance on the Son of God is completed.

So the soldiers come to one thief and it may be with the Roman battle-ax they chop his legs and break the bones and there is a cry and a shudder and the blood gushes out and he is dead. They came to the other thief likewise and broke his bones and ended that poor life. But when they came to Jesus they found He was dead already. Oh, they must not break the bones of the Lord Jesus for it was a rule of the passover lamb that not a bone of him should be broken. And so a soldier took a spear and thrust it into the side of the Lord Jesus and there flowed out blood and water. Do you suppose that soldier understood that he was fulfilling the Old Testament Scripture which said, "They shall look on Him whom they pierced"? No, but, thank God, the Scripture is fulfilled and Christ has died "according to the scriptures" as the Gospel said He must die (I Cor. 15:3,4). Now we know the meaning when the Scripture says God "hath made Him to be sin for us, who knew no sin; that we might be made the righteousness of God in Him" (II Cor. 5:21).

Christ died the spectacularly accused and condemned sinner and now we may live the forgiven children of God counted blameless and taken into God's family for Jesus' sake.

Let us always remember, "Christ died for our sins according to the scriptures."

We may not know, we cannot tell
What pains He had to bear.
But we believe it was for us
He hung and suffered there.

There was no other good enough
To pay the price of sin,
He only could unlock the gate
Of Heaven and let us in.

The Burial of the Lord Jesus

When Jesus died on Calvary's cross, a great host of people stood about. There were His disciples. There was Mary the mother of Jesus. There were the good women who followed Him from Galilee. There were the mockers and the haters, and there, too, surely were some shamed to take a stand but greatly moved to love and trust the Saviour.

Of course, those bodies must be taken down from the cross for the chief priests will not allow that any accursed body still hangs on the tree when the sun goes down and then begins that annual high Sabbath of the passover lamb.

What will they do with those bodies? I suppose the bodies will be thrown with the garbage into the valley of Gehenna, or it may be that bodies like these would be buried in the pauper's grave with money furnished by those thirty pieces of silver which Judas gave back to the high priest.

But near the cross two men stop in earnest conversation. Both of them are members of the Sanhedrin, that supreme court in religious affairs for Israel. One is Nicodemus who came to Jesus by night and to whom Jesus preached the Gospel that you must be born again. The other is Joseph of Arimathaea, also a counselor and a good man, and he is a disciple of Jesus "but secretly for fear of the Jews." I can imagine that with burning eyes he said to Nicodemus, "Nick, you and I are cowards. We ought to have taken a stand for Jesus."

Oh, I think they did not vote to have Jesus killed, but they did not boldly claim that they believed in Him as the Saviour and Messiah. Now that poor, torn, abused body is about to be taken down from the cross.

So they agreed and went to Pilate and begged the body of Jesus. And when Pilate had been told that Jesus had been some time dead, he consented. And now I can imagine that with stepladders and with cloth tenderly wrapped around that poor body now growing cold, they withdrew the nails and spikes and let down the body of Jesus.

It was just a little ways down around the hill. And Joseph said, "I have a tomb hewn out in solid rock. We will bury the body there." And Nicodemus said, "I will buy the hundred pound of sweet spices and the fine linen to wrap the body in." And so they stopped, we suppose, in that garden just below the hill and there was a cistern. There they washed the poor, dusty, bloodstained body of the Saviour. There were

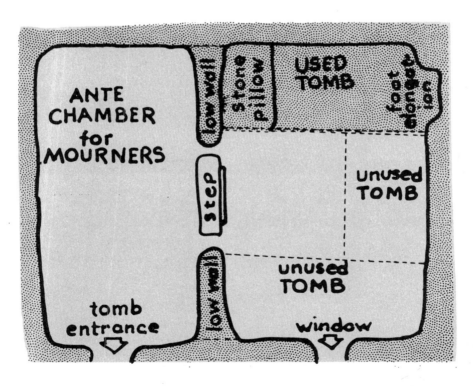

big stripes down His back that had bled. The crown of thorns on His head had punctured the skin more than once. And there in His side was the great gash where the spear went in. The hands and feet were torn by the spikes where Jesus had hung for nearly six hours.

Then the body was taken tenderly to Joseph's tomb there in the garden. I have seen that tomb hewn back into the solid rock. I suppose the body of Jesus was longer than the body of Joseph, for it seems that they needed to chisel out at the foot to make more room for the body of Jesus. And there they wrapped His body in spices and bitter herbs, as the manner of the Jews is to bury; and laid it in that grave.

The chief priests knew that Jesus had plainly promised that He would rise from the dead. So they said to Pilate, "Set a watch over the tomb lest His disciples come by night and steal the body away." Ah, they hoped to thwart the power of the Spirit of God that would raise Jesus from the dead. So Pilate set soldiers to guard it. He set a Roman seal on the door of the sepulchre.

For three days and three nights the body of Jesus lay there. We suppose He was crucified and died Wednesday afternoon, because He had plainly told the people that as Jonah was three days and three nights in the belly of the whale so the Son of man shall be three days and three nights in the heart of the earth. So Thursday, Friday and Saturday Jesus lay in that grave. Sometime before Sunday morning He would rise from the dead. Ah, dear Lord Jesus, the work is done! "Christ died for our sins according to the scriptures; And. . .he was buried, and . . .he rose again the third day according to the scriptures."

Someone may say, "I am not sure whether it was the Garden Tomb under Gordon's Calvary or whether it was the tomb in the Catholic Church of the Holy Sepulchre, where Jesus lay." Never mind. I have seen them both. They are both empty! The Lord Jesus is risen from the dead! My Saviour.

Where we believe our Lord lay.

The Resurrection of Jesus Christ

A minister said that years ago he stood in Philadelphia before a famous painting of the Saviour on the cross. He stood deeply moved. A lad came up and stood looking at the picture. "Yes," said the boy, "they killed Him. He hadn't done anything wrong and they nailed Him there and let Him die!" The man and the boy looked on the picture with deep emotion. As the minister turned to leave, the boy came running after him and said, "Mister, He didn't stay dead! He didn't stay dead!"

No, praise the Lord, the Saviour did not stay dead!

> Low in the grave He lay—
>   Jesus my Saviour!
> Waiting the coming day—
>   Jesus my Lord!
>
> Up from the grave He arose,
> With a mighty triumph o'er His foes;
> He arose a Victor from the dark domain,
>   And He lives forever with His saints to reign.
> He arose! He arose!
> Hallelujah! Christ arose!

The three days in the grave are part of the plan of the Lord Jesus. Already it was foretold in the Old Testament, the Lord Jesus said it, "Thou wilt not leave My soul in hell [the place of the dead]; neither wilt Thou suffer thine Holy One to see corruption" (Ps. 16:10). No, that body of Jesus would never decay.

"As it began to dawn toward the first day of the week,

came Mary Magdalene and the other Mary to see the sepulchre." They brought spices to pack about that dear body to keep down corruption, to keep down the stink, they thought. But, behold, "the angel of the Lord descended from heaven, and came and rolled back the stone from the door, and sat upon it. His countenance was like lightning, and his raiment white as snow: And for fear of him the keepers did shake, and became as dead men." The angel said to the women, "Fear not ye: for I know that ye seek Jesus, which was crucified. He is not here: for He is risen, as He said. . . go quickly, and tell His disciples that He is risen from the dead; and, behold, He goeth before you into Galilee; there shall ye see Him: lo, I have told you."

These women saw Jesus. They ran to tell the disciples. Meantime, what about these soldiers? They fell over like they were dead at the startling sight of the glorious angel. The Roman seal didn't matter to the angel. It was broken, that great stone wheel was rolled back from the door and an angel sat upon it.

The soldiers reported to the chief priests that Jesus had risen. They bribed the soldiers to say, "His disciples came and stole Him away while we slept."

When Mary heard that loved voice, she said, "Master!" and went to embrace His feet. CHRIST IS RISEN INDEED!

We are told that Mary saw Jesus and thought He was the gardener, and she said, "Where have you laid Him? If you will tell me, we will take the body away." Ah, but it was Jesus, and He called her name and she knew Him.

Peter and John came early to the sepulchre on the words of the women. John outran Peter, but Peter boldly walked into the sepulchre and saw the burial clothes there.

The disciples had remained, abiding in that Upper Room where the Lord's Last Supper was spread, and there on that first day of the week Jesus came. Oh, how astonished they were! But Jesus said, "Have you anything here to eat?" And they brought Him a piece of broiled fish and honeycomb. He ate the fish and picked out the bones. He ate the honeycomb and licked His fingers. They could still not believe it. He must be a ghost! No, Jesus said, "Put your hands upon Me and see. Don't you feel My flesh and bones? A ghost, a spirit does not have flesh and bones."

Two men were on their way to Emmaus, and they came upon a Stranger there. He said to them, "Why are you so sad and downcast?"

They did not know He was the resurrected Saviour. They said, "Don't You know the things that happened in Jerusalem? Jesus was a Man mighty in word and deed and we had hoped He was the One who would deliver Israel and now He is dead." Then Jesus said to them, "O fools and slow of heart to believe all that the prophets have spoken: Ought not Christ to have suffered these things, and to enter into His glory? And beginning at Moses and all the prophets, He expounded unto them in all the scriptures the things concerning Himself."

As they went on they stopped to have a meal. And they begged Jesus, this unknown Stranger to them, to stay and eat. But as He broke the bread and blessed it, they recognized, "This is Jesus!" How glad they were. And when Jesus left them, they rushed back to Jerusalem to tell the disciples that Jesus is alive, we met Him in the way.

Again and again Jesus appeared to them. He was seen of all the apostles. He was seen at one time of over five hundred

Christians. He met some disciples fishing by the Sea of Galilee. And finally, when He was going to Heaven in a public ascension, He led the disciples out to the Mount of Olives and gave them again the Great Commission and blessed them.

But the angel promised He is coming again.

Then Jesus is alive from the dead. That proves, first of all, He is a living Saviour. Second, it proves that we who put our trust in Him shall also arise from the dead. Those of our loved ones who died in the faith—they are not gone. When Christ returns, they will return with Him to get their resurrection bodies. And we may look forward to the happy day when we will gather with all our loved ones again, those who have been saved and will meet with Jesus when He calls us out at the rapture. Christ is alive from the dead!

The Saviour Goes to Heaven, Promising to Return

After His resurrection from the dead, the Lord Jesus for some forty days appeared again and again to the disciples. Oh, how glad they were to know He was alive, He had risen from the dead. All the disciples saw Him. Above five hundred disciples saw Him at one time. They saw Him eat before them. They put their hands upon Him and felt His flesh and bones. They heard His voice. There could be no doubt the Lord Jesus was alive from the dead.

In those forty days He gave the Great Commission again and again. Then one day He led the disciples out to the Mount of Olives and gave them the Great Commission once more and lifted up His hands and blessed them. Suddenly, as He blessed them, He was taken up, up, up into the sky and a cloud received Him out of their sight!

Jesus had told the disciples that He was going away. He said, "In My Father's house are many mansions: if it were not so, I would have told you. I go to prepare a place for you. And if I go and prepare a place for you, I will come again, and receive you unto Myself; that where I am, there ye may be also." Many times the Lord Jesus made it clear that He must go back to Heaven for a season and that later He would return for His own to accomplish a great series of events in His second coming and then reign on the earth for a thousand years before He turned the kingdom over to the Father.

Now He had gone up into Heaven and they stood staring up after Him. Oh, Jesus was gone!

Suddenly there stood by them two men in white apparel. They looked like men, but actually they were angels of God. And they said, "Ye men of Galilee, why stand ye gazing up into heaven? this same Jesus, which is taken up from you into heaven, shall so come in like manner as ye have seen Him go into heaven."

This same Jesus! They didn't say there would come wars. They didn't say there would come the Holy Spirit upon you. They didn't say there would come death and trouble. No. They said this same Jesus, Himself, will personally come again.

First, what the angels are saying is that the promises of the ages are to be fulfilled, and that He will return literally to reign on the earth.

A cloud received Him out of their sight, and we are told, "Behold, He cometh with clouds; and every eye shall see Him, and they also which pierced Him: and all kindreds of the earth shall wail because of Him. Even so, Amen" (Rev. 1:7). He is coming the same way He went away, as He left from the Mount of Olives, so the Scripture says.

Zechariah 14:4 tells us about the second coming. "And His feet shall stand in that day upon the mount of Olives, which is before Jerusalem on the east. . . ."

We know from many Scriptures that Jesus will come to destroy the wicked, to fight the Battle of Armageddon, to put down the kingdoms of this world, and to set up His own kingdom. We know that He will sit on the throne of David. We know that as the Seed of Abraham, He will inherit and rule the land of Canaan. Ah, in that time the Bible says that the earth shall be filled with the knowledge of the Lord as the waters cover the sea. We are told that the lion and bear shall feed together. And the lion shall eat straw like the ox. We learn that they will neither hurt nor harm in all God's holy mountain at that time. There will be a thousand years of that reign before the Lord turns the kingdom over to the Father.

But there are preliminary incidents of the second coming before Christ returns physically to the earth to set up His kingdom. We are told that "the Lord Himself shall descend

Our Lord goes away, promising to return again.

from heaven with a shout, with the voice of the archangel, and with the trump of God: and the dead in Christ shall rise first: Then we which are alive and remain shall be caught up together with them in the clouds, to meet the Lord in the air: and so shall we ever be with the Lord" (I Thess. 4:16,17).

And again, in teaching us of the resurrection, Paul is inspired to say, "Behold, I shew you a mystery; We shall not all sleep, but we shall all be changed, In a moment, in the twinkling of an eye, at the last trump: for the trumpet shall sound, and the dead shall be raised incorruptible, and we shall be changed. For this corruptible must put on incorruption, and this mortal must put on immortality" (I Cor. 15:51-53).

Before the Lord reigns on the earth, He will come to take out of the graves and out of the sea, the bodies of all the born-again Christians. And He will bring those spirits back to receive their bodies raised from the dead. "And the dead in Christ shall rise first: Then we which are alive and remain shall be caught up together with them in the clouds, to meet the Lord in the air."

We learn that there is to be a wedding feast in Heaven. And it will be like the king who had made a marriage feast for his son, which Jesus told about in Matthew 22. We are told there will be a judgment seat of Christ and that Christians will receive rewards for their works and will receive the things they have done in the body. Although we are saved, not all Christians will have the same rewards. Some whose works are like wood, hay and stubble, will see them burned. These Christians will be "saved so as by fire." And some whose works are like gold, silver and precious stones, will receive a wonderful reward, as the Scripture tells us in I Corinthians 3:10-15.

Yes, and every Christian must stand before the judgment seat of Christ to receive the things done in the body, whether they be good or bad (II Cor. 5:10).

On this earth there will be a great tribulation time, and then Christ will return with saints and angels to set up His kingdom on the earth.

Now this series of events all will come to pass in what we call the second coming of Christ. In His first coming there was His birth, His ministry, and His death on the cross, and His resurrection. In His second coming there will be the rapture of the saints caught up to meet Christ in the air, and our judgment and rewards in Heaven with Jesus, and the wedding feast, and then we will come back to the earth with Christ.

When will all of this happen? Nobody knows. The one thing the Lord made clear most often, the one thing He emphasized was, "But of that day and hour knoweth no man, no, not the angels of heaven, but My Father only" (Matt. 24:36).

When He told the parable of the wedding and the virgins who were ready, waiting for the bridegroom to come, they did not know when. And when he came, some were not prepared. And He said, "Watch therefore, for ye know neither the day nor the hour wherein the Son of man cometh."

So the first part of the events of the second coming, when Christ will come to call out His own from the world, and raise the Christian dead and change the Christian living, that is a secret known only to God. And Christians should be prepared for it.

Oh, Jesus said, "But of that day and hour knoweth no

man, no, not the angels of heaven, but My Father only" (Matt. 24:36). But every Christian ought to live in the view of this glad hope. The Bible calls it a "blessed hope." Jesus is coming. We do not know when, but it may be at any moment. And let us pray as John the apostle prayed, "Even so, come, Lord Jesus."

A Christian gentleman went to one of the judges of the state of Georgia and said, "Judge, I hear that you and your wife are going to be separated."

"Sir," said the judge indignantly, "that is an insult. My wife and I have lived together for more than half a century. We are not like the modern type—we expect to stay together till the end of our days. What do you mean, sir, when you say that we are to be separated?"

"Well, Judge," said the gentleman, "your wife is a Christian, and you are not—and that means eternal separation one day."

The judge's anger cooled and he looked at his friend seriously, saying, "My God, man, I never thought of it that way!"

The Wonderful Enduement of
Power at Pentecost

After Jesus had risen from the dead, He met with the disciples again and again for forty days. And He gave them the Great Commission. They were plainly commanded to go into all the world and preach the Gospel to every creature. And they were commanded to teach those whom they won to Christ to be baptized and then to carry out the same Great Commission themselves. And the day Jesus ascended to Heaven, He repeated that Great Commission to them again, and He gave explicit instructions.

He said, "And that repentance and remission of sins should be preached in His name among all nations, beginning at Jerusalem. . .And, behold, I send the promise of My Father upon you: but tarry ye in the city of Jerusalem, until ye be endued with power from on high" (Luke 24:47-49).

It is stated again in Acts, chapter 1. "And, being assembled together with them, commanded them that they should not depart from Jerusalem, but wait for the promise of the Father, which, saith He, ye have heard of Me. For John truly baptized with water; but ye shall be baptized with the Holy Ghost not many days hence" (vss. 4,5).

Oh, they were to be filled, covered, surrounded, baptized, anointed with the Spirit of God, in order to carry out the Great Commission. They were to have power. And so He said, "It is not for you to know the times or the seasons, which the Father hath put in His own power. But ye shall receive power, after that the Holy Ghost is come upon you."

Now these disciples had been commanded to tarry in Jerusalem, to wait there. So we learn that "these all continued with one accord in prayer and supplication, with the women, and Mary the mother of Jesus, and with His brethren."

I suspect that they fasted and prayed during that time, too, for Jesus had told them that they would not fast while the bridegroom was with them, but when the bridegroom was taken away, they would fast. So now, with all their hearts they waited and prayed that God would do as He promised, would endue them with power from on High.

Already, the day Jesus rose from the dead, He had breathed upon them and said, "Receive ye the Holy Ghost." And so the sweet Spirit of God had now moved in to dwell in the bodies of every Christian in the world.

Now it was with them as the Apostle Paul later would say, "What? know ye not that your body is the temple of the Holy Ghost which is in you, which ye have of God, and ye are not your own? For ye are bought with a price: therefore glorify God in your body, and in your spirit, which are God's" (I Cor. 6:19,20).

Yes, they had been born again by the Spirit of God. They now were indwelt by the same Holy Spirit. And day by day they could have help, as you and I can have help, in their study of the Bible, they can have comfort in their sorrows, and light on their path. Oh, but they needed more. They needed, as we all need, to have a special enduement of power to carry out the Great Commission and get the Gospel to everybody around us.

To preach the Gospel is not enough. For we learn that "the letter killeth, but the spirit giveth life" (II Cor. 3:6). We know that God's work must have God's power if it is to succeed.

So they waited in the Upper Room. In ten days the Feast of Pentecost came. At that time Jerusalem would be crowded with visitors from far and near. And that day, after they had waited ten days in prayer, the Spirit of God came upon them. "And they were all filled with the Holy Ghost."

There were about 120 of them who waited and prayed, and God's power came on all of them.

They were commanded to get the Gospel to every creature, but, behold, here are people from fifteen or sixteen countries. There are Jews who speak Latin from Rome. There are Jews who speak Arabic. There are Jews from various countries and languages. They had come back to Jerusalem to worship at Pentecost. Well, God in lovingkindness gave the power to these Spirit-filled disciples to talk to these who came, and talk to them in their own tongue in which they were born. People heard the Gospel.

And then Peter stood and preached and three thousand people were saved that day. Oh, what a wonderful time of revival and blessing. What a wonderful start now God has made with these few Christians to get the Gospel out to every creature!

Tongues of fire hover over the disciples.

And people were amazed. They came and said, "Peter, aren't these people drunk?"

"No," Peter told them. It was only nine o'clock in the morning. And with the light wine they had then, people would not be drunk by that time. No, they were not drunk.

"Well, what was this then, this great stir?"

And Peter replied, "But this is that which was spoken by the prophet Joel; 'And it shall come to pass in the last days, saith God, I will pour out of My Spirit upon all flesh: and your sons and your daughters shall prophesy, and your young men shall see visions, and your old men shall dream dreams: And on My servants and on My handmaidens I will pour out in those days of My Spirit; and they shall prophesy: And I will shew wonders in heaven above, and signs in the earth beneath; blood, and fire, and vapour of smoke. . .' " (Acts 2:16-19).

Well, many Jews wanted what these Spirit-filled Christians had. And they came and asked Peter, "Men and brethren, what shall we do?"

And Peter told them to repent, and then to be baptized, committing themselves to Christ and to the new life and power. And he said, "And ye shall receive the gift of the Holy Ghost. For the promise is unto you, and to your children, and to all that are afar off, even as many as the Lord our God shall call."

These disciples had the same Saviour we have. Yes, and we have the same Gospel to take to sinners which they had. Oh, then, we, too, need, and may have, this mighty power of God, this enduement of power, to witness for Jesus.

It came again to these. We learn that after a great flood-tide of power and many saved, they were threatened and perhaps hindered in their witnessing, and they met and prayed again. "And when they had prayed, the place was shaken where they were assembled together; and they were all filled with the Holy Ghost" (Acts 4:31).

And God has given us a command, too. In Ephesians 5:18, "And be not drunk with wine, wherein is excess; but be filled with the Spirit." We, too, need the power of God to witness for Him and carry out the Great Commission which He has commanded us.

Paul and Barnabas Called to Be Missionaries

ACTS 13

When Stephen was stoned at Jerusalem in the midst of a great persecution of the Christians, Christians scattered out in every direction and went preaching the Word. Some of them went to Antioch of Syria, three hundred miles north of Jerusalem, and had great revivals and many were saved. From Jerusalem the apostles sent Barnabas down to Antioch. There you remember that fiery young convert, Saul of Tarsus, had been converted as he went to Damascus. He began to preach with such great energy and power that he had to run for his life. Then he went to Jerusalem. Barnabas spoke up for him. He encouraged the apostles and other Christians to receive this man now, who had before been arresting Christians and bringing them to trial, to receive a beating or to be put to death. Then he preached in Jerusalem with great power. Again his life was threatened; so he went off to Tarsus where he grew up. There he stayed for some time.

Is Paul done with preaching? No. Down in Antioch Barnabas remembered that young man. "Oh, God can use him here," he said. "He ought not quit preaching!" So Barnabas went to Tarsus and got Saul and brought him to Antioch.

One day they had a good prayer meeting. Some earnest Christians met to pray about the Lord's work. Among those present were Simeon (called Niger); Lucius of Cyrene; Manaen who had been brought up with Herod the tetrarch; and

Saul. As these earnest men fasted and prayed, God's Spirit laid upon their hearts: "Separate me Barnabas and Saul for the work whereunto I have called them."

Well, they fasted and prayed some more. Then sure that God had heard them, they put their hands upon Paul and Barnabas and the Spirit of God was on them and "being sent forth by the Holy Ghost, departed unto Seleucia."

Where will they go for the missionary journey? I can well believe that Barnabas said, "Let's go to the island of Cyprus.

Ready to go; ready to stay; ready to do Thy will.

I lived there. I had property there which I gave to the Lord's work under the apostles at Jerusalem. Let's go there."

Good old Barnabas! His real name was Joses, but the apostles were so pleased by his liberality, faithfulness and zeal that they called him "Barnabas, the son of consolation."

The little party sailed to Cyprus. John Mark, nephew of Barnabas, went along, perhaps to run errands, carry the baggage, secure food and such matters for these two missionaries.

They landed at Salamis and preached the Word of God in the synagogue there. Then they went through the island to Paphos. A certain sorcerer lived there, a false prophet, a Jew named Bar-jesus or Elymas. This Elymas worked with Sergius Paulus, a Roman deputy, governor. Sergius Paulus was a prudent man. He called in Paul and Barnabas to tell them the Word of God.

Elymas the sorcerer argued with them against the Christian religion, and sought to turn Sergius Paulus away from the truth.

With burning eyes, Paul stood before the sorcerer and rebuked him. Filled with the Holy Ghost, Paul said, "O full of all subtilty and all mischief, thou child of the devil, thou enemy of all righteousness, wilt thou not cease to pervert the right ways of the Lord? And now, behold, the hand of the Lord is upon thee, and thou shalt be blind, not seeing the sun for a season." At once a mist fell upon him and darkness, and he went about seeking someone to lead him by the hand. The Roman deputy, Sergius Paulus, saw that God was in this, so he trusted the Saviour and was saved.

Then Paul and Barnabas left the port of Paphos and sailed away to Perga in Pamphylia.

But John Mark, I am sorry to say, was a little tired of the rigorous missionary life. I suppose he was homesick for Mother; so he went back to Jerusalem, while Paul and Barnabas went on their missionary journey.

I can imagine that Paul had said, "Barnabas, we went to your old home, Cyprus. I lived in Tarsus in Pamphylia before I went to Jerusalem for an education. Don't you think we might go back to my old country and begin a mission work there?"

So they went to Perga in Pamphylia and then to Antioch in Pisidia. (This is a different Antioch than the one in Syria.)

Since Paul and Barnabas were Jews, and since Jews knew about the Old Testament Scriptures and the promised Messiah and the true God, they naturally went first to the synagogue on the Jewish Sabbath. As they sat there, leaders in the synagogue asked them, "Ye men and brethren, if ye have any word of exhortation for the people, say on."

Paul stood up and preached to them the wonderful story of how God had dealt with Israel, and how at long last God sent John to foretell it, and how Jesus came and how the Jewish leaders crucified Him. Then Paul told how He arose from the dead. He said, "Be it known unto you therefore, men and brethren, that through this man is preached unto you the forgiveness of sins: And by Him all that believe are justified from all things, from which ye could not be justified by the law of Moses."

Paul spoke very sharply to these Jews. Then Gentiles came to beg Paul and Barnabas that they might hear the Word also. These Jews and proselytes followed Paul and Barnabas.

The next Sabbath day, what a crowd came to the synagogue! But the Jews, seeing the multitudes that heard, were jealous and they spoke up against Paul, contradicting and blaspheming. Paul and Barnabas told them plainly, "It was necessary to bring the Word of God to you, but now since you have proven yourselves unworthy, we will turn to preach to the Gentiles also."

When the Gentiles heard this, they were glad.

Many were saved. When the Jews rose up so strongly against Paul and Barnabas, they shook the dust off their feet and came to Iconium, leaving some good Christians there who were filled with the Holy Spirit.

From this time on, in his missionary work, the Apostle Paul and those with him preached first to the Jews, who already had the Old Testament Scriptures and ought to be ready for the Messiah, then they turned to preach the same

Gospel to the Gentiles everywhere, because Christ died for the sins of the whole world, both Jew and Gentile. God wants everyone to hear the Gospel and He wants all who will to be saved.

Missionary Joys and Troubles

Paul and Barnabas started their mission work on the island of Cyprus where Barnabas had lived and served. Then they went up to what we now call Asia Minor, to Pamphylia and the cities in that area. The Apostle Paul grew up at Tarsus and was educated there before going to Jerusalem. And the work of Paul and Barnabas as Spirit-filled evangelists and missionaries—those true to Christ and who preach and witness as they ought—is a work of joy but also a way of persecution and trouble. You will find out from these missionaries.

In Iconium, "they. . .so spake, that a great multitude both of the Jews and also of the Greeks believed." Many were saved. Praise the Lord! "They. . .so spake" means they preached in the power of the Holy Spirit, so that God saved people—Jews in the synagogue as well as many Greeks.

But the great blessing and power of God here brought trouble. Don't be surprised at that. The Lord Jesus was persecuted and hated and condemned and crucified. He told us, "The servant is not greater than his lord. If they have persecuted Me, they will also persecute you" (John 15:20). Remember that in Jerusalem Peter and John were beaten, and Peter and James were put in jail, and James was beheaded. Then Stephen was stoned to death. We need not be surprised when Satan raises up opposition to strong, plain Bible preaching, preached in the power of God.

So we read, "But the unbelieving Jews stirred up the Gentiles, and made their minds evil affected against the

brethren." On the one side, here are Spirit-filled Christians witnessing for God and getting people saved. On the other hand, part of the crowd held with the unregenerate Jews who didn't want to accept Jesus as Saviour. Finally the crowd started to rush the place where Paul and Barnabas stayed; they wanted to beat them up and to stone them to death! They knew about it, so Paul and Barnabas fled to nearby Lystra and Derbe, cities of Lycaonia, and preached the Gospel all around there.

Where God's mighty power is on the preachers and other witnesses who are winning people to Christ, often God works a miracle of healing, too. So it was here. There was a man in Lystra, a cripple from the day he was born, who never had walked a step. He heard Paul speak. When Paul looked at him he perceived the man had faith. So he called out with a loud voice, "Stand upright, brother, on thy feet." The young man leaped and walked! The first steps he had ever taken in his whole life!

My, how the people were affected! They knew about that man. These heathen people said, "The gods are come down to us in the likeness of men." And they called Barnabas, Jupiter; they said Paul was Mercurius because he was the chief speaker. And these poor, ignorant people thought their heathen gods had shown themselves, so the priest of Jupiter brought oxen and garlands and would have done sacrifice with the people. But Paul and Barnabas tore their clothes in distress and ran among the people and said:

"Sirs, why do ye these things? We also are men of like passions with you, and preach unto you that ye should turn from these vanities unto the living God, which made heaven, and earth, and the sea, and all things that are therein: Who in times past suffered all nations to walk in their own ways. Nevertheless He left not Himself without a witness, in that He did good, and gave us rain from heaven, and fruitful seasons, filling our hearts with food and gladness."

The people were astonished and stopped their intended worship.

But the fight of wicked men was not over. Here came Jews from Antioch and Iconium where Paul and Barnabas had preached before, and they persuaded the people. And that poor, changeable crowd joined with them and they stoned Paul and dragged him out of the city, supposing he was dead.

I can imagine that Barnabas and other Christian friends followed out there in great distress. They gathered around the poor, bruised, beaten body of Paul. Was he dead? No, he stirred. Oh, they knelt beside him. They gave him strong hands and lifted him up. Paul was alive! They took him into the city. I am sure they bathed his wounds and put ointment on his bruises and fed him. And by the next day Paul was able to go with them, and he and Barnabas went to Derbe where he had preached before. They taught there for a while, then they returned to Iconium and to Antioch.

What did they tell the new Christians? They exhorted them "to continue in the faith, and that we must through much tribulation enter into the kingdom of God." Young Christians should know that if one lives godly in Christ

Jesus, one will have some persecution, but one can always have God's help.

But Paul, Barnabas, what will you do with these young Christians in all these towns where you have preached? Why, they started new churches! They selected the most mature spiritual men in each case for elders or leaders in the churches. Oh, with what fasting and praying Paul and Barnabas held up these young Christians in heathen countries! But the work was permanently blessed of God, and Paul and Barnabas went through that whole country preaching and teaching. Then back to Antioch and Syria from where they had started. There they reported to the godly men who prayed with them and sent them away and all rejoiced that God had "opened the door of faith unto the Gentiles." There Paul and Barnabas stayed for a long while preaching and teaching the disciples.

There are many joys and there are many sorrows and temptations for a great soul winner. God give us a heart to suffer for His sake if need be.

Must One Keep the Mosaic Law to Be Saved?

ACTS 15

It is strange but sad that we poor ignorant people tend to think more of the outward routine of religion than the spiritual lessons they are supposed to teach. So in New Testament times, even when Jews got saved, they hated to give up the passover supper, the circumcision of their boys, and the priesthood and Temple at Jerusalem.

People are oftentimes like that now. Some feel that one must be baptized in order to be saved. Some who have gone to mass and confessed to a priest think that after they are saved, they still need to go to that unscriptural sacrifice regularly.

You need not be surprised to find that everywhere Paul and Barnabas went and many, many people were saved, some went among these converts saying that now if you are going to be a Christian, you must be circumcised and must keep the law of Moses.

Isn't that strange? We know that no one was ever saved by keeping the law of Moses. We know that circumcision is a picture of being born again and marked as set aside for Christ. We know that all the sacrifices simply picture Jesus our Saviour dying on the cross. The atoning death of Jesus is the great saving fact, not those other sacrifices which pointed to it, and which pictured it.

Those people won to Christ by Paul and Barnabas were only young Christians. They had not had time to grow much in grace, nor to grow great Christian character. They were easy to mislead. Even in Jerusalem, many of the Christians still held on to the outward rites of the Jewish ceremonial law, and they thought other converts should do so also. In fact, most of the Jewish Christians had not understood that Gentiles could be saved also.

So teachers went among the new converts which Paul and Barnabas had won, and these teachers taught them they must be circumcised or they could not be saved.

What a stir it caused!

At Antioch in Syria there was a great dissension. Christian Jews who came down from Judaea kept teaching the people they must be circumcised in order to be saved. Paul and Barnabas saw that that discussion there would not get the matter settled; they must go to Jerusalem and call together the apostles and get all the leaders agreed on this matter.

So these two went down to Phenice and Samaria declaring how God had saved so many Gentiles. They came on to Jerusalem and called together the apostles and elders and told all the wonderful things God had done in saving thousands of both Jews and Gentiles in the cities of what is now Asia Minor. But even in Jerusalem some of the Jews, who were Pharisees and converted but still holding to some of the ceremonial law, insisted "that it was needful to circumcise them, and to command them to keep the law of Moses."

Well, the apostles and elders came together in a great council in Jerusalem to decide this thing. I am glad they settled it clearly, too, being made to remember how easy it is to be saved by simple faith in Christ without the ceremonies and law.

First, Peter stood and gave a testimony. He told how God had selected him to go to the household of Cornelius and there preach the Gospel. He reminded the people how he didn't want to go. He had never been in a Gentile home. He had never preached to a Gentile. But God let a great sheet down from Heaven in a vision, with all kinds of animals on it. And God had said, "Rise, Peter; kill, and eat."

Peter was astonished, for here were animals the Jews would never eat. They were not to eat pork, for instance.

They were not to eat catfish or any fish without scales. So Peter protested in his vision and said, "I have never eaten that which is unclean!"

But God repeated the lesson again—the sheet let down from Heaven and the command to rise, kill and eat. After three times God told Peter, "What God hath cleansed, that call not thou common." Peter told how Cornelius and his family and loved ones were all saved; how God gave them a wonderful fullness of the Spirit and power to witness, as He had given to the disciples at Pentecost. So there was unquestionable evidence a Gentile could be saved without keeping any of the law of Moses.

And I think Peter said with great pathos, "Now therefore why tempt ye God, to put a yoke upon the neck of the disciples, which neither our fathers nor we were able to bear? But we believe that through the grace of the Lord Jesus Christ we shall be saved, even as they."

When Peter had finished, Paul and Barnabas stood up and told how wonderfully God had saved multitudes under their preaching, both Jews and Gentiles alike.

After that, James, who lived in Jerusalem (James the brother of our Lord Jesus, who wrote the book of James), reminded them:

"Simeon hath declared how God at the first did visit the Gentiles, to take out of them a people for His name. And to this agree the words of the prophets; as it is written, After this I will return, and will build again the tabernacle of David, which is fallen down; and I will build again the ruins thereof, and I will set it up: That the residue of men might seek after the Lord, and all the Gentiles, upon whom My name is called, saith the Lord, who doeth all these things. Known unto God are all His works from the beginning of the world. Wherefore my sentence is, that we trouble not them, which from among the Gentiles are turned to God: But that we write unto them, that they abstain from pollutions of idols, and from fornication, and from things strangled, and from blood. For Moses of old time hath in

every city them that preach him, being read in the syn-agogues every sabbath day."—Vss. 14-21.

So good men were sent with a letter to be read by Christians everywhere, showing that Gentile converts were not to be circumcised nor were they to keep ceremonial laws.

We are glad that one who trusts in the Lord Jesus for forgiveness has everlasting life at once, without keeping any of the ceremonial law.

Paul and Silas:
Another Missionary Journey

ACTS 15,16

After some time at Antioch in Syria, Paul wanted to go back to visit every city where they had ministered in order to encourage the converts. Barnabas would like to go, but he wanted to take his nephew Mark who had quit them after going with them to Cyprus before. Paul doubted whether the young man would be reliable help. Because of this disagreement between Paul and Barnabas, Barnabas took his nephew Mark and went back to his old home country, the island of Cyprus. We hear no more about him in the Bible, though we know that he must have done good work wherever he went. He was a good man.

Then Paul took Silas and began another missionary journey. The brethren recommended him prayerfully to the grace of God and he went through Syria and Cilicia confirming the churches.

He came to Derbe and Lystra where he had preached before and where he had been stoned. There they found a young man, Timothy, who would later be of great help to the Apostle Paul. His mother was a Jewess, his father a Greek, a Gentile. So that there would be no question among the Jews, Paul had Timothy circumcised and took him with him.

How glad these Gentile converts in all the cities were when Paul could show them the letter written by the apostles and elders at Jerusalem declaring they need not be circumcised nor need they keep the ceremonial laws. When they trusted Christ in their hearts they were saved. It was good to have

"In stonings,
often."

the argument settled in the churches; and they grew in the faith.

Now they had been to the principal cities where they had preached before. Some way the Holy Spirit impressed them they should not stay in the little province of Asia. They would have gone into Bithynia but the Holy Spirit reproved it. They went on over to the coastline to Troas and there a vision appeared to Paul in the night, "There stood a man of Macedonia, and prayed him, saying, Come over into Macedonia, and help us." Ah, Paul told those who were with him; they agreed it was the call of God. They must go over the strait that separates Asia and Europe into Greece.

What a great day that was! Now in the future the Gospel will go on through Greece and Rome, into Spain, and eventually to England and throughout Europe. What a great difference it would have been had the Gospel gone on through Asia to India, China and Japan through the missionary journeys of Barnabas and Paul and Silas! Had that been the case, America might not have been blessed with the great Christian heritage. And many of us might not have known the Saviour. But God has determined the Gospel will go into Europe.

They went into Macedonia, which is part of Greece, and came through Troas, Samothracia and Neapolis to the great city of Philippi.

Where would they find some friendly hearts to hear the Gospel? They learned that a prayer meeting was often held by certain women on the Sabbath day out by the riverside. And there Paul and Silas went.

There was a businesswoman named Lydia, a seller of purple, who evidently ran an important business in the city of Thyatira. As she heard Paul, her heart was touched and she turned to trust the Lord Jesus and was baptized and her household. Then Paul and Silas and friends moved into the home of this important businesswoman and stayed with her awhile.

On the streets one day a young woman came by. I suppose her eyes were wild, for she was demon-possessed. She was a fortuneteller and the evil spirits helped this slave girl to make money for the men who owned and used her.

In some strange way she was attracted to Paul and his party. She called out openly, "These men are the servants of the most high God, which shew unto us the way of salvation." Every time she saw Paul and his companions on the street she would cry out.

Paul's spirit burned within him. Oh, that he could cast out that demon and save that poor devil-possessed girl!

One day God gave him faith and he turned to that evil spirit and said, "I command thee in the name of Jesus Christ to come out of her." That spirit came out that same hour. Now the girl was no more wild, no more devil-possessed. She would tell no more fortunes. She would no more make money as a slave girl.

Now when her masters who had made money by her evil spirit saw that the hope of their gain was gone, they caught Paul and Silas and brought them down to the judges, saying, "These men, being Jews, do exceedingly trouble our city, And teach customs, which are not lawful for us to receive, neither to observe, being Romans."

The heathen multitude rose up against Paul and Silas and the judges had them bound and beaten and turned over to the jailer for safe keeping. The jailer put Paul and Silas in the basement and made their feet fast in the stocks. Certainly they could not get away now!

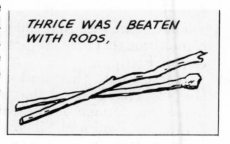

THRICE WAS I BEATEN WITH RODS,

At midnight Paul and Silas sang and prayed to God. I do not know how discouraged they may have been the first part of the night, but now they prayed and sang praises. Suddenly an earthquake began to shake the old jail. Bars were broken off the windows, doors were popped open, the stocks that held the men were broken, and all the prisoners were free.

When the jailer was dumped out of bed and awakened in the middle of the night by an earthquake, he was astonished. Seeing the doors were all open, Oh, he thought, surely some of the prisoners will get away and I will be blamed for it. So he drew his sword to kill himself. . . .but Paul stopped him. "We are all here. Do yourself no harm."

The jailer came in, deeply convicted of his sins. These men claimed to speak for the most high God. Now, he asked, what must he do to be saved? They answered back that classic statement which has been the theme of every gospel preacher in the world: "Believe on the Lord Jesus Christ, and thou shalt be saved." And the same plan is good for your family and everybody else who will trust Christ.

The jailer was saved. How penitent he was! He had beaten these men of God until the blood ran down their backs. He penitently washed their stripes. Now he must openly claim his salvation. So he was baptized the same hour of the night.

Yes, and all his family trusted Christ and all were baptized. What a happy ending to that sad time!

Yes, it costs something to be a missionary, or to be a Spirit-filled witness. But isn't it wonderful that God takes the part of His servants and that no one need suffer more than God allows us to suffer in His dear name and for the good of others.

There has been such a commotion in the city, but Paul and Silas have not really broken any laws. So the rulers of the city sent word that they need stay in jail no longer.

But Paul indignantly sent them word, "Come and bring us out of jail yourselves. You have had us beaten openly, uncondemned and we are Roman citizens. We demand you come and bring us out honorably."

Oh, how scared those officers were when they found they had beaten Roman citizens without condemnation! They came and begged Paul and Silas to leave town quietly.

Well, they first visited the other Christian brethren, and went back to the house of Lydia and were comforted, and others were happy. And they went on their missionary journey to other cities.

Paul loved the young Christians he left at Philippi. And what a tender letter he was inspired to write them in the book of Philippians!

The Gospel in Great Cities
of Greece

In the Bible, the country of Greece is known by two names. The northern part was called Macedonia; the southern part, including Athens and Corinth, was called Achaia.

God seems to have gotten much of the world ready for the coming of the Saviour. So, "when the fullness of the time was come, God sent forth His Son, made of a woman, made under the law, To redeem them that were under the law, that we might receive the adoption of sons" (Gal. 4:4,5).

Under Alexander the Great, the armies of Greece had conquered the then known world. And everywhere Greek art, culture and the common language—Koine Greek—was spread. Then when Rome conquered the same countries and took over rulership, the Greek language was still spoken everywhere.

Thus it is interesting that Luke, who went with Paul on some of his missionary journeys, was inspired to write the book of Luke and Acts in Koine Greek. Then Paul, who won so many souls in missionary journeys, along with Barnabas and then with Silas and others, wrote letters back to the churches he had founded: I and II Corinthians, Galatians, Ephesians, Philippians, Colossians. And he wrote letters to Timothy, Titus and Philemon, and then before going to Rome, wrote to the people at Rome. And all these epistles enclosed in the New Testament were written in the Greek language. We think probably he wrote also the book of Hebrews to Christian Jews.

But God has gotten the country ready. Now Paul could go from one province to another without being stopped at custom houses and without having to learn a new language. Everywhere he could preach to a group of Jews and others who understood the Greek language.

After leaving Philippi, Paul and Silas went to Thessalonica. There Paul preached and a great many were saved. He preached first in the synagogue to the Jews for three Sabbath days, for the Jews met to worship on their Sabbath. But he preached to Gentiles, also, and a great multitude of these were saved.

It is not surprising that Satan caused wicked men and those of heathen religions to rise up against Paul and others. They said that since Paul preached Jesus as King, he was against the Roman governor. They took Jason, one of the converts, before the judges. They took a peacebond of Jason and let the people go.

Now where will Paul and Silas go? They will go to Berea, another city nearby. "These were more noble than those in Thessalonica, in that they received the word with all readiness of mind, and searched the scriptures daily, whether those things were so" (Acts 17:11).

When a Sunday school class is called "The Bereans" or when a church is called "The Berean Church," they should mean that they study the Scriptures and try to go by the Bible.

Paul and Silas had many converts in Berea—some high class, honorable Greeks and many men, as well as Jews. But when the unconverted Jews in Thessalonica heard that the Gospel was being preached in Berea, they came and started an uproar there also. So Paul was slipped out and sent down to Athens, while Timothy and Silas remained for the time in Berea.

Athens was the center of heathen culture in all the world. There the great artists and sculptors lived. There the great philosophers and teachers gathered pupils about them. Paul finds himself in that situation. Yes, Athens was, in some sense, the center of the heathen worship of the world.

Paul sent word for Silas and Timothy to come to him quickly. There in Athens his heart was stirred with the idolatry. On Mars' Hill, about half way up the famous Acropolis, was built the world famous temple to Venus and other temples. And there on Mars' Hill were gathered the various heathen philosophers, teachers and idols, representing all kinds of gods. Paul's spirit was so stirred within him that in the Jewish synagogue and in the market place and wherever little crowds gathered, he disputed with them and with the heathen philosophers.

Some of them brought Paul upon Mars' Hill and urged that he tell them about his religion and doctrine. So there Paul faced the heathen philosophers and idolaters and preached that famous sermon which is recorded in Acts 17. He had found an idol dedicated "TO THE UNKNOWN GOD," and there he began to preach about Jesus, Creator and Saviour, yet a Saviour who was unknown to these heathen philosophers and leaders.

A few people, not many, were converted. No church was founded at Athens. And Paul did not write an inspired letter to them to become part of the Bible.

But Paul was determined to get the Gospel to the great cities of the world. Yonder sixty miles west on the peninsula was Corinth, a city of a quarter of a million people. It was a great city with many peoples and languages, and much idolatry and wickedness. There went Paul to preach the Gospel.

He told us later that he went to Corinth with much fear and trembling. Evidently he had deeply pondered why his results in Athens were not spectacular, not as pronounced as in other centers. And he made a holy vow to preach Jesus Christ and Him crucified alone.

He went to Corinth and there an angel of God stood by him and said, "Fear not, Paul, for no man shall lift his hand against you to do you hurt." When he was arrested and brought before the judgment seat, the judge dismissed the case.

Paul stayed for eighteen months in that great city and won

thousands of people. First, he preached in the synagogue and later out next door. The master of the synagogue himself was converted, along with many others. Later Paul will go back to Ephesus and will preach there for three years with great blessing.

But Paul had a burning love for the Jews. Though called to be an apostle to the Gentiles, he some way could not get the people of Jerusalem off his mind. So he determined to go back there and take gifts prepared for the poor Christians who had lost homes and jobs and had come to great poverty because of their faith.

Ah, but Paul, trouble awaits you at Jerusalem. He was warned by the Holy Spirit not to go; nevertheless he was determined to go and was willing to die, if need be, to take the Gospel to Jerusalem.

Paul and the Idol Makers
at Ephesus

ACTS 18,19,20

After a blessed year and a half at Corinth, Paul took ship and sailed back to Asia Minor, to Ephesus, a great city of that province of Asia, now in Asiatic Turkey. It was one of the seven churches of Asia, addressed later in the book of Revelation.

Paul took with him Aquila and Priscilla, tentmakers with whom he had lived and labored in Corinth. There Paul preached in a Jewish synagogue. Leaving Aquila and Priscilla in Ephesus, Paul went to all the churches of the area strengthening the disciples.

At this time, Apollos, a preacher from Alexandria, Egypt, came to Ephesus. Some way he had heard the Gospel by someone converted under John the Baptist. He was a remarkable preacher, who showed powerfully from Old Testament Scriptures that Jesus is the Christ. He spoke with great power of the Holy Spirit. But Apollos had not been present at Pentecost, and we suppose he had never heard that every convert should have the enduement of power to witness for Christ.

Aquila and Priscilla, who had long worked with God's great Apostle Paul, took this mighty preacher aside and taught him "the way of God more perfectly." Apollos knew the mighty Gospel, as did all the disciples of John, and he learned that he should teach all Christians to be filled with the Spirit.

EPHESUS: The most complete city ever excavated and dating back to the 11th century BC was the leading city of culture and religion of Ancient Asia.

Apollos went out to Corinth with a good recommendation by the brethren, and Paul came back to Ephesus.

First in the synagogue, for three months Paul preached mightily. Then he disputed daily in the school of Tyrannus. Through all the province the Gospel was spread. Paul preached anywhere and everywhere he could.

Some vagabond Jews, exorcists, saw the wonderful results when Paul cast out devils. As they watched him, they thought, He just uses the name of Jesus, and the demons come out as He commands them. So they tried it. Among them were seven sons of Sceva, a Jewish priest. They said, "We adjure you by Jesus whom Paul preacheth!" But the demon in the afflicted man cried out, "Jesus I know, and Paul I know; but who are ye?" and he leaped upon these pretenders and routed them quickly.

Fear came on both Jews and Greeks. People which used curious arts brought their books and burned them. It amounted to thousands of dollars. Revival spread far and wide, and many were saved.

At Ephesus there was a great idol statue of Diana, a Greek goddess. Foolish tradition was that this idol came down from Heaven. It was taught that Diana was a goddess of fertility and so one who would multiply crops and increase flocks and guarantee children. So this idol was greatly worshiped throughout the whole area.

A group of silversmiths, thinking to make a good thing out of this superstition and idol worship, made silver shrines, images of this Diana of the Ephesians, and sold them. This brought them much money. But Paul was saying that there be no gods, which are made with hands, that Diana was no God. The Christian religion was truth and heathen religions were all false.

At this the idolmakers raised a big to-do. They organized something like a labor union, they gathered together the workmen and said, "You know that by this craft of idol making we have our wealth. Moreover, Paul and the Christians, by making light of Diana of the Ephesians, have turned away much people." At hearing this, they were full of wrath. They determined to end this preaching of the Christians. The rabblerousing silversmiths set the people crying out, "Great is Diana of the Ephesians."

People caught Gaius and Aristarchus, men of Macedonia who had traveled with Paul, and rushed them into that giant theater. Paul wanted to go in but the disciples suffered him not. And the noble, important men, who were his friends, urged Paul not to go before that mob. Alexander was put forth and beckoned with his hand to speak, but because he was a Jew, the crowd interrupted him and for two hours they cried out, "Great is Diana of the Ephesians."

"Great is Diana of the Ephesians!"

The townclerk, representative of the Roman government, came out to appease the people. He said, "Every man knows the city of the Ephesians is a worshiper of the great goddess Diana and of the image that fell down from Jupiter. That cannot be spoken against, so do nothing rashly. You have arrested these men, who have robbed no temples, nor blasphemed your goddess. Now why don't you get lawyers and sue them if they have hurt your trade? But for this day's uproar, we are in danger to be called

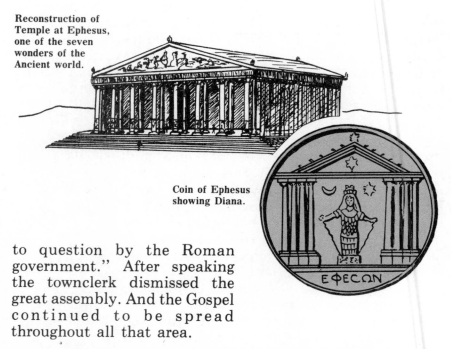

Reconstruction of
Temple at Ephesus,
one of the seven
wonders of the
Ancient world.

Coin of Ephesus
showing Diana.

to question by the Roman government." After speaking the townclerk dismissed the great assembly. And the Gospel continued to be spread throughout all that area.

Now Paul had preached in and around Ephesus for some three years. He went back through Macedonia. Later in Asia at Troas in an upper chamber a young man named Eutychus sat in the window. As Paul preached long, this young man went to sleep and fell out the third-story window and was taken up for dead. But Paul fell upon him, embraced him and said, "Don't be troubled; his life is still in him." Paul talked on till break of day.

Paul let the ship depart and he walked some nineteen miles across the peninsula to Assos. Sailing on, they came to Miletus, a seaport town close to Ephesus. There Paul sent word to the elders of that city to come to meet him, and he gave them a marvelous message. He reminded them how he had taught them publicly and from house to house. He warned them solemnly that some, even of their own people, would backslide and lead into false doctrine. So they must beware. Then he said, "Therefore watch, and remember, that by the space of three years I ceased not to warn every

The Great Theatre

"And the whole city was filled with confusion: and having caught Gaius and Aristarchus, men of Macedonia, Paul's companions in travel, they rushed with one accord into the theatre, And when Paul would have entered in unto the people, the disciples suffered him not." (Acts 19:29,30).

one night and day with tears." Paul told these preachers, most of whom he had won to Christ, that he would see their face no more. And out on the seashore they embraced each other and wept and Paul departed.

But Paul had had a marvelous ministry of some three years at Ephesus.

Paul Must Go to Rome

At Corinth Paul had written the inspired letter to the Romans. How often he had planned to visit Christians at Rome, but was hindered.

God had led Paul to preach in great cities like Athens, Corinth, Ephesus and Rome, spreading the Gospel as far as possible. He was God's "apostle to the Gentiles." More and more he must leave to other disciples and apostles the preaching to the Jews at Jerusalem and elsewhere. He knew many Christians at Rome. My, how many of them are named in the 16th chapter of Romans: he sent greetings to them all!

Paul wrote the people at Rome, "Whensoever I take my journey into Spain, I will come to you." Yes, Paul would come to Rome, but he did not know he would come as a prisoner and that the Roman government would pay for his travel. Paul had many indications that there would be serious persecution and trouble if he went to Jerusalem, yet he felt he must go.

"And now, behold, I go bound in the spirit unto Jerusalem, not knowing the things that shall befall me there: Save that the Holy Ghost witnesseth in every city, saying that bonds and afflictions abide me. But none of these things move me, neither count I my life dear unto myself, so that I might finish my course with joy, and the ministry, which I have received of the Lord Jesus, to testify the gospel of the grace of God. And now, behold, I know that ye all, among whom I have gone preaching the

kingdom of God, shall see my face no more."—Acts 20:22-25.

He had another warning in Acts 21. At Tyre, Paul tarried with certain disciples seven days, and they "said to Paul through the Spirit, that he should not go up to Jerusalem."

Again, when they came to Caesarea, a prophet named Agabus "bound his own hands and feet, and said, Thus saith the Holy Ghost, So shall the Jews at Jerusalem bind the man that owneth this girdle, and shall deliver him into the hands of the Gentiles."

So all his party begged Paul not to go up to Jerusalem. And Paul would not heed the warning of the Holy Spirit. He said, "What mean ye to weep and to break mine heart? for I am ready not to be bound only, but also to die at Jerusalem for the name of the Lord Jesus."

I think Paul was mistaken. But I can well understand how his heart was so burdened for the Jews at Jerusalem, and how he wanted to preach to them, and could not see why they would not listen to him.

"*FIVE TIMES RECEIVED I FORTY STRIPES SAVE ONE.*

At Jerusalem the Christian brethren were so excited to see Paul! His great ministry throughout many provinces had been reported with great pride and joy. Some Jewish Christians were so anxious for Paul to appear to be a good Jew that they had him join in with the sacrifice of others who had taken a Nazarite vow. Paul did.

But in the Temple, radical, unconverted Jews saw him and thinking he had brought a Gentile into the Temple, they cried out against him, seized him and was beating him when soldiers came from the fortress and took him away. He begged for a chance to speak to the people as he stood on the stairway, and they were astonished that he spoke Hebrew.

But the Pharisees insisted on having Paul come to meet before the Sanhedrin. Paul was brought before that Jewish supreme court in spiritual matters and there told the story of

Agrippa said to Paul, "Almost thou persuadest me to be a Christian."

his conversion. He had been a faithful, earnest Pharisee. He had represented the Sanhedrin, going out to arrest Christians and giving witness before them as they were tried. He had held the garments of those who stoned Stephen. He had proved himself a good Jew. But now he had truly been converted.

He reminds them that God had said to him in a trance, "Make haste, and get thee quickly out of Jerusalem: for they will not receive thy testimony concerning me" (Acts 22:18), and Paul had argued with the Lord.

My, what a riot in the Sanhedrin! What an uproar! The chief captain brought Paul into the castle and suggested he be examined by scourging. But when he learned that Paul was a Roman citizen, he dared not do that.

The chief Roman captain then commanded the Sanhedrin to come before Paul and make their accusation. There Paul appealed to the Pharisees. He knew it was a divided group. The Sadducees did not believe in the resurrection, nor in angels and spirits. The Pharisees did. So Paul said, "I am a Pharisee, the son of a Pharisee: of the hope and resurrection of the dead I am called in question." That caused a big argument among the Sanhedrin. So the soldiers delivered Paul from their hands and brought him back to the castle. That night the Lord stood by him and said, "Be of good cheer, Paul: for as thou hast testified of me in Jerusalem, so must thou bear witness also at Rome."

But certain of the Jews met and took a solemn vow they would neither eat nor drink until they killed Paul. They would ask again that Paul be brought before the Sanhedrin. They would then immediately fly on him and kill him.

Paul's nephew heard of their plotting and came to tell Paul, then the centurion. Paul must be gotten out of Jerusalem. The centurion ordered a company of horsemen and foot soldiers to go with Paul down to the coast and up to Caesarea where the governor had more offices.

So they slipped away by night and Paul was brought before Governor Felix at Caesarea. Jews came down from Jerusalem and hired a lawyer to accuse Paul. Then Paul stood before Felix the governor, and his wife Drusilla, and preached to them about faith in Christ. "And as he reasoned of righteousness, temperance, and judgment to come, Felix trembled, and answered, Go thy way for this time; when I have a convenient season, I will call for thee."

Oh, that convenient season never came! Felix put off the matter because he hoped that Paul would bribe him in order to be set free. Poor Felix trembled but did not get saved!

Then after two years with Paul in jail at Caesarea, Festus came into the governor's place over Judaea and left Paul bound.

The Jewish leaders wanted Paul brought back to Jerusalem for trial, but Festus said they should come to see him there. And when they again accused him falsely, Paul insisted, "I appeal unto Caesar." Paul had Roman citizenship which was a great honor. He had a right to appeal to the emperor at Rome to get justice. And now Festus agreed he would send him to Rome.

Then Agrippa, governor of another province, came to visit at Caesarea. There Paul stood before him and preached the Gospel. He said, "King Agrippa, believest thou the prophets? I know that thou believest." Agrippa said to Paul. "Almost thou persuadest me to be a Christian." Paul answered, "I would to God, that not only thou, but also all that hear me this day, were both almost, and altogether such as I am, except these bonds."

Agrippa said to Festus, "This man might have been set at liberty, if he had not appealed unto Caesar."

But Paul is going to Rome.

Paul Faces Shipwreck and Savages; Arrives at Rome

ACTS 27,28

Paul was one of relatively few people who had the rights and privileges of citizenship at Rome. Some people bought the right of citizenship with great price, but Paul inherited that.

So he appealed to Caesar: now there is nothing Festus can do but send him to Rome and there be tried under Caesar.

A Roman centurion or captain named Julius was put in charge of Paul and several other prisoners. They found a ship sailing from Adramyttium, not far from Caesarea which is on the coast. Aristarchus, a good friend of Paul's, a Macedonian, was with them.

The ship sailed north and stopped briefly at Sidon where Paul was allowed to go meet some friends and refresh himself. Then they sailed "under Cyprus, because the winds were contrary." They stopped at Myra, a city of Lycia, in what is now Asia Minor. There the centurion found another ship sailing for Rome and they transferred to that ship. Many people were aboard—276 including the sailors, soldiers, prisoners and passengers.

The home port of the ship was Alexandria, but they were carrying freight and people to Rome. They sailed slowly many days, came near Cnidus, then sailed under Crete and on by Salmone, on the eastern tip of the island of Crete. Then on the southern coast they came to "The fair havens" near Lasea.

THRICE I SUFFERED
SHIPWRECK,

A NIGHT AND A DAY I HAVE
BEEN IN THE DEEP;

Sail ships cannot always go in all kinds of weather, so it was customary for good ships to lay up in harbor during the very heavy winter weather, that time of fasting for the atonement which came from the tenth of the seventh month (our October). But the owner and captain of the ship felt the little harbor was crowded and "not commodious to winter in" and felt he must get on his way as far as he could toward Rome.

Paul warned them, "Sirs, I perceive that this voyage will be with hurt and much damage, not only of the lading and ship, but also of our lives." But both the centurion and captain of the ship felt pressed to go ahead. So when the wind blew softly from the south, they sailed out, hoping to find a better harbor at Phenice on the western end of Crete.

However, they had not sailed long until a mighty gale of a wind came. It was very customary that at this time a great gale would blow on the Mediterranean and they called it "Euroclydon." My, what excitement on the ship! what fear among the passengers! what concern of the captain and the sailors! With difficulty they pulled in the boat they had been trailing; they undergirded the ship with ropes.

They sailed around the little island of Clauda. The ship was in such distress and seemed so likely to sink that they lightened the ship and threw overboard all the freight and as much extra things as they could to lighten the ship. The tempest continued day after day. You can imagine what distress the people were in.

But one day the Apostle Paul stood in the midst of them

all and called their attention to himself and said:

"Sirs, ye should have hearkened unto me, and not have loosed from Crete, and to have gained this harm and loss. And now I exhort you to be of good cheer: for there shall be no loss of any man's life among you, but of the ship. For there stood by me this night the angel of God, whose I am, and whom I serve, Saying, Fear not, Paul; thou must be brought before Caesar: and, lo, God hath given thee all them that sail with thee. Wherefore, sirs, be of good cheer: for I believe God, that it shall be even as it was told me."

However, he told them they must be cast upon an island. The storm continued and the ship was driven before the wind. The sails were furled with perhaps just enough sails left to keep the ship headed straight before the wind.

There was some evidence they must be drawing near to land. So they sounded with a weight on a cord and found the sea was twenty fathoms or 160 feet deep. They went a little further and found it was fifteen fathoms, or only 90 feet deep. They were coming close to some land. What would they do? The ship would pound on the rocks on the shore. So they cast four anchors out of the stern, and wished for the day.

The sailors thought they might escape out of the ship, so they let down a boat. Paul called this to the attention of the centurion and to the soldiers saying, "The sailors must stay with us; they only can control the ship as we go into shore." So the soldiers cut off the ropes from the boat which the sailors were about to let down to the sea, and let the boat fall off.

Daylight came. Paul besought the people, "You have gone fourteen days without eating; now everyone take food and eat. This is for your good health. I promise that not a hair of the head shall fall from any of you." So Paul took bread and gave thanks and ate, and the people also were encouraged to eat.

How will these 276 people get to land? When they had eaten all they wanted, they threw overboard everything else that might help weight the ship down. When it was day, they discovered a little creek with a shore. They thought they might run the ship into that little creek. So taking up the anchors, they committed themselves unto the sea and loosed the rudder bands, put up the mainsail and made toward shore. The ship ran aground and stuck fast, but the hinder part of the ship began to brake with the violence of the waves.

The soldiers who were taken along to guard the prisoners counseled together. "We must kill these prisoners, lest some should swim out and escape." But the centurion, willing to save Paul, kept them from harming any of the prisoners, and commanded those who could swim to come ashore; those who could not swim could get a board or broken piece of the ship and be washed up on the shore. So it was that the last one on that ship was saved alive, as Paul had foreseen they would be.

These must wonder, Where are we now? They were on the island of Melita, now called Malta. We suppose the people were only partly civilized. They are called "barbarous people." They came now to this people wet, cold and frightened, and were shown kindness. They kindled a fire and gave some covering because of the cold.

Paul went out to do his part, gathering sticks for the fire. And in the sticks was a viper, deadly poisonous. As Paul threw the sticks on the fire, this poisonous snake fastened on his arm. Oh, they thought, he will surely die! The barbarians thought perhaps Paul was a criminal who had gotten by with his sin at sea, but now vengeance from God had caught up with him. But while they watched, Paul shook the snake off into the fire and felt no harm. When they saw no harm had come to him, they changed their minds and said that he was a god.

Here is the first case we know of where the promise of Jesus in the Great Commission in Mark 16:18 came to pass. There we are told that a certain sign should follow them that have faith, and "they shall take up serpents; and if they drink any deadly thing it shall not hurt them." Paul was not putting on a show. Rather, this is only another instance of God's loving care for that preacher who trusted Him and laid his life on the altar.

They are in the midst of winter. Now in the stormy Mediterranean in midwinter, no ship will set out to finish the journey to Rome. So Paul makes himself useful.

The chief man of the island was Publius, who was very kind to these strangers that had been cast from the troubled sea onto the shores of his island. He took them in and lodged them courteously. The father of Publius lay sick of a fever and a bloody flux. Paul entered in and prayed, and laid his hands on him, and God healed him. Then many others who had diseases came and were healed.

After three months, they departed in a ship of Alexandria, which had wintered in the isle, and in this they sailed on toward Rome.

Landing at Syracuse, they tarried there three days. From there they came to Rhegium. After one day the south wind blew and they came up the coast of Italy to Puteoli. There Paul found Christian brethren and was allowed to stay with them for seven days. Then brethren in Rome heard about Paul's coming, and they came down to meet him as far as the Appii forum. When Paul saw them, he thanked God and took courage.

When Paul landed at Rome, he and the other prisoners were delivered by the centurion Julius to the captain of the praetorian guard, the emperor's guard. But Paul was allowed to dwell in his own house with a soldier who kept him.

After three days Paul called for Jewish leaders to meet him. He explained how he had been accused of blasphemy because he preached the Gospel. Although there were some Christians in Rome and Paul had mentioned a good many of them in his letter, Peter was not there and they did not know much about Paul. They heard him. Some believed and some did not.

Paul stayed for two years there preaching, as he had done elsewhere. He first preached to Jews. They spoke the same language. They both knew the Old Testament Scriptures. But then when many Jews rejected the Saviour, Paul preached to the Gentiles. He was called the apostle to the Gentiles.

Paul went to Rome but it was not the journey he expected to take, was it? No. He had written to them after he had been to Jerusalem, "When therefore I have performed this, and have sealed to them this fruit, I will come by you into Spain. And I am sure that, when I come unto you, I shall come in the fulness of the blessing of the gospel of Christ" (Rom. 15:28,29).

But this time Paul did not come to Spain, so we take it that after these two years, Paul was released from prison. He went preaching again and saw Philemon, as he promised to do in a letter (Philem. 22). I suppose he went back to visit with the Philippian Christians as he had promised (Phil. 1:26). We suppose he was arrested again after he had been to Spain and other places.

At last Paul will die in a Roman prison from where he wrote to Timothy and others from his cell.

Yes, Paul got to Rome, and eventually died in Rome. But what a ministry he had!

The Apostle Paul at Rome

Paul had long hoped and prayed that he might go to Rome, the capital city of the world. From there the Gospel could be scattered everywhere. He already knew some people at Rome. He had mentioned them in his letter to the church at Rome. Some friends came down the Appian Way to meet him, and Christians in Rome told Paul they had heard some things about Christ and this Way, but knew little about it.

Paul was a prisoner, but he was allowed to rent a house and live there with a soldier to keep him and care for him.

Paul called for the Jewish leaders in Rome to come to see him. And there he presented the Gospel to them. Some were willing to accept it and some were not. Paul very sternly pressed upon them that if they would not accept the Gospel he would turn to the Gentiles, who would hear it.

Tradition is that Peter was at Rome, and that here Peter was crucified and that he became the first pope at Rome. No. When Paul wrote the book of Romans and addressed his letter to some twenty-eight people or families at Rome, he did not mention Peter. When Paul arrived in Rome, others met him but no mention of Peter. Peter was not there.

Paul wrote letters from Rome. In these letters he mentioned others who were with him, but he did not even mention Peter, for Peter was not there.

In II Timothy 4:10,11 Paul said, "Demas hath forsaken me, having loved this present world. . . .Only Luke is with me." Peter was not at Rome. Rather, he was over in the ancient Babylon area preaching to the multitude of Jews who had been there since the captivity. His letters of I and II Peter were written from Babylon. We remember that Peter was the apostle to "the circumcision," that is, to the Jews, but Paul was the apostle to the Gentiles.

We have a record of Paul those two years in his own house in Rome. But there is indication that Paul was later arrested again. Likely he had been back to see the Philippian brethren and Philemon whom he had written, asking him to prepare him a place. Doubtless he had gone on to Spain, as he before had intended to do. Now he was arrested and we think again put in the Mamertine Prison under the palace, where it seems Paul was later beheaded. He wrote Timothy from there, "I am now ready to be offered, and the time of my departure is at hand. I have fought a good fight, I have finished my course, I have kept the faith." So Paul died at Rome, doing more to get out the Gospel than any of the other apostles.

While in Rome we have often gone down into the Mamertine Prison, now covered by a little church. We have walked down into that damp dungeon where he must have been a prisoner for many months. What a miserable place! He urged Timothy to bring the books to read in his solitary hours and the coat he had left at Troas, to defend him from the damp cell and the cold of winter. And he urged him to come before winter. I hope Timothy got to see the Apostle Paul before he was beheaded.

Paul is a restless spirit! We seldom have it recorded "he slept," or "sat," or "stood." He is a man of motion! He is always "coming" or "going." He is always speaking and preaching.—W. B. Riley.

Exiled on Patmos, the Apostle John Writes the Last Book in the Bible

We learn some details of the great ministry of the Apostle Paul in the book of Acts and in the letters which Paul wrote to the churches. God does not give us many details in the ministry of the other apostles, except for some years in Jerusalem itself, where the apostles stayed.

Then in the 12th chapter of Acts, the Apostle James was beheaded by King Herod.

In chapter 13, Paul and Barnabas started the first missionary journeys.

We learn that after a great ministry in Jerusalem, Peter went to Babylon to minister to the many thousands of Jews of the ten tribes which did not return from the Babylonian Captivity. And so the first and second epistles of Peter were written from there.

Thomas went to India.

On the cross Jesus gave the care of his mother to John the Beloved: "Son, behold thy mother" and, "Mother, behold thy son." So John took Mary to his home and cared for her like a loving son would care for his mother. Eventually when John moved to Ephesus, he took Mary with him. A foolish tradition says that Mary went bodily to Heaven. Oh, no! She lived and died at Ephesus and is buried there.

John continued to preach until he was the last apostle alive. He preached so plainly that the Roman government exiled him, i.e., condemned him to live on the Island of Patmos in the Aegean Sea, off the coast of what is now Asiatic Turkey.

We must remember that it costs something to be a faithful preacher of Jesus Christ. It cost John. He had written the three epistles or letters of I John, II John, III John about the year 90, and John is now about ninety years of age. Then as he kept preaching, he was exiled to Patmos. On that beautiful little island God moved his heart and revealed to him what he should write down, word for word, the last book in the Bible—the book of Revelation. We know it is the last book of the Bible and that none were written after that, because Revelation 22:18 says, "If any man shall add unto these things, God shall add unto him the plagues that are written in this book."

Can you see the old man, weighted down with so many years, we suppose the last man alive who had looked on the face of Jesus, had put his hands upon Him, had leaned on His breast at the supper, and the one who was called "the disciple whom Jesus loved."

God has a final word for us all. A number of churches in what is now Asia Minor (the seven churches of the little province of Asia it was then) had made inquiry from John. So he wrote for the messengers or pastors of these churches these letters to the seven churches.

The book of Revelation first tells how John, on the Lord's Day, was in the Spirit, and Jesus Christ appeared to him in His glory and told him words he must write down. John wrote. Then he writes the seven messages to the seven churches in chapters 2 and 3.

God then gave John the outline of what will happen in the far future after Jesus comes and calls His saints into the air to meet Him. There will arise, Jesus said, "the man of sin," "the beast." He will be the one pictured in Daniel as a dictator to restore the Roman Empire. He will claim to be God on earth. He will set out to make people worship him. He will have such a world dictatorship that none can buy nor sell without his mark upon their bodies or hands. He will set out

to kill out the Christians, those converted during the tribulation time.

But at long last the seven years of trouble, the tribulation of Israel will come to an end, and Christ Himself will return and will deliver Jerusalem. He will bring the armies of Heaven with Him and smite the Man of Sin and his millions of devil-possessed soldiers in the valley of Armageddon. What a sight!

We are told how John saw Jesus coming riding on a white horse, crowned with many crowns, and the armies of Heaven following Him on white horses. And His name is called the Word of God. Oh, Lord Jesus, come!

Then God told John how, after that battle of Armageddon, Christ would come to sit on His throne. There will be a thousand years of blessed peace, the millennium when Christ will reign personally on the earth, then the last rebellion, and there will be the great white throne judgment of the unsaved dead out in space. This earth will be purged with fire and planted in a new Garden of Eden. And God Himself will come down to make His home with men on earth.

Oh, can't you see that Golden City coming down from God out of Heaven! Streets of gleaming gold! Great walls of jasper! Every gate a separate pearl! Can't you imagine the River of Life flowing with trees of life on either side, and the trees bearing twelve manner of fruit, a new fruit every month! And the leaves will be for the healing of the nations!

What about the sun, moon and stars? We will need no more sun, for the Lord God Himself is the Light of that wonderful city. There will be no night there, for no one will have need to rest. We will never grow tired. God will wipe away all the tears of those who had broken hearts and suffered for Him.

Then God says, "Now we must close this canon of inspiration and no one must ever change it." So He said, "John, before we close this, we must give another sweet invitation to the unsaved."

I can imagine John said, "Lord Jesus, I have taken some carbon or soot and mixed it with olive oil to make ink. I have gotten some quill pens ready. Here is a parchment or skin that I must write on to keep it permanently. All right, Lord Jesus, tell me what You wish me to write."

The Lord Jesus said, "Write, John, 'And the Spirit and the bride say, Come. And let him that heareth say, Come. And let him that is athirst come. And whosoever will, let him take the water of life freely.' "

Oh, the Lord couldn't close the canon of inspiration without giving another sweet call to sinners to trust Him and be saved!

John closed with a farewell and said, "Even so, come, Lord Jesus."

Yes, and let all of us too say, "Come, Lord Jesus! Come!"

Sinners Face Jesus at the Last Judgment of the Unsaved Dead

REVELATION 20

There are many warnings in the Bible that sin must come to judgment.

"Be sure your sin will find you out," Moses said in Numbers 32:23.

"The way of transgressors is hard," reads Proverbs 13:15.

"The wages of sin is death," declares Romans 6:23.

There is the solemn warning of Galatians 6:7,8: "Be not deceived; God is not mocked: for whatsoever a man soweth, that shall he also reap. For he that soweth to his flesh shall of the flesh reap corruption. . . ."

In Isaiah 45:23 we learn that God has sworn, "That unto Me every knee shall bow, every tongue shall swear."

Romans 14:11,12 repeats that, "For it is written, As I live, saith the Lord, every knee shall bow to Me, and every tongue shall confess to God. So then every one of us shall give account of himself to God." That solemn promise is repeated again in Philippians 2:10,11.

Judgment is coming, and no one can escape it.

There are several kinds of judgment given in the Bible. Jesus said, "The Father. . .hath committed all judgment unto the Son." Every human being in the world must account to Jesus Christ.

First, there is the judgment of Christians, which will take place at the rapture. We are caught up to meet Jesus in the air, then we must all stand before the judgment seat of

Christ. First Corinthians 3:10-15 tells of that judgment when some Christians will receive a reward because their works are like gold, silver and precious stones that abide, while others will suffer loss because their works are like wood, hay and stubble, yet they will be saved "yet so as by fire." Second Corinthians 5:10 speaks also of that judgment of Christians when we receive the things done in the body. But that is not the judgment of the unsaved dead which we discuss here.

Remember, as far as the eternal doom of our souls is concerned, that is all settled. For John 5:24 says, "Verily, verily, I say unto you, He that heareth My word, and believeth on Him that sent Me, hath everlasting life, and shall not come into condemnation; but is passed from death unto life." Some translations give that "and cometh not to judgment." My sins are already judged in Jesus. He has paid my debt. Thank God, I am forgiven! But I must still give an account for the deeds done in the body. And there are more rewards for some than for others.

Then there is another judgment when the Lord Jesus returns to this earth and sends His angels out to gather together all the Jews. Then rebels will be purged out and the other Jews will see Jesus and be converted, a whole nation in a day. What a grand time of salvation that will be! But the rebels will be purged out.

Then there is a judgment discussed in Matthew 25, when Jesus comes to sit on the throne of His glory. All the Gentile population not slain in the battle of Armageddon will be gathered before Jesus and judged, divided as the sheep and the goats. Those who took the part of Christ and the Christians and have trusted Jesus, will be counted sheep, and He will say, "Come, ye blessed of My Father, inherit the kingdom prepared for you from the foundation of the world." But Gentiles who have not taken the part of Christ and of Christians will go away into everlasting punishment.

But the great white throne judgment is the final judgment of every sinner who turns down Jesus Christ and dies unsaved.

First, we must remember there are two Bible resurrec-

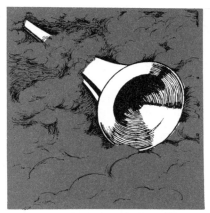

tions. The first resurrection is of the Christians. At the rapture, the Scripture says, "For the Lord Himself shall descend from heaven with a shout, with the voice of the archangel, with the trump of God: and the dead in Christ shall rise first: Then we which are alive and remain shall be caught up together with them in the clouds, to meet the Lord in the air: and so shall we ever be with the Lord" (I Thess. 4:16,17).

Then Christians will reign with Christ for a thousand years on this earth. We call that the millennium, which is just another word for "thousand." The Bible says at the end of the thousand years, ". . .the rest of the dead lived not again until the thousand years were finished"; then they will be raised.

Now we read the story of that great judgment of the unsaved dead when they are brought out of graves, out of the sea, and their spirits out of Hell to be judged.

"And the devil that deceived them was cast into the lake of fire and brimstone, where the beast and the false prophet are, and shall be tormented day and night for ever and ever. And I saw a great white throne, and Him that sat on it, from whose face the earth and the heaven fled away; and there was found no place for them. And I saw the dead, small and great, stand before God; and the books were opened: and another book was opened, which is the book of life: and the dead were judged out of those things which

were written in the books, according to their works. And the sea gave up the dead which were in it; and death and hell delivered up the dead which were in them: and they were judged every man according to their works. And death and hell were cast into the lake of fire."—Rev. 20:10-15.

First, note the resurrection of the bodies of these unsaved people. Some have moldered into dust in far-off lands; they will be raised up. Some will have gone down in shipwreck into the sea and been eaten by creatures in the ocean, yet their bodies will be reassembled and resurrected. God has promised to do that.

Then the spirits of the unsaved dead will be brought out of Hell. Surely they will not want to come, for they must face Jesus and they must face the record of their sins. But come they will. They will be brought out and Hell will be emptied for a little while as these are brought to face Jesus Christ, sitting on a great white throne.

But where will it be? Out in space. This is the time when God will burn over this earth and purge it with fire so that every trace of man's habitation will be destroyed. Then God will plant in the earth a new Garden of Eden and start over again. But in that judgment out in space all the unsaved will be assembled to be judged.

What about Christians? Yes, we will be there, because we will be witnesses. The Scripture says about the rapture, ". . .so shall we ever be with the Lord." So we will go where He goes. Then Jesus said, "The men of Nineveh shall rise up in the judgment with this generation, and shall condemn it: for they repented at the preaching of Jonas" (Luke 11:32). So saved people will be there to give witness against those who heard the Gospel but would not be saved. Now God has record books open. It is not left to somebody's frail memory. Every deed is recorded. Every idle word that men uttered must come to judgment here.

Just as God is so careful to reward every good deed, and since not a cup of cold water is offered in Jesus' name but will receive a reward; so now not even an idle word can escape public exposure at this last judgment. God's record books have it all down. The books will be opened and people will be judged out of the books according to their works.

Notice nothing is said here about regeneration, for none of these people have been regenerated. Nothing is said here about the Gospel of salvation by grace, for these have all turned down the Gospel. Nothing is said here about the atoning blood of Jesus, for all these have rejected that atoning blood. Now God can only talk to them about their works, since none would trust the Saviour and His atoning death for their sins.

So here is a sad, sad record that men had forgotten. Oh, that will be a time when the skeletons will come out of the closets, a time when chickens will come home to roost. That will be a time when people remember the sins they had long forgotten. That will be the time when at long last God's perfect judgment meets to every man what his sin has deserved.

Is there no hope for these to be saved who come before this judgment? No. None at all. They have already rejected the Saviour. And as the tree falls, so shall it lie. These have already hardened their hearts against God. When there was a time for repentance, they would not repent. There was a time when God offered them mercy and pleaded but they rejected mercy, and so set themselves against Christ and against God that now there is no further hope.

Now at long last comes the sad word. They open another book, the Book of Life. Let anyone search it who will. Ah, but each one in this crowd will have to say, "My name is not there! Oh, my name is not there!" So everyone whose name was not written in the Book of Life will be cast into the lake of fire.

Let this be a solemn time of heart-searching for all who read these words. Will you put your trust in Jesus? If you will, then He will be your Redeemer. He will forgive you. He paid your debt. Now you can be forgiven and set free!

O sinner, trust Christ today!

The Last Invitation in
The Bible

We have read wonderful stories from all the Bible. When we come to the last book in the Bible, we find that the Lord Jesus gave the very words of Scripture to John the beloved disciple. John was in exile, imprisoned out on the island of Patmos, for his testimony. There the Lord Jesus gave him the words in the book of Revelation.

He told John about the beautiful golden city coming down from God out of Heaven, the Heavenly Jerusalem. He called it "bride, the Lamb's wife." He warned that no one was to add any part to this inspired Bible after the book of Revelation, and if one were to take from the words of this prophecy, he would suffer great curses.

Then coming to the end of the divine canon of revelation, the Lord Jesus must give another invitation to sinners. I can imagine that He said, "John, let us write another sweet invitation to sinners to trust in Christ and be saved." I can think that John said, "All right, Lord. I have made some ink with soot and olive oil. I have parchment ready on which to write, and a good quill pen. What shall I write?" The Lord Jesus answered, "Write, The Spirit and the bride say, Come. And let him that heareth say, Come. And let him that is athirst come. And whosoever will, let him take the water of life freely."

What a wonderful invitation! All the way through the Bible we have found how God loves sinners, how God gave His Son to die for sinners, and that "whosoever believeth in Him [or trusteth in Him] should not perish, but have everlasting life." Now here is the invitation again. Every poor sinner is invited to come to Jesus for forgiveness. The Holy Spirit bids people come. The Heavenly Jerusalem, the Lamb's bride, is prepared and ready.

Jesus said, "In My Father's house are many mansions: if it were not so, I would have told you. I go to prepare a place for you. And if I go and prepare a place for you, I will come again, and receive you unto Myself; that where I am, there ye may be also." So the Heavenly City says, "Come." And "let him that heareth say, Come."

Oh, dear Christian who reads this, make sure that your loved ones are invited to come and trust in Christ, too. And who is to come? "Whosoever will." How simple it is. Simply take the cup of salvation. It is free. Salvation is already paid for. God loves you. The moment your heart turns to Him and trusts in Him, He forgives all your sins.

The sweet promise of Romans 10:13 is: "For whosoever shall call upon the name of the Lord shall be saved."

If you who read this are conscious that you are an unconverted, unforgiven sinner, then I beg you to turn to Jesus in your heart now, trust Him to forgive you and claim Him as your Saviour.

Here is an invitation. Can you say yes to this? If you can sign this, copy it in a letter and mail it to the author.

Evangelist John R. Rice
THE SWORD OF THE LORD
P. O. Box 1099
Murfreesboro, Tennessee 37130

Dear Brother Rice:

I have enjoyed your Bible Story Book and I realize that I am a poor sinner who needs to be converted. I realize that God wants to save me. I believe Jesus died for me, so here and now I put my trust in Jesus, I take Him as my Saviour, and set out to live for Him and write to let you know.

Signed _____

Address _____

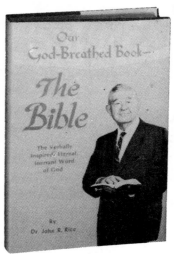